Corporate Social Responsibility and Natural Resource Conflict

This book examines the possibilities and limitations of corporate social responsibility in minimising the violent conflict often associated with natural resource exploitation. Through detailed and penetrating empirical analysis, the author skilfully asks why previous corporate social responsibility practices have not always achieved their aims.

This theme is explored though an analysis of two of the most complex and protracted conflicts linked to natural resources in the Asia Pacific region: Bougainville (Papua New Guinea) and West Papua (Indonesia). Drawing on first-hand accounts of corporate executives and communities affected by resource conflict, this book documents the translation of global corporate social responsibility into local peace. Covering topics as diverse as post-colonialism, law, revenue distribution, security, the environment and customary reconciliation, this ambitious text reveals how and why current corporate social responsibility initiatives may be unable to assist extractive companies avoid social conflict. The study concludes that this is attributable to the failure of extractive companies to respond to the social and environmental issues of most concern to local host communities. The idea is that extractive companies could actively contribute to peace building if they were to engage with the interdependencies between business activity and the root causes of conflict.

What sets this book apart is that it offers a holistic framework for extractive companies to engage with the complexity of resource conflict. 'Interdependent Engagement' is an integrated model of corporate social responsibility that encourages extractive companies to deal with the underlying causes of resource conflict, rather than applying solutions or critiques of their symptoms.

Kylie McKenna is a Research Fellow at the Australian National University, Australia.

Routledge Research in Sustainability and Business

Corporate Social Responsibility and Natural Resource Conflict

Kylie McKenna

Routledge
Taylor & Francis Group

LONDON AND NEW YORK

First published 2016
by Routledge
2 Park Square, Milton Park, Abingdon, Oxon OX14 4RN

and by Routledge
711 Third Avenue, New York, NY 10017

First issued in paperback 2017

Routledge is an imprint of the Taylor & Francis Group, an informa business

British Library Cataloguing in Publication Data
A catalogue record for this book is available from the British Library

Library of Congress Cataloguing in Publication Data
Names: McKenna, Kylie, author.
Title: Corporate social responsibility and natural resource conflict / Kylie McKenna.
Description: New York, NY : Routledge, 2016. |
Includes bibliographical references and index.
Identifiers: LCCN 2015021518| ISBN 9781138783287 (hardback) |
ISBN 9781315768755 (ebook)
Subjects: LCSH: Social responsibility of business. | Natural resources–Management.
Classification: LCC HD60 .M39 2016 | DDC 658.4/083–dc23
LC record available at http://lccn.loc.gov/2015021518

ISBN 13: 978-1-138-10430-3 (pbk)
ISBN 13: 978-1-138-78328-7 (hbk)

Typeset in Goudy
by Out of House Publishing

For my dear friends,
John Braithwaite, Gill Hewitt, Nagasuri, Shubhavyuha,
Sudrishti and Viraja – with sincere appreciation for your love
and support.

Contents

Illustrations

Figures

Tables

Acknowledgements

This book is one outcome of years of education, travel, friendship and inspiration. It began as a PhD thesis under the supervision of John Braithwaite at the Australian National University (ANU). My PhD experience was incredibly rewarding and I was completely blessed to share these years with my mentor and friend in John. My colleagues at the Regulatory Institutions Network (RegNet) provided significant support. My thanks to Suza Akila, Valerie Braithwaite, Lennon Chang, Hilary Charlesworth, Jo Ford, Neil Gunningham, Budi Hernawan, Hiroko Inoue, Aderito Soares and Cheryl White for the contributions you all made to this project and my time at RegNet. Sincere thanks in particular to Budi Hernawan who continued to read drafts of this work and provided wonderful feedback.

I am grateful to the examiners of my PhD thesis (Glenn Banks, Daniel Franks and Fiona Haines) who provided insightful advice on how to revise my thesis for publication. I revised and revised again (!) this manuscript as a Research Fellow at the State, Society and Governance in Melanesia Program (SSGM), also at the ANU. The bright and encouraging smiles of the SSGM academics, professional staff, students and visitors (including the wonderful participants who have attended the Pacific Research Colloquium over the years) have made this work an enriching experience. Sincere thanks in particular go to those who provided feedback on earlier drafts: Matthew Allen, Sinclair Dinnen, Jenny Munro, Gordon Peake and Anthony Regan. I also note my SSGM colleagues who have been tremendous sources of friendship and encouragement, especially: Kerryn Baker, Claire Cronin, John Cox, Meabh Cryan, Melissa Demian, Susan Dixon, Richard Eves, Miranda Forsyth, Shaun Gessler, Nicole Haley, Peta Jones, Lia Kent, Sarah Logan, Stephanie Lusby, David Oakshott, Tim Sharp, Graeme Smith, Ceridwen Spark, Almah Tararia, Pyone Myat Thu and Anita Togolo.

This research would not have been possible without the financial support of World Vision Australia that provided me with a stipend and fieldwork funding for my PhD research. I am also grateful for the funding provided to me through SSGM, RegNet, as well as the ANU RSAP, Vice-Chancellor and IARU travel funds.

I am incredibly grateful to the participants in this research who gave so generously of their time. Whether the interview was conducted in the burnt-out shell of a building up at Panguna, or in the head office of an extractive company in China, I learnt so much from every Bougainvillean, Papuan and corporate executive who participated in this research. I thank those who hosted me during fieldwork, showed me around their countries and shared many memorable experiences. My thanks also to the Autonomous Bougainville Government, the National Research Institute of PNG and my interpreters Clarence, Hubert, John, Octovianus and Petrus.

My thanks go to my family and my parents in particular, Jenny Barratt and Paul McKenna. From my days as a rugby league player for the Guildford Owls on an all-boys team, my Mum and Dad have always encouraged me to do what I enjoy, no matter how unconventional and unlikely. I also thank my Nanny and Grandpop who have been the best grandparents anyone could ever ask for.

In its essence, this book is about our connection with one another and how engaging with our interdependence can enable us to be more open and responsive. It has been my friends who have shown me the beauty, complexity and love that can flow from this. With thanks to Gambhiraja, Gill Hewitt, Jim Pescud, Jenny Tierney, Kitty Rahilly, Maryann Athaide, Nagasuri, Nyrelle Finch, Sarah Goode, Satyagandhi, Shubhavyuha, Sudrishti, Viraja, Yasokaruna and the wider sangha of the Sydney Buddhist Centre.

Glossary and abbreviations

ABG	Autonomous Bougainville Government
adat	customary or indigenous
AGA	Applied Geology Associates
ALP	Australian Labor Party
AMDAL	*Analisis Mengenai Dampak Lingkungan* (Integrated Environmental and Social Impact Assessment)
ARCO	Atlantic Richfield Company
BCL	Bougainville Copper Limited
Bel Kol	cooling of the heart
BP	British Petroleum or 'beyond petroleum'
BRA	Bougainville Revolutionary Army
BRF	Bougainville Resistance Forces
Brimob	*Korps Brigade Mobil* (Mobile Brigade)
Bupati	Regency Head
CEO	chief executive officer
CRA	Cozinc Rio Tinto Australia
CSR	corporate social responsibility
EIA	environmental impact assessment
EIS	environmental impact study
Freeport	PT Freeport Indonesia
GDP	gross domestic product
hak ulayat	indigenous land rights
ICBS	integrated community-based security
ICG	International Crisis Group
JATAM	*Jaringan Advokasi Tambang* (mining advocacy network)
Kiap	administrative field officer
Komnas HAM	*Komisi Nasional Hak-Hak Asasi Manusia* (Indonesia's National Commission for Human Rights)
LEMASA	*Lembaga Musyawarah Adat Suku Amungme* (the Amungme Tribal Council)
LEMASKO	*Lembaga Musyawarah Adat Suku Kamoro* (the Kamoro Tribal Council)
LNG	liquefied natural gas

LPMAK	*Lembaga Pengembangan Masyarakat Amungme dan Kamoro* (the Amungme and Kamoro Community Development Organisation)
merdeka	freedom or liberation
MNC	multinational corporation
MRP	*Majelis Rakyat Papua* (Papuan People's Council)
NGO	non-governmental organisation
NPLA	New Panguna Landowners Association
OPIC	Overseas Private Insurance Corporation
OPM	*Organisasi Papua Merdeka* (Free Papua Movement)
PLA	Panguna Landowners Association
PNG	Papua New Guinea
PNGDF	Papua New Guinea Defence Force
PTFI	PT Freeport Indonesia
RAV	resettlement affected villages
reformasi	democratic reform movement at time of fall of President Suharto
rekognisi	recognition
SEIA	Summary Environmental Impact Assessment
SIA	social impact assessment
suku	tribe
tanah negara	state-owned land
TBO	*Tenaga Bantuan Operasi* (civilians who provide assistance to the Indonesian military)
terra nullius	land belonging to no one
TIAP	Tangguh Independent Advisory Panel
TNI	*Tentara Nasional Indonesia* (Indonesian military)
Tongoi Papua	Freeport Union for indigenous workers
UN	United Nations
US	United States
WALHI	*Wahana Lingkungan Hidup Indonesia* (Indonesian Forum on the Environment)
wantok	one talk or language

1   The challenge of corporate social responsibility and conflict

In every organisation or company, the management should be connected with us. It took so many years to understand that. Nobody understood that at the time ... but they do now.

(B18, landowner group chairman, interview with Kylie McKenna, Bougainville, 2010)

In April 2010 I travelled to Arawa, the old mining town of the Panguna mine in the Autonomous Region of Bougainville, Papua New Guinea (PNG). During my stay in Arawa I visited the house of an elderly landowner of land taken by the Panguna mine who had a long history of involvement in the Panguna Landowners Association (PLA). During the operating years of the mine, the PLA lobbied for a greater share of the wealth derived from the project for landowners, and compensation for the environmental damage it caused. I had only arranged to speak with this one landowner, but during our meeting about ten people from his family joined us. They sat across from the elderly man and me in silence, listening to every word he recounted of his experiences of the past, and his hopes for Bougainville's future. During our discussion, he spoke of the unfairness of the Australian Administration that supported a mining agreement that was not considered to represent the specific interests of the people of Bougainville. The landowner spoke of lobbying mine operator, Bougainville Copper Limited (BCL), and the PNG Government for more compensation, and the unwillingness of the corporate executives at the time to listen to the grievances of local people. He spoke of communication problems between landowners and BCL's Village Relations Department, of the murder and rape of women by migrants to Bougainville from other parts of PNG and the feeling of becoming a stranger on his own land.

The story I heard that day reflected upon an extremely painful past. But as images of the past were invoked, the elderly landowner also drew my attention to possible futures for the Panguna mine. He went on to talk about a belief that BCL has learned from the mistakes of the past, and his certainty that if Bougainvilleans truly want independence from PNG, the mine must be reopened.

In a deceptively simple way, this story encompasses many of the lessons learned during the course of this study. Drawing on the thoughts of over 90 stakeholders,[1] ranging from multinational resource company executives (including corporate social responsibility [CSR] professionals, company directors and indigenous employees) to local landowners, this book explores the theme of how extractive companies might amend CSR practices to facilitate peaceful development. As the landowner alluded in his comments to the connection between local people and corporations, this study focuses on the interdependence that exists between large extractive companies and the societies in which they operate. The purpose is to investigate the productive possibilities that might emerge from engaging with this interdependence, rather than denial of it. The aim is to contribute to understandings of how large extractive companies can not only avoid the violent conflict that is so often associated with this industry, but can actually facilitate the peaceful extraction of natural resources.

Resource conflict

Conflict relating to natural resources is a defining feature of contemporary global armed conflict. Research conducted by the United Nations (UN) estimates that at least 40 per cent of intrastate conflicts, that is, conflicts that occur within the boundaries of a nation-state, have a link to natural resources (UNEP, 2009, p. 30). Numerous studies have sought to explain this dynamic. Termed the 'resource curse' or the 'paradox of plenty', scholars in this field argue that instead of contributing to peace and prosperity, an abundance of natural resources has a tendency to be associated with poor economic growth, poverty, corruption, state weakness, authoritarianism and repression, all of which increase the likelihood of armed conflict (Bannon & Collier, 2003; Collier & Hoeffler, 2005; Ross, 2001, 2003; Sachs & Warner, 2001).

A prominent explanation for the resource curse is that the presence of natural resources provides both an incentive for warring groups to compete and sell off the resource, as well as the financial means to purchase weapons (Collier & Hoeffler, 2005). Civil war is expensive and the tools of war have to be financed (Bannon & Collier, 2003, p. 3). Consequently, rebel movements can be characterised, in part, as business organisations. Without a source of finance, they 'will wither away or be capable of only limited and low-level violence – more of an irritant than a serious threat to an established government' (Bannon & Collier, 2003, pp. 3–4).

While there is general consensus in the literature that economic drivers can and do contribute to conflict, there is less agreement as to how influential they are relative to the social and environmental impacts that large-scale resource developments create, such as the influx of 'economic migrants' and disruptions to 'traditional' ways of life (Hook & Ganguly, 2000, p. 65). This has become known as the 'greed vs. grievance' debate, where the motivations of rebel movements are categorised as either 'loot' or 'justice' seeking (Ballentine & Nitzchke, 2003, p. 2). The data assembled for this book suggest that resource conflicts can be characterised by a combination of both these motivations. Some individuals are motivated by greed, while others simply want an end to the social and environmental disruptions caused by large extractive projects. For still others, possibly most, the motivations of both greed and grievance merge in ways that are difficult to disentangle.

Beyond notions of greed and grievance attention has also been drawn to the ways in which natural resource exploitation becomes linked in particular ways to identity and social change. Aspinall (2007, p. 950) argues that the separatist conflict in Aceh, Indonesia, was not determined by 'any intrinsic qualities of natural resource extraction'. Rather, 'the key factor was the presence of an appropriate identity based collective action frame' (Aspinall, 2007, p. 950). The crux of Aspinall's argument is that 'what determines rebellion is not the presence of a natural resource industry and its material effects, but rather how it is interpreted by local actors' (2007, p. 953).

Similarly, Escobar (2006) argues that most conflicts over natural resources involve economic, ecological and cultural dimensions, each of which is transformed through resource exploitation:

> it entails the transformation of local diverse economies, partly oriented to self-reproduction and subsistence, into a monetized, market-driven economy. It involves changes of complex ecosystems into modern forms of nature ... And it is changing place-based, local cultures into cultures that increasingly (have to) resemble dominant modern cultures, with their individualistic and productive ethos and market orientation.
>
> (Escobar, 2006, p. 7)

These transformations have been documented empirically internationally, such as in Banks' (2008, p. 23) argument that 'what appear to be "resource" conflicts in Papua New Guinea are actually better conceived as conflicts around identity and social relationships', as well as in Watts' (2004) interest in the agency of extractive industries in reconfiguring relationships between territory, identity and rule in the Niger Delta.

Notwithstanding the connections between resource wealth and armed conflict, the natural resource curse should not be considered a *fait accompli* (Bannon & Collier, 2003, p. 11). For example, while diamonds can be linked to economic and social collapse in Sierra Leone, they were 'critical to Botswana's success in becoming the fastest-growing economy in the world and a middle income county' (Bannon & Collier, 2003, p. 11). Resources can result in social conflict and division but the case of Botswana also shows that they can be a basis on which to reduce poverty and promote development.

The responsibilities of extractive companies

Recognition of the potential for natural resources to ease poverty and contribute positively to economic and social development has led to the search for new frameworks on how to maximise the positive potential, while mitigating the risks. Examples include the Extractive Industries Transparency Initiative and the

Voluntary Principles on Security and Human Rights, which target the elimination of corruption and human rights violations. More recent frameworks are wider reaching, aiming to capture 'the ingredients successful countries have used' (NRGI, 2010) to translate resource wealth into development. Much of the analysis to date, however, has been targeted at resource-abundant governments. As a result, existing recommendations largely focus on strategies that might redress or avoid the governance failures associated with resource wealth, such as economic overreliance on natural resources and revenue sharing regimes.

A notable example of a recent framework to guide responsible resource exploitation is the Natural Resource Charter (NRC). The NRC is a global initiative drafted by prominent economists including Michael Spence and Paul Collier. The NRC offers guidelines or 'precepts' to manage natural resources 'in a way that generates economic growth, promotes the welfare of the population, and is environmentally sustainable' (NRGI, 2010, p. 1). Ten of the twelve precepts outlined in the NRC are directed at the governments of resource producing states, while the remaining two target the home governments of extractive companies and extractive companies themselves. There is just one 'precept' for extractive companies, which is quite broad and lacks practical detail. It simply asks companies to 'follow best practice in contracting, operations and payments' (NRGI, 2010, p. 2).

There is also interest in the role that extractive companies could play in responding and potentially resolving recourse conflict in their areas of operation. This interest has been precipitated by three factors: (1) the expanded global reach of corporations and larger revenue base of some companies in comparison to the annual gross domestic product (GDP) of the developing states in which they operate; (2) the prominence and visibility associated with this wealth globally has been associated with increased expectations of social responsibility; and (3) the change in global approaches to conflict resolution which 'has seen a move away from zero sum orientations' towards an emphasis on 'the critical need for negotiation and cooperation' (Jamali & Mirshak, 2010, pp. 444–5). Extractive companies therefore, 'are at once being called to task for exacerbating armed conflicts and being called upon to participate in their prevention and resolution' (Berman, 2000, p. 28).

Corporate social responsibility

One avenue for the engagement of extractive companies in responding to resource conflict has been the expansion of the theorisation and practice of CSR to encompass conflict analysis and peace building.[2] 'CSR' has become recognisable shorthand for the onus on business to consider the consequences of business activity on the societies and environments in which they operate. Despite over 50 years of scholarship on CSR, there is no universally accepted definition (Dahlsrud, 2008). Moreover, various models of CSR have evolved over time, such as community relations and community development, adding further ambiguity to defining this field (Kemp, 2009, 2010).

Attempts to address the negative impacts of business on society are not a new phenomenon. Some analysts (Cheney et al., 2007, p. 4) trace the origin of such initiatives back to the late 1870s when corporate activities were beginning to be identified as having detrimental impacts on society. Corporate responses to these concerns have a similarly long history. For example, during what is known as the 'progressive' era in the United States (US) (from 1900 to 1920) industrialists were believed to have 'found themselves in the awkward position of advocating a system of factory labour that, by many critics standards, was proving to be a detriment to society' (Cheney et al., 2007, p. 4). In response, corporations began implementing employee welfare programmes designed to 'curb growing dismay over the negative impact of industrialization on community and family life' (Cheney et al., 2007, p. 4).

Despite these early forays into social responsibility, the core expectation of business remained to maximise profits for shareholders (Carroll, 1991, p. 39). It was not until the 1970s that this view changed dramatically. At this time the establishment of a new generation of regulatory agencies in the US began to identify not just shareholders, but also the environment, employees and consumers as company 'stakeholders' (Carroll, 1991, p. 39). In this way, from the 1970s onwards, expectations of the responsibilities of business widened.

Within the extractive industries, CSR gained particular momentum in the 1980s when an unprecedented number of extractive companies began to champion the concept (Hilson, 2012, p. 131). According to Hilson, only a few years earlier most extractive company chief executive officers (CEOs) and directors were indifferent to CSR, and some companies preferred to pay fines for non-compliance to environmental regulations than embrace the concept. This uptake has been mirrored by a dramatic rise in voluntary initiatives, codes of conduct and industry guidelines seeking to define CSR 'best practice' within the extractives industry (Kepore & Imbun, 2011). Reasons for its adoption are manifold but primarily 'represent a bid to legitimize the sector after decades of environmental disasters and the trampling of indigenous rights' (Gilberthorpe & Banks, 2012, p. 185).

The drivers of CSR in the extractives industry

Adoption of CSR by the extractives industry raises questions regarding who and what are driving CSR? And what is the role of non-business actors such as states and 'communities' in framing the CSR agenda? In regard to states, Hamann and Kapelus (2004, p. 89) argue the main reason CSR gained higher status in mining companies in South Africa was that the state implemented a scorecard that measured 'companies' performance against a range of so-called black economic empowerment criteria'. CSR as a response to state pressure problematises notions of CSR as 'voluntary' self-regulation. In some areas, performance on these issues has become a 'prerequisite for companies' access to mining licenses' (Hamann & Kapelus, 2004, p. 89), such as compensation payments outlined in formal agreements between developers, the state and 'landowning communities' (Imbun, 2007, p. 178).

In contrast to state pressure, Idemudia and Ite (2006, p. 196) argue the key driver for extractive companies to adopt CSR in Nigeria was the need to secure a 'social license to operate' as well as the high incidence of hostage taking, sabotage and violent conflict. This motivation meant that CSR policies in the region were largely a defensive strategy to avoid reputation damage and costs associated with community conflict (Idemudia & Ite, 2006, p. 196).

Different again, a unique characteristic of CSR in PNG is acknowledgement of local agency in shaping the CSR agenda. While broader critiques often neglect the role of indigenous actors in informing CSR policies and programmes (Gilberthorpe, 2013), Papua New Guineans have been described as holding a 'shopping list mentality' (Imbun, 2007, p. 178), where it is common for indigenous communities in PNG to expect mining companies to provide road infrastructure, education and health services and other development needs (Kepore & Imbun, 2011, p. 230).

While community demands are acknowledged by both extractive companies and analysts as genuine (Imbun, 2007, p. 190), less clear is the weight of local power in contrast to the underlying business imperatives of CSR. To the extent that business organisations determine the budget and scope of CSR activities (Kepore & Imbun, 2011, p. 222) it is likely that 'standards of appropriateness regarding the nature and level of corporate social action' (Marquis et al., 2007, p. 926) will vary from one resource producing community to another.

Models of CSR

In spite of the diversity of influences of CSR, it is recognised that its character as a 'defensive' strategy has evolved over time. CSR in the Niger Delta has advanced 'into a full-blown and an expected organizational practice' (Idemudia & Ite, 2006, p. 196). This is reflected in the doubling of CSR budgets and significant contributions by extractive companies to social development infrastructure (Idemudia & Ite, 2006, p. 196). Contemporary CSR among extractive companies, therefore, is recognised as encompassing more than 'just' philanthropy, sponsorships and donations (Kemp, 2010, p. 2).

To encapsulate the diversity of CSR and its underlying motives within the extractives industry, Kemp (2009, pp. 203–5) distinguishes three theoretical and professional approaches. The first is 'public relations' which focuses on corporate reputation management through formal communication, such as websites and corporate reports. 'Public relations' is the most 'traditional' dimension of community affairs 'in the sense that they have long been accepted as work that large mining companies do' (Kemp, 2010, p. 5). The second approach is 'community relations' which focuses 'on building relationships in order to meet business objectives' (Kemp, 2009, p. 205). Kemp argues the current discourse focuses primarily, although not exclusively, on 'external engagement and bridging', rather than 'internal organizational change'. Finally, the 'community development' model 'invokes poverty reduction and human development goals and infers value-based commitments to social justice, equity and inclusion where benefits flow even to the most vulnerable' (Kemp, 2009, p. 199).

The strength of Kemp's three-dimensional model is that it allows a more nuanced framing of CSR. For example, if we were to map these approaches according to public participation, community development would represent 'high end' participation with a goal to 'empower', whereas public relations would be at the lower end of a participation spectrum with a goal to 'inform' (IAP2, n.d.). The use of more specific terms such as community development allows the opportunity to more accurately identify the audience and purpose of corporate–community policies and practices. In spite of these strengths, Kemp herself acknowledges that this nuance can add further complexity to an already contested field since, 'whether companies are practicing public relations, community relations or community development is not an easy distinction to make given the often overlapping nature of these activities' (Kemp, 2010, p. 2).

In practice, CSR generally manifests as corporate commitments in the form of socio-economic development projects, employee volunteering, community–business partnerships, social and environmental impact assessments, the adoption of discretionary codes of conduct (such as labour standards, human rights and environmental protection) and, as highlighted above, can incorporate formal agreements between states and communities. In this book, the use of the term CSR is also maintained because, as will be explained further, the 'social' in CSR enables an important window for theoretical and empirical analysis.

CSR and conflict

While CSR generates benefits for local communities that are often welcome and much needed, there is an increasing awareness that there could be limits to the value of expanding the scope of CSR to encompass conflict resolution and peace building. Counter to normative arguments in favour of corporations engaging with conflict and peace, analysts have noted the unsatisfactory results of CSR globally, given that resource conflicts 'continue to emerge under improved conditions of "socially responsible resource development"' (Gilberthorpe & Banks, 2012, p. 186). The fact that CSR has been embraced by extractive companies and that the sector has been acknowledged for transforming the defensive character of CSR globally begs the question: why is it that despite a commitment to CSR, violent conflict surrounding extractive sites has not abated, and in some contexts, has actually increased (Idemudia & Ite, 2006)?

Idemudia (2010, pp. 837–9) outlines three structural factors that have constrained CSR effectiveness in Nigeria: the capital-intensive nature of the oil industry (which only creates a small amount of local employment); the logic of capitalist production and profitability (whereby multinational corporations [MNCs] choose profitability over meaningful contributions to conflict prevention that may incur costs); and a skewed CSR agenda (whereby companies largely pursue micro-CSR activities, for example, building schools and roads, rather than macro-CSR issues, for example, fighting corruption or acknowledging the resource curse). Idemudia (2010, p. 839) argues 'while attention to micro-CSR issues might address some aspects of local grievances that drive violence in the region, it is unable to deal with the root causes of grievances'.

Also in reference to the unsatisfactory results of CSR in Nigeria, Frynas (2005, p. 581) argues that there is mounting evidence of a gap between the stated intentions of the business community in relation to CSR, and its actual impact in the real world. Frynas (2005, p. 598) provides five reasons for this outcome: subservience of CSR to corporate objectives; failure to involve the beneficiaries of CSR; lack of human resources; social attitudes of company staff; and failure to integrate CSR projects into larger development goals.

Poor CSR results have also been identified in PNG. While the rise of CSR in the country 'has meant safer technologies and better stakeholder engagement, there is little evidence of any real socio-economic development at the grassroots' (Gilberthorpe & Banks, 2012, p. 185). Gilberthorpe and Banks (2012, p. 185) explain this as a consequence of the strategic business model of CSR, which places greater emphasis on meeting ' "performance standards" than on the specificities of the social contexts in which strategies are implemented'. As a result, CSR has generated 'ill-conceived and inappropriate development programmes that generate inequality, fragmentation, and social and economic insecurity' (Gilberthorpe & Banks, 2012), all of which do 'little to ameliorate the social risks that were and remain a key rationale for the adoption of these social responsibilities in the first place' (Gilberthorpe & Banks, 2012, p. 186).

A further critique of CSR extended in this book 'is the general absence of justice in the CSR narratives' (Hamann & Kapelus, 2004, p. 87). Hamann and Kapelus argue that the criterion of social justice needs to be applied in any assessment of CSR narratives and practices. Inclusion of fairness would mean that 'companies can only claim to be socially responsible if their direct, indirect, and cumulative impact on society benefits the most vulnerable and worst off' (Hamann & Kapelus, 2004, p. 87). Drawing on a case study of platinum and chrome mining in South Africa, the authors acknowledge that companies provide important education, health and social business development resources but have 'had little impact on the root causes of social problems surrounding the mine' (Hamann & Kapelus, 2004, p. 87).

Business and peace

Notwithstanding these limitations, some analysts suggest the scope of CSR should be widened even further to encompass a proactive role for business in the promotion of peace building. Avenues for corporate engagement in peace building can be categorised into two forms: indirect action (intended to soften the adverse effects of violence) and direct action (intended to stop violence or prevent a situation from becoming violent) (Oetzel et al., 2007, pp. 341–3).

Regarding the 'indirect' roles that corporations can play in peace building, Fort and Schipani (2004, p. 11) argue that corporations are engines that produce jobs, and with them the economic and social benefits that follow from employed individuals. They identify three connections linking business and peace building:

- standard ethical business practices may reduce bloodshed;
- legal rules undergirding corporate governance may be reconsidered to include peace as a governance *telos*; and
- business could become a more important dimension of foreign policy.

Through these links, Fort and Schipani identify four specific contributions business can make to peace, 'fostering economic development, exercising track two diplomacy, adopting external evaluation principles, and nourishing a sense of community' (Fort & Schipani, 2004, p. 4). Such contributions, they argue, can contribute to the development of a more harmonious environment.

Similarly, Gerson (2001, p. 103) argues that business has an important role to play in peace building as 'conflict settlement requires the injection of hope born of employment and economic opportunity' and 'only the private sector can provide this over the long term'. The heart of Gerson's argument is that jobs and economic opportunity offer hope to the 'seemingly disinherited', with new incentives to maintain stability and break the cycle of violence (Gerson, 2001, p. 109). In addition to the benefits of employment and economic opportunity, Gerson claims that the characteristics of business logic can be useful in any conflict management process, through 'the provision of managerial know-how and expertise to enable all the actors in the field – the World Bank, the UN, and civil society – to operate in a more streamlined and synergistic fashion' (Gerson, 2001, p. 107).

Other analysts suggest that business is already playing a direct role in peace building through pre-existing commitments to CSR. As Sherman (2001, p. 3) argues, 'more than is commonly recognized, some private sector actors have undertaken policies that seek to promote human rights and environmental health and to mitigate or avoid conflict in host communities'.

While corporations are not generally imagined as peace builders, analysts also suggest there could be a 'business case' for engagement to this end (Oetzel *et al.*, 2007, pp. 336–7). Corporations could gain a comparative advantage through: the reduction of employee turnover rates; avoidance of costs associated with loss of assets or interruption to business activities; the reduction of insurance risk premiums; improved relations with communities and host governments; and preferential opportunities for expansion (Oetzel *et al.*, 2007, pp. 336–7); minimizing safety risks to employees; cost savings from expenditure on security and the destruction of property; and even preventing the loss of ability to operate (Laplante & Spears, 2008; Rettberg, 2007). Nonetheless, peace can also present costs for business such as new taxation requirements to support post-conflict reconstruction efforts (Rettberg, 2007, p. 465) and increased competition. This places limits on the value of appealing solely to the profit motive of firms as a means of encouraging engagement in peace building.

Critics and the search for an alternative framework

Given that there are opportunities and incentives for business in peace building, yet identified limitations to CSR, it is important to question the value of expanding corporate responsibilities to include violence and peace. Hilson (2012, p. 132) argues that in considering new roles for business in conflict, it is important to remember why businesses are operating in difficult investment environments in the first place, such as the numerous economic incentives it may provide, tax breaks, low royalty payments, as well as lax regulatory environment and pollution control requirements (Kepore & Imbun, 2011, p. 221). More broadly, Kemp (2010, p. 10) asks to what extent participatory, people-centred development can be undertaken by a profit-orientated organisation.

This is an important question for two reasons. First, struggles over natural resources often pit rich against poor, or majority against minority, within regions, countries and transnationally (Escobar, 2006, p. 7). Second, resource conflicts are often characterised by the interplay of 'capitalistic economic models, on the one hand, and some sort of mobilization around, or in defence of, local cultures on the other' (Escobar, 2006, p. 7). To understand resource conflicts, therefore, we must draw attention not only to the unequal distribution of income and material resources but also to 'what could be called "cultural distribution conflicts", namely, those that arise from the relative power, or powerlessness, accorded to various cultures and cultural practices in historical context' (Escobar, 2006, p. 8).

That is why this book maintains a focus on the interdependence between business and society in previous theorisations of CSR (Porter & Kramer, 2006), while advocating corporate engagement with justice claims beyond material redistribution of benefits. The aim is to explore whether this type of engagement can result in a greater alignment between CSR and peace building, and what this may look like in practice.

Bruno Latour's (2005) *Reassembling the Social* has been instrumental in the development of the arguments presented in this book. As his theory of the social posits, 'it cannot be construed as a kind of material or domain' (Latour, 2005, p. 1). Latour's analysis of the 'social' calls into question what he considers the default position of sociology that draws on terms such as 'society', 'social order', and 'social practice' to distinguish it from other domains such as economics, geography, biology, psychology, law, science and politics (Latour, 2005, p. 3). Latour argues that there is 'no distinct domain of reality to which the label "social" or "society" could be attributed' (2005, p. 4). His aim is thus to redefine sociology not as the 'science of the social', but as the tracing of associations (Latour, 2005, p. 1).

Latour's understanding of the 'social' as a 'very peculiar movement of re-association and reassembling' (Latour, 2005, p. 6) enables a more holistic and complex account of CSR. This is because Latour argues for an analysis of the 'social' itself, rather than relying on a variety of other concepts such as 'globalisation' and 'power' to explain isolated dynamics. This study takes a Latourian approach by conceptualising the 'social' within CSR as 'a type of momentary association which is characterized by the way it gathers together into new shapes' (Latour, 2005, p. 65). While not dismissing the importance of other paradigms, these are only able to provide partial critiques of the interaction between the field of CSR and the context in which it is implemented. This can result in the sidelining of other important factors, which may play a role in the outcome of CSR policies and programmes. As Escobar (1995, p. xviii) argues, 'local talk about development is not only about development per se, but about history and culture – about the State, citizenship, difference, knowledge, and exploitation'.

Investigating the use of the 'social' enables a conceptualisation of CSR as interdependent with the political, economic, legal and cultural context in which it is implemented. When the 'social' is scrutinised, rather than taken for granted in the analysis of CSR, one can begin to see how the field is both contributor to, and participant in, a specific context. From this perspective, CSR cannot operate somewhere above 'society' in order to then contribute to 'it'. Reframing CSR with reference to Latour's concept of the social, CSR can no longer be understood – as it currently is – as an engagement between a neutral outside organisation and some abstract notion of society. Rather, large resource sites are understood as deeply embedded in a diverse range of actors and institutions with their own histories, interests and agendas. This includes, for example, national governments that set the rules of corporate–community engagement and are ultimately responsible for regulating the behaviour of corporations, and the national military, which might become involved through the provision of security.

Likewise, it is important to note that extractive companies are not homogeneous entities either. While classical and neoclassical theories depicted the firm as 'simply a set of production units responding to competitive initiatives in accordance with the law of diminishing returns' (Yeung, 2005, pp. 307–8), alternative conceptions portray the firm as a 'dynamic and evolving organization constructed through ongoing social relations and discursive struggles among social actors' (Yeung, 2005, p. 309). The most important point from Yeung's (2005, p. 307) analysis for the purpose of this study is that the 'firm serves as a relational institution that connects spatially differentiated actors in different places and regions'.

Another theoretical insight that has informed the analysis of CSR in this study is the question of the types of justice claims it aims to target. Nancy Fraser (2008) illuminates the importance of this question by outlining a three-dimensional theory of justice. Fraser (2008, p. 16) defines justice in general as parity of participation whereby 'justice requires social arrangements that permit all to participate as peers in social life'. Fraser (2008, p. 16) suggests there are three obstacles to participatory parity, each representing a distinct species of injustice that subsequently requires a different remedy (outlined in Table 1.1).

The purpose of drawing on Fraser's three-dimensional theory of justice is not to highlight the contradictory nature of these claims when they are made simultaneously, but to illustrate the type of justice claims that CSR has been designed to redress. This book argues that CSR has primarily been structured according to a distributive justice framework through the delivery of material resources

Table 1.1 Fraser's three-dimensional theory of justice

Injustice	Source of injustice	Remedy
Distributive injustice or maldistribution of resources	Economic structures, e.g., class structure of society	Redistribution
Status inequality or misrecognition	Institutionalised hierarchies of cultural value	Recognition
Exclusion from the community of those entitled to representation/unequal voice in public deliberations and fair representation in public decision-making	Political constitution of society/ boundaries of the political community/the procedures that structure public processes of contestation	Representation

Source: Summarised from Fraser (2008, pp. 16–18).

to communities affected by an extractive project (for example, the allocation of money through a landowner trust fund, or the provision of funding for new infrastructure or services). While material resources are far from inconsequential, armed conflicts are often also characterised by claims for cultural and political justice and the most effective remedy might be a wise balance between redistribution, recognition and redistribution.

In combining a more complex understanding of the 'social' with the heterogeneity of justice discourses, we are plunged into larger debates about economic development and the problem of whether industrialisation can be achieved in a way that promotes social justice and environmental sustainability. In other words, it calls into question the processes which Escobar (1995, p. xii) refers to as 'tales of growth and capital' that are 'inherited by development economics from classical political economy, and elsewhere as "the Western Economy"'. Without this consideration, dominant Western principles of development as progress, industrial growth and consumption go unhindered which can undermine 'many, if not most, of the current proposals for sustainability and for moving to a post-carbon age' (Escobar, 1995, p. xii).

While the approach to CSR outlined in this book does not offer an 'alternative to development' per se, it could represent one step in the search for replacements. It is argued that one of the ways this might be made possible is through a stronger focus on mutuality and justice by the key agents of industrial growth: large extractive companies. Two explanations offered in this book for why CSR has not been successful in facilitating this process to date are: an ambiguous understanding of the 'social', and a disproportionate focus on distributive justice.

This analysis is more optimistic than previous accounts of extractive industries, such as Filer's (1990, p. 3) 'time bomb hypothesis', which suggests mines across PNG will generate the same volatile mixture of grievances and frustrations, leading to a major conflict after approximately 15 years of operation. Nonetheless, the analysis is critical in tone and is connected to what is referred to as 'transition studies' (Escobar, 1995, p. xix), in that it calls for a 'radical cultural and institutional transformation' (Escobar, 1995, p. xx). Therefore, while the analysis is not based on a perspective of the resource curse as inevitable, it complements broader assertions for 'a new, holistic culture, or even the coming of an entirely new era beyond the modern dualist (for example, Macy 2007; Goodwin 2007), reductionist (for example, Kauffman 2008), and economic (for example, Schafer 2008) age' (Escobar, 1995, p. xx).

To substantiate these arguments it is important to consider the roles and impacts of extractive companies in real conflicts. Otherwise, advocating potential roles for business in peace is at best hypothetical, and at worst, may produce more harm than good.

The scope of the study: Bougainville and West Papua compared

The empirical focus of the research presented here is the business activities of three large extractive companies and their corporate partners operating in Bougainville (PNG) and West Papua[3] (Indonesia):

- Bougainville Copper Limited (BCL); the operator of the Bougainville copper mine located in Panguna, Autonomous Region of Bougainville, PNG. Ownership of BCL consists of 53.58 per cent Rio Tinto, the PNG Government 19.06 per cent, and public shareholders 27.36 per cent (Bougainville Copper Limited, 2012).
- PT Freeport Indonesia (PTFI, referred to hereafter as 'Freeport'); operator of the Ertsberg and Grasberg copper and gold mines located in Papua Province, Indonesia. Freeport is owned by Freeport-McMoRan Copper & Gold, 90.64 per cent and the Indonesian Government 9.36 per cent (Freeport-McMoRan Copper & Gold, n.d.). Rio Tinto also has a significant joint venture interest in the Grasberg mine, entitling the company to '40 per cent share of production above specified levels until 2021 and 40 per cent of all production after 2021' (Rio Tinto, 2008).
- BP (British Petroleum or 'beyond petroleum'); operator of the Tangguh Liquefied Natural Gas (LNG) project located in the Bintuni Bay area of West Papua Province, Indonesia. BP Berau Ltd (100 per cent owned by BP) operates Tangguh 'with two other wholly-owned BP subsidiaries – BP Muturi Holdings B.V. and BP Wiriagar Ltd. – giving the company a 37.16% share in Tangguh LNG' (BP, 2015).

Bougainville and West Papua experienced two of 16 recorded civil wars around the world linked to natural resource development during the period 1990–2002 (Ross, 2003, p. 18). Yet these locations have been under-represented in scholarly studies of the role of CSR in resource conflict, despite the fact that they witnessed two of the most protracted and complex conflicts in the Asia-Pacific region. Much of the existing CSR literature focuses on Africa and in particular, the case of Shell in Nigeria (Akpan, 2006; Ite, 2004; Omeje, 2005; Pegg, 1999; Watts, 2004; Zalik, 2004).

By connecting the motivations, intentions and constraints of executives from large extractive companies with local perspectives, this research builds on existing scholarship to provide a detailed account of the social consequences of this field of business practices. In this sense the aim is to contribute to knowledge of the causes of resource conflict in Bougainville and West Papua specifically, as well as to elucidate lessons that might be learned from these particular conflicts for the development and implementation of beneficial CSR in other locations.

Bougainville and West Papua are particularly valuable cases to examine as they both provide a 50-year longitudinal perspective over which to consider how CSR might be reconceptualised to more effectively contribute to peaceful development. The history and current context of the conflicts in Bougainville and West Papua have been the subject of significant and distinguished study in which the connections between the relevant MNCs and the dynamics of the two conflicts have been identified (Ballard, 2001; Ballard & Banks, 2009; Braithwaite *et al.*, 2010a, 2010b; Filer, 1990; Regan 2003, 2010). The intention of the research presented in this book is not to attempt to rewrite or duplicate this work. Rather, by combining prior research with new fieldwork, the aim is to analyse the potential for the association between resource development and armed conflict to be somehow transformed to facilitate peace.

It is important to recall, however, that CSR has evolved considerably since the entry of two of the case study companies into Bougainville and West Papua. The point of this analysis is neither to berate the case study companies, nor to pinpoint which model of CSR they may have deployed at each historical moment. Rather, the purpose is to explore the potential possibilities that might emerge through corporate engagement with their associations with sources of conflict and the various measures they may draw on to mitigate and/or resolve these. Moreover, the case studies of Bougainville and West Papua are not highlighted because there are gaps in the existing literature about the details of the two conflicts, but rather the case studies have been selected as mechanisms through which to consider the possibilities that exist for large corporations to contribute to peace.

The findings presented draw on Merry's (2006) notion of 'de-territorialized ethnography'. In an era of globalisation, the research sites of social scientists are rarely fixed in single or discretely bounded locations. This development has increasingly required scholars to stretch the methodological traditions of their disciplines in an effort to connect international regulation with local justice (Merry, 2006). Merry (2006, p. 29) suggests that a useful way of exploring the impact of placeless global phenomena (such as international human rights discourse) is to 'locate sites where global, national, and local processes are revealed in the social life of small groups'. That is why this study spans nine countries, yet encompasses a detailed focus on two particular sites. In total, 93[4] people participated in this study[5] (for a breakdown of participants in the Bougainville and West Papua cases, see Appendices 1 and 2) across six main phases of data collection[6] with distinct aims and findings (see Appendix 3).

Limits and conclusion

The stakeholders in the two case studies were numerous and I did not interview all of them. Indonesian, Australian and PNG Government officials are another group of stakeholders who could have been included in this research. Their views as the regulators who set the terms and conditions of resource extraction would add another layer of verification and would likely provide additional (divergent) perspectives. Data were also not collected from individuals associated with the Indonesian and PNG sides of the two conflicts. Many Indonesian and PNG nationals have been directly affected by the conflicts and most likely hold views about how the wealth derived from the three resource projects should be equitably shared. While the absence of these voices represents a gap in the data collected in this study, documenting the perspectives of local communities most directly affected by resource development has been consciously prioritised. As will become evident throughout the remaining chapters, local communities are often excluded from decision-making and it is their voices that are least likely to be heard. One of the aims of this research has been to begin to address this type of marginalisation. However, this is not to say that other perspectives are less valid and Chapter 11 will further explore some of the implications of this empirical constraint.

An important limitation of the data collected for the West Papua case specifically is that the researcher did not visit local communities surrounding BP's Tangguh LNG project. During her visit to West Papua in June 2010, protests were taking place across both Papua and West Papua provinces. Based on local advice about the likelihood of the protests turning violent, a decision was made not to travel to the western province. The consequence is that the West Papua data include significantly more voices from non-governmental organisation (NGO) workers in comparison to the Bougainville case. While several Papuans with direct experience of this project were interviewed, the findings presented on the Tangguh project are not as substantial as they are for the BCL and Freeport cases. Nonetheless, this small data set and synthesis of secondary materials can be used as a basis for further research on the social and environmental impacts of Tangguh. Further, considering the dearth of contemporary primary data about Papuan perspectives on the Tangguh project, even the small amount of data presented in this book represents a worthwhile contribution to knowledge.

By reframing CSR in terms of interdependence throughout the rest of this book, a way in which CSR might be reconfigured to incorporate some of the goals of peace building will be discussed. The first step in this journey begins with an introduction to the cases of Bougainville and West Papua.

Notes

1 See Appendices 1 and 2 for a breakdown of participants.
2 This study draws on a broad definition of 'peace building' as the creation of a 'struc-ture of peace based on justice, equity and cooperation' (Gawerc, 2006, p. 49). The term itself has a relatively short history, only becoming popularised in 1992 follow-ing Boutrous Boutros-Ghali's document, *An Agenda for Peace, Preventive Diplomacy, Peacemaking and Peace-Keeping*. Boutros-Ghali originally defined peace building as applicable only to 'post-conflict' situations with a particular emphasis on projects that bring states involved in international conflict together (Boutous-Ghali, 1992). Since the early 1990s, however, the term 'post-conflict' has been problematised as conflict is seldom 'solved' (D'Costa & Ford, 2008, p. 11). Consequently, the term peace building now encompasses a broader range of activities and actors, with relevance to all phases of a conflict (Gawerc, 2006, p. 439). This may include, for example, 'establishing dispute resolution mechanisms and cooperative arrangements as well as meeting people's basic economic, social, cultural and humanitarian needs' (Reith & Zimmer, 2004, p. 5). It is in this broader sense that the term peace building will be used throughout this book.
3 Various names have been used for West Papua which may be more familiar to the reader including: West New Guinea, Irian Jaya, West Irian and Papua. Comprising the Bird's Head Peninsula (West Papua Province) and the remaining and larger areas of the island (Papua Province), this book uses the name 'West Papua' to refer to the entire territory.
4 Including seven participants from the corporate headquarters of multinational extract-ive companies beyond the case study companies.
5 To accommodate confidentiality concerns, an indication of the types of people inter-viewed has been supplied in Appendices 1 and 2. Yet where there is any even slight worry that reference to types of people (for example, a 'religious leader') for both cases might compromise the informants' confidentiality, only coded identification (for example, B6, WP17) will be used.
6 For a more substantial discussion of the methodology used in this study, see McKenna (2012).

Bibliography

Akpan, W. 2006. 'Between responsibility and rhetoric: Some consequences of CSR practice in Nigeria's Oil Province', *Development Southern Africa*, vol. 23, no. 2, pp. 223–38.

Aspinall, E. 2007. 'The construction of grievance: Natural resources and identity in a separatist conflict', *Journal of Conflict Resolution*, vol. 51, no. 6, pp. 950–72.

Ballard, C. 2001. 'Human rights and the mining sector in Indonesia: A baseline study'. London: International Institute for Environment and Development. <http://pubs.iied.org/pdfs/G00929.pdf> [accessed 7 May 2015].

Ballard, C. & Banks, G. 2009. 'Between a rock and a hard place: Corporate strategy at the Freeport mine in Papua, 2001–2006', in B. P. Resosudarmo & F. Jotzo (eds.), *Working with Nature against Poverty: Development, Resources and the Environment in Eastern Indonesia*. Singapore: ISEAS Publishing, pp. 147–77.

Ballentine, K. & Nitzschke, H. 2003. *Beyond Greed and Grievances: Policy Lessons from Studies in the Political Economy of Armed Conflict*. New York: International Peace Academy.

Banks, G. 2008. 'Understanding "resource" conflicts in Papua New Guinea', *Asia Pacific Viewpoint*, vol. 49, no. 1, pp. 23–34.

Bannon, I. & Collier, P. (eds.) 2003. *Natural Resources and Violent Conflict: Options and Actions*. Washington, DC: World Bank, Washington.

Berman, J. 2000. 'Boardrooms and bombs', *Harvard International Review*, vol. 22, no. 3, pp. 1–28.

Bougainville Copper Limited. 2012. 'Bougainville Copper Limited'. <www.bcl.com.pg/about-us/about-the-company/> [accessed 13 July 2015].

Boutros-Ghali, B. 1992. 'An agenda for peace: Preventive diplomacy, peacemaking and peace-keeping'. <www.unrol.org/files/a_47_277.pdf> [accessed 22 May 2015].

BP. 2015. 'Tangguh LNG'. <www.bp.com/en_id/indonesia/bp-in-indonesia/tangguh-lng.html> [accessed 13 July 2015].

Braithwaite, J., Braithwaite, V., Cookson, M. & Dunn, L. 2010a. *Anomie and Violence: Non-Truth and Reconciliation in Indonesian Peacebuilding*. Canberra: ANU Press.

Braithwaite, J., Charlesworth, H., Reddy, P. & Dunn, L. 2010b. *Reconciliation and Architectures of Commitment: Sequencing Peace in Bougainville*. Canberra: ANU Press.

Carroll, A. B. 1991. 'The pyramid of corporate social responsibility: Toward the moral management of organizational stakeholders', *Business Horizons*, July–Aug., pp. 39–48.

Cheney, G., Roper, J. & May, S. K. 2007. 'Overview', in S. K. May, G. Cheney & J. Roper (eds.), *The Debate Over Corporate Social Responsibility*. Oxford: Oxford University Press, pp. 3–12.

Collier, P. & Hoeffler, A. 2005. 'Resource rents, governance, and conflict', *Journal of Conflict Resolution*, vol. 49, no. 4, pp. 625–633.

Dahlsrud, A. 2008. 'How corporate social responsibility is defined: An analysis of 37 definitions', *Corporate Social Responsibility and Environmental Management*, vol. 15, no. 1, pp. 1–13.

D'Costa, B. & Ford, J. 2008. 'Terminology matters: Statebuilding, nationbuilding and peacebuilding'. Centre for International Governance and Justice, Issues Paper 6. <http://regnet.anu.edu.au/sites/default/files/CIGJ-IssuesPaper6-full.pdf> [accessed 25 May 2015].

Escobar, A. 1995. *Encountering Development: The Making and Unmaking of the Third World*. Princeton: Princeton University Press.

Escobar, A. 2006. 'Difference and conflict in the struggle over natural resources: A political ecology framework', *Development*, vol. 49, no. 3, pp. 6–13.

Filer, C. 1990. 'The Bougainville rebellion, the mining industry and the process of social disintegration in Papua New Guinea', in R. J. May & M. Spriggs (eds.), *The Bougainville Crisis*. Bathurst: Crawford House Press, pp. 73–112.

Fort, T. L. & Schipani, C. A. 2004. *The Role of Business in Fostering Peaceful Societies*. Cambridge: Cambridge University Press.

Fraser, N. 2008. *Scales of Justice: Reimagining Political Space in a Globalizing World*. Cambridge: Polity Press.

Freeport-McMoRan Copper & Gold. n.d. 'Grasberg Minerals District'. <www.fcx.com/operations/grascomplx.htm> [accessed 13 July 2015].

Frynas, J. G. 2005. The false developmental promise of corporate social responsibility: Evidence from multinational oil companies', *International Affairs*, vol. 81, no. 3, pp. 581–98.

Gawerc, M. I. 2006. 'Peace-building: Theoretical and concrete perspectives', *Peace & Change*, vol. 31, no. 4, pp. 435–78.

Gerson, A. 2001. 'Peace building: The private sector's role', *American Journal of International Law*, vol. 95, no. 1, pp. 102–19.

Gilberthorpe, E. 2013. 'In the shadow of industry: A study of culturization in Papua New Guinea', *Journal of the Royal Anthropological Institute*, vol. 19, no. 2, pp. 261–78.

Gilberthorpe, E. & Banks, G. 2012. 'Development on whose terms? CSR discourse and social realities in Papua New Guinea's extractive industries sector', *Resources Policy*, vol. 37, no. 2, pp. 185–93.

Goodwin, B. 2007. *Nature's Due: Healing our Fragmented Culture*. Edinburgh: Floris Books.

Hamann, R. & Kapelus, P. 2004. 'Corporate social responsibility in mining in Southern Africa: Fair accountability or just greenwash?' *Development*, vol. 47, no. 3, pp. 85–92.

Hilson, G. 2012. 'Corporate social responsibility in the extractive industries: Experiences from developing countries', *Resources Policy*, vol. 37, no. 2, pp. 131–7.

Hook, J. & Ganguly, R. 2000. 'Multinational corporations and ethnic conflict: Theory and experience', *Nationalism and Ethnic Politics*, vol. 6, no. 1, pp. 48–71.

Idemudia, U. 2010. 'Rethinking the role of corporate social responsibility in the Nigerian oil conflict: The limits of CSR', *Journal of International Development*, vol. 22, no. 7, pp. 833–45.

Idemudia, U. & Ite, U. E. 2006. 'Corporate–community relations in Nigeria's oil industry: Challenges and imperatives', *Corporate Social Responsibility and Environmental Management*, vol. 13, no. 4, pp. 194–206.

Imbun, B. Y. 2007. 'Cannot manage without the "significant other": Mining, corporate social responsibility and local communities in Papua New Guinea', *Journal of Business Ethics*, vol. 73, no. 2, pp. 177–92.

International Association for Public Participation (IAP2). n.d. 'IAP2: Good public participation results in better decisions'. International Association for Public Participation, Louisville. <www.iap2.org/> [accessed 7 May 2015].

Ite, U. 2004. 'Multinationals and corporate social responsibility in developing countries: A case study of Shell of Nigeria', *Corporate Social Responsibility and Environmental Management*, vol. 11, no. 1, pp. 1–11.

Jamali, D. & Mirshak, R. 2010. 'Business–conflict linkages: Revisiting MNCs, CSR, and conflict', *Journal of Business Ethics*, vol. 93, no. 3, pp. 443–64.

Kauffman, S. A. 2008. *Reinventing the Sacred: A New View of Science, Reason, and Religion*. New York: Basic Books.

Kemp, D. 2009. 'Mining and community development: Problems and possibilities of local-level practice', *Community Development Journal*, vol. 45, no. 2, pp. 198–218.

Kemp, D. 2010. 'Community relations in the global mining industry: Exploring the internal dimensions of externally oriented work', *Corporate Social Responsibility and Environmental Management*, vol. 17, no. 1, pp. 1–14.

Kepore, K. P. & Imbun, B. Y. 2011. 'Mining and stakeholder engagement discourse in a Papua New Guinea mine', *Corporate Social Responsibility and Environmental Management*, vol. 18, no. 4, pp. 220–33.

Laplante, L. & Spears, S. 2008. 'Out of the conflict zone: The case for community consent processes in the extractive sector', *Yale Human Rights and Development Law Journal*, vol. 11, no. 1, pp. 69–116.

Latour, B. 2005. *Reassembling the Social: An Introduction to Actor-Network Theory*. Oxford: Oxford University Press.

McKenna, K. 2012. 'Interdependent engagement: Corporate social responsibility in Bougainville and Papua'. PhD Thesis, Australian National University, Canberra.

Macy, J. 2007. *World as Lover, World as Self: Courage for Global Justice and Ecological Renewal*. Berkeley: Parallax Press.

Marquis, C., Glynn, M. A. & Davis, G. F. 2007. 'Community isomorphism and corporate social action', *Academy of Management Review*, vol. 32, no. 3, pp. 925–45.

Merry, S. E. 2006. *Human Rights & Gender Violence: Translating International Law into Local Justice*. Chicago: University of Chicago Press.

NRGI (Natural Resource Governance Institute). 2010. The Natural Resource Charter, 2nd edn. New York: NRGI. <http://naturalresourcecharter.org/> [accessed 7 May 2015].

Oetzel, J, Getz, K. & Ladek, S. 2007. 'The role of multinational enterprises in responding to violent conflict: A conceptual model and framework for research', *American Business Law Journal*, vol. 44, no. 2, pp. 331–58.

Oetzel, J., Westermann-Behaylo, M., Koerber, C., Fort, T. L. & Rivera, J. 2010. 'Business and peace: Sketching the terrain', *Journal of Business Ethics*, vol. 89, supp. 4, pp. 351–73.

Omeje, K. 2005. 'Oil conflict in Nigeria: Contending issues and perspectives of the local Niger Delta people', *New Political Economy*, vol. 10, no. 3, pp. 321–32.

Pegg, S. 1999. 'The cost of doing business: Transnational corporations and violence in Nigeria', *Security Dialogue*, vol. 30, no. 4, pp. 473–84.

Porter, M. E. & Kramer, M. R. 2006. 'The link between competitive advantage and corporate social responsibility', *Harvard Business Review*, vol. 84, no. 12, pp. 78–92.

Regan, A. J. 2003. 'The Bougainville conflict: Political and economic agendas', in K. Ballentine & J. Sherman (eds.), *The Political Economy of Armed Conflict: Beyond Greed and Grievance*. Boulder, CO: Lynne Rienner, pp. 133–66.

Regan, A. J. 2010. *Light Intervention: Lessons from Bougainville*. Washington, DC: US Institute of Peace Press.

Reith, L. & Zimmer, M. 2004. 'Transnational corporations and conflict prevention: The impact of norms on private actors'. Centre for International Relations/Peace and Conflict Studies, University of Tübingen. <https://publikationen.uni-tuebingen. de/xmlui/bitstream/handle/10900/47310/pdf/tap43.pdf?sequence=1&isAllowed=y> [accessed 25 May 2015].

Rettberg, A. 2007. 'The private sector and peace in El Salvador, Guatemala, and Colombia', *Journal of Latin American Studies*, vol. 39, no. 3, pp. 463–94.

Rio Tinto. 2008. 'Operations & financial report'. <www.riotinto.com/annualreport2007/ operationsfinancialreview/copper_group/operations/grasberg/index.html> [accessed 13 July 2015].

Ross, M. 2001. 'Does oil hinder democracy?' *World Politics*, 53, April, pp. 325–61.

Ross, M. 2003. 'The natural resource curse: How wealth can make you poor', in I. Bannon & P. Collier (eds.), *Natural Resources and Violent Conflict: Options and Actions*. Washington, DC: World Bank, pp. 17–42.

Sachs, J. D. & Warner, A. M. 2001. 'Natural resources and economic development: The curse of natural resources', *European Economic Review*, vol. 45, pp. 827–38.

Schafer, P. 2008. *Revolution or Renaissance: Making the Transition from an Economic Age to a Cultural Age*. Ottawa: University of Ottawa Press.

Sherman, J. 2001. 'Private sector actors in zones of conflict: Research challenges and policy responses'. International Peace Academy Workshop Report. <www.fafoarkiv.no/ nsp/ipa-report.pdf> [accessed 13 July 2015].

United Nations Environment Programme (UNEP). 2009. *From Conflict to Peacebuilding: The Role of Natural Resources and the Environment*. <www.unep.org/pdf/pcdmb_ policy_01.pdf> [accessed 7 May 2015].

Watts, M. 2004. 'Resource curse? Governmentality, oil and power in the Niger Delta, Nigeria', *Geopolitics*, vol. 9, no. 1, pp. 50–80.

Yeung, H. W. C. 2005. 'The firm as social networks: An organisational perspective', *Growth and Change*, vol. 36, no. 3, pp. 307–28.

Zalik, A. 2004. 'The Niger Delta: "Petro violence" and "partnership development"', *Review of African Political Economy*, vol. 31, no. 101, pp. 401–24.

Zandvliet, L. 2005. *Opportunities for Synergy: Conflict Transformation and the Corporate Agenda*. Berghof Research Center for Constructive Conflict Management. <www.berghof-foundation.org/fileadmin/redaktion/Publications/Handbook/Articles/zandvliet_handbook.pdf> [accessed 7 May 2015].

2 Conflict in Bougainville and West Papua

Introduction

This chapter introduces the geographic, cultural and historical background to the Bougainville and West Papua conflicts. In particular, the chapter highlights the way in which the peoples of Bougainville and West Papua became connected to the nation-states of PNG and Indonesia respectively, and the role of natural resources in these processes. This is not to suggest that natural resources have been the only 'connector' in these relationships, nor that resource extraction occurs amid untouched, peaceful and homogeneous societies. My purpose in tracing the connections between resource development and nationalism in the two case studies is to provide a springboard for considering a whole range of other connections between actors and institutions that feed into the creation of conditions vulnerable to conflict. As argued by Latour, 'the first feature of the social world is this constant tracing of boundaries by people over some other people' (2005, p. 28). This 'tracing' evolves over time whereby groups of people are constantly formed and re-formed in relation to ideas, people, processes and objects. Examples identified in the Bougainville and West Papua cases include: trade; religion; employment; colonialism; geopolitics; law; elections; money; copper; gold; natural gas; pipelines and pylons.

What follows is a broad, not necessarily linear introduction to the land and peoples of Bougainville and West Papua. The aim is to sketch some of the dynamics that have tied 'Bougainvillean' and 'Papuan' societies to larger nation-states. The history, geography and anthropology of Bougainville and West Papua have been the subject of significant and distinguished study (Ballard, 2001; Ballard & Banks, 2009; Braithwaite *et al.*, 2010a, 2010b; Denoon, 2000; Filer, 1990; Regan, 2003, 2010; Ogan 1996, 2005; Oliver, 1973, 1991). It is with some hesitancy that I characterise this chapter as an historical introduction. Such analysis has been undertaken with much greater rigour, depth and excellence elsewhere. The value of this work, I hope, rests in its comparative analysis, and connections made with broader, international theory on CSR, resource conflict and peace building. Making these connections results in inevitable trade-offs in terms of local integrity. However, it is my firm belief that the significance of the local is most starkly drawn when connected to issues of broad significance. What can be learned from the Bougainville and West Papua cases that might assist in the creation of peaceful, prosperous futures for people in those locations, as well as far beyond? All this is to say that any historical scholar would no doubt find the following summary lacking. It is my intention to write generally, dealing in greater depth with points and issues that resonate directly with the themes of this book. It should certainly not be read as a holistic account or authority either in terms of history or anthropology. Those seeking such detail are encouraged to consult the sources cited.

Bougainville and PNG

The Autonomous Region of Bougainville is located in the South-West Pacific (see Figure 2.1). It comprises two main islands, Buka and Bougainville, and numerous surrounding smaller islands.[1] Bougainville is the larger of the two main islands, while Buka is smaller but densely populated. Together, Bougainville and Buka are about 250 km long and approximately 64 km across at their widest point (Oliver, 1973, p. 7). Bougainville is geologically, linguistically and culturally a part of the Solomon Islands chain, but was controversially integrated into the largest nation of the Pacific Islands, PNG. Bougainville is located 1,000 km from Port Moresby (the capital of PNG) making it PNG's most geographically remote province. Despite Bougainville's small size, the province is both environmentally and culturally diverse, consisting of approximately 40 different land systems (Oliver, 1973, p. 8) and 25 distinct languages (Regan, 2010, p. 7).

Bougainville was first colonised by Germany in 1884 in an effort to spread the German presence in the Pacific east from PNG and into the northern part of the Solomon Islands. While Britain was extending its colonial footprint into the southern end of the Solomons, two Anglo-German declarations in 1886 'divided the Solomons so that Buka and Bougainville, the Shortlands Choiseul, Isabel, Ontong Java and part of the Floridas came under German protection' (Griffin, 2005, p. 75). A convention in 1899–1900, dealing mainly with the sovereignty of Western Samoa, then resulted in a multi-faceted agreement that moved the German protected area 'back south of Bougainville to what is the boundary of Papua New Guinea today' (Griffin, 2005, p. 75). Germany therefore maintained control of the islands of Buka and Bougainville, while the rest of what is now known as the Solomon Islands were recognised as British Territory (see Griffin, 2005). This division led to Bougainville's administrative separation from the northern part of the Solomon Islands, despite the existence of strong geographic, cultural and trade ties between the two.

The administration of Bougainville brought new foreign influences, and the islands became stages for a variety of colonial struggles. In 1905, Germany established its first government station on Bougainville, which was followed by the development of copra plantations (Denoon, 2000, pp. 11–15). Yet the stronger foreign influence during this period were the Catholic missionaries who were encouraged by the German Administration as an inexpensive means of pacification, to complement the presence of the European plantation owners (Ogan, 1996, p. 34). According to Oliver (1991, p. 93), the arrival of Europeans had

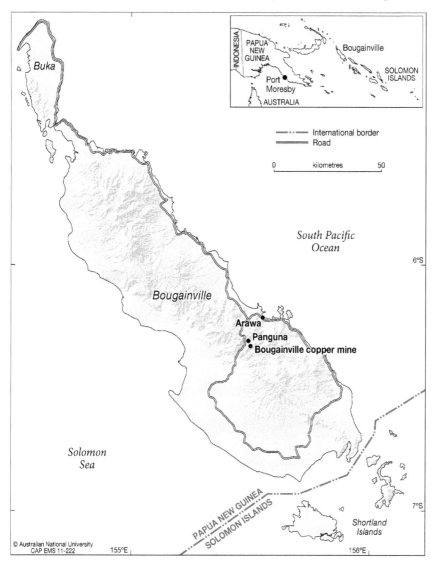

Figure 2.1 Map of Bougainville

both positive and negative consequences for the people of Bougainville. On the one hand, Europeans brought medical services and discouraged murder and warfare. On the other hand, new diseases were introduced and new tensions emerged through the employment of males on colonial plantations far from their place of origin (Oliver, 1991, p. 93).

At the start of the First World War, German control of Bougainville was disrupted by the arrival of an Australian expeditionary force (Braithwaite *et al.*,

2010b, p. 10). Formal control of Bougainville was later granted to Australia by the League of Nations in 1921 as part of its mandate over German New Guinea. Australian government activity during this period was limited and foreign rule was again disrupted following Japanese occupation in 1942.[2] The presence of the Japanese on Bougainville slowly built up from mid-1942 when there were rarely more than 50 Japanese personnel, to a maximum of 65,000 in 1943 (Regan, 2010, p. 10).

Following the Second World War, Australia[3] administered Bougainville as a part of the Trust Territory of New Guinea until PNG's eventual independence from Australia in 1975. During the post-war period, Australia became more strategically aware of the importance of New Guinea to security back home (Oliver, 1991, p. 78). The Australian Government believed that 'a more prosperous, better educated, and politically sophisticated indigenous population [of New Guinea] would provide a stronger shield against future aggression' (Oliver, 1991, p. 78). Mandated by the UN, the two previously separate territories of Papua (the southern half of what is now PNG) and New Guinea (the eastern half) had been brought together under Australian administration (National Museum of Australia, n.d.). This was subject to the requirement that its peoples would be protected and their rights and interests assured (Oliver, 1991, p. 78). Australian administration subsequently raised the hopes of villagers on Bougainville, who expected economic development and similar lifestyles to those of the Australians (Denoon, 2000, pp. 14–16).

Hopes that Australia would introduce better living standards were short-lived. Australia was criticised for removing the education policy introduced by the Germans, and for ineffective attempts to foster political participation (Denoon, 2000, p. 13). Although Australia sought to harness participation through the introduction of Local Government Councils, from the late 1950s they were poorly funded and the Administration was not trusted (Denoon, 2000, p. 13). This mistrust was partly attributable to work on the plantations, which were plagued by paternalism, racism and physical violence (Ogan, 1996, p. 39). The suffering experienced by Bougainvilleans during the Second World War was laid at the feet of the Australian Administration who were seen as either unwilling or unable to extend protection to Bougainvilleans (Oliver, 1991, p. 77). Ill feeling towards the Australian Administration continued into the 1960s, when 1,000 Nasioi[4] asked a UN visiting mission to transfer the mandate from Australia to the US (Denoon, 2000, p. 15).

Cultures and land

Bougainville was not a homogeneous society prior to European influences. According to Oliver, whatever cultural uniformity may have prevailed on Bougainville at the time of human settlement diversified greatly over time (1991, p. 95). Bougainville cultures are characterised by both similarities and variations. Echoing Latour's (2005, p. 27) notion of 'no group, only group formation', Bougainville's cultures are in a constant process of change (Ogan, 2005, p. 47).

Prior to colonisation, Bougainvilleans comprised small 'stateless' societies characterised as clan-based, land-holding groups made up of just 50 to 200 people (Regan, 2010, p. 8). There was no 'state-like' entity on Bougainville that provided stability and order (Regan, 2010, p. 12). Further, there was no pre-colonial 'tribal' solidarity and no pan-Bougainville identity (Denoon, 2000, p. 10). Instead, the principle of 'reciprocity' between societies provided social balance (Regan, 2010, p. 12). While groups were often hostile to one another, 'ties of kinship and common cult practices sometimes served to bind separate tribes into somewhat larger unities, but usually not for long at a time' (Oliver, 1991, p. 102). These larger social networks were 'made up of [a dozen or two] kinsfolk interrelated by *matrilineal*[5] ties, in which kinship is traced through women rather than through men' (Oliver, 1991, p. 104). In spite of these wider ties, Bougainvilleans tend to identify most strongly with their clan-based localised landowning group (Regan, 2010, p. 11).

Preceding colonisation, Bougainvilleans were mostly subsistence farmers, obtaining most of their food from their own gardens and supplementing this with fishing and hunting (Oliver, 1991, p. 95). Food gathering was labour intensive, with Siwai women spending 'about ten hours daily at it and men generally less' (Oliver, 1991, p. 96). Bougainvilleans also made use of magic to make crops grow and to attract fish, although this was only done once all practical knowledge, labour and skills had not achieved the desired results (Oliver, 1991, pp. 100–1). Trade through the exchange of goods was also common between inlanders and coast dwellers to provide access to resources that they themselves could not produce (Oliver, 1991, p. 101).

Bougainville's cultural diversity extends to principles of land tenure. According to Oliver (1991, p. 106), it is unlikely that any two Bougainvillean societies operate according to exactly the same principles. While a small proportion of land on Bougainville is 'alienated' by government or private acquisition, all other land in PNG (including Bougainville) is recognised by the PNG Government as customary owned[6] (Regan, 2010, p. 11). Land in Bougainville is thus owned 'under longstanding indigenous practices and norms that vary considerably between language and culture groups' (Regan, 2010, p. 11).

Mining and identity

In spite of Bougainville's cultural diversity, a more common or shared Bougainvillean identity began to emerge from the early twentieth century, and especially from the 1950s onwards (Regan, 2010, p. 13). Initially, Bougainvillean identity politics centred on colonial neglect under the Australian Administration, spurred by the presence of many 'outsiders' from elsewhere in PNG who came to Bougainville to work on colonial plantations (Regan, 2010, pp. 10–13). However, the general feeling of Australian neglect later became coupled with specific grievances related to mineral exploration and development.

The emergence of an identity via comparison to 'outsiders' advanced in the 1960s. Rich deposits of copper ore were discovered at Panguna, central

Bougainville in 1964.[7] This discovery led to the development of what became one of the world's largest open-cut mines. The Panguna mine was operated by BCL, and owned by Cozinc Rio Tinto Australia (CRA). CRA held majority ownership with 53 per cent; 28 per cent was floated on the Australian Stock Exchange; and 19 per cent was bought by the Australian Government for the future independent State of PNG (Dorney, 2000, p. 42). A large number of shares were also reserved for purchase by Bougainvilleans; however, it is unclear how many actually benefited (Braithwaite et al., 2010b, p. 12).

The establishment of the mine was opposed by many inhabitants of BCL's mine lease areas (Bedford & Mamak, 1977), which comprised about 33,700 acres of land (Brown, 1974, p. 26). Others resented the lack of consultation with the Bougainville leadership, despite the fact that there was no political entity to represent Bougainvilleans until the early 1970s (Regan, 2010, p. 11). Compounding early concerns related to increasing numbers of outsiders,[8] the development of the mine also led to the arrival of thousands of economic migrants who continued to adhere to ethnic and tribal alliances instead of developing class solidarity with other workers (Imbun, 2000). Illustrating the link made by Escobar (2006) between natural resources and the defence of local cultures, this worried the native residents who were anxious about the long-term viability of their traditions.

Mining-related grievances intensified once production at Panguna began in 1972. New concerns about large-scale mining developed, particularly with regard to the inequitable distribution of mining royalties and compensation. Little wealth was returned to Bougainville. In Chapter 4 we will see that this was due in large part to a requirement in PNG law, which 'had treated subsurface minerals as the property of the state' (Regan, 2010, p. 13). This legal view conflicted with indigenous land tenure systems, which rarely distinguished between surface and sub-surface rights, nor allowed those who did not share a cultural relationship to a tract of land to draw benefits from it permanently. Nonetheless, the legal view prevailed and this was reflected in the profit shares of the minerals produced at the mine. Only 5 per cent of the PNG Government's royalty of 1.25 per cent would be distributed among landowning groups (Ogan, 1999, p. 5).

The distribution of wealth to different parties subsequently enmeshed BCL in the processes that led to Bougainville's long-term political incorporation into PNG. Production of the mine began just prior to the election of the Australian Labor Party (ALP) as the Government of Australia. Under the leadership of Gough Whitlam, the ALP supported early independence for PNG. In this context, mining on Bougainville was then seen by the Australian Government as one way to create an economic base to finance an independent PNG nation. This was despite the fact that several years earlier, some Australian officials had recognised that Bougainville did not culturally belong to the New Guinea grouping (Denoon, 2000, p. 8).

Beyond economic inequality between Bougainville and PNG and between Bougainvilleans who enjoyed employment at the mine and those who didn't, mining brought social change. Disruptions were caused by what Filer refers to as the 'economic stratification of the landowning community' (1990, p. 116) that resulted in the distortion of the social structures of village life. In particular, village leaders could not match the new forms of cash income for young mine employees, or 'playboys' (Howley, 2002, p. 29). As a consequence, Howley (2002, p. 30) claims that young people began to discover a new socialisation process increasingly focused on imitating peers rather than aspiring to the cultural values of the elders in the community. The greatest impact of these changes was on the status of women in the community who had previously made significant contributions to social control (Regan, 1998, p. 275).

In the years immediately before PNG gained independence in 1975, there was talk of secession on Bougainville (Regan, 2010, p. 15). While Bougainville leaders attempted a unilateral declaration of independence in September 1975, there was no international recognition for their separatist agenda (Regan, 2010, p. 15). Further, support among Bougainvilleans for independence was not unanimous. Some welcomed large-scale mining and saw the benefits that could flow from integration into an independent PNG. These benefits proved significant as by the late 1980s, Bougainville was considered one of the most well-developed provinces of PNG.

A 'special case'?

Consideration as to whether the Bougainville conflict could have been prevented has generated debate as to whether there was anything to distinguish Bougainville from other districts of PNG at the time (Denoon, 2000, p. 27). Although there was some pro-independence sentiment on Bougainville, for example, Denoon (2000, p. 27) claims that in the 1960s similar expressions of political secessionism had been made elsewhere in PNG, including East New Britain, Papua, the Highlands and Trobriand Islands. Others such as Griffin (2005) argue that Bougainville was a 'special case', because of the dark skin colour[9] of the people of Bougainville, the island's isolation from Port Moresby as well as a belief in the superiority of the island's natural resources.

Debate as to whether there were specific warnings that mining-related grievances could escalate into a civil war extends into analyses of the Bougainville conflict itself. Regan (2010, p. 17) argues that the conflict was not initially about independence. Instead, as discussed earlier, concerns mainly focused on mine revenue shares as well as employment opportunities for Bougainvilleans.

According to Regan (2010, pp. 17–18), the origins of the conflict stemmed from complaints relating to mining revenue distribution and preferential employment treatment for two main groups of Bougainvilleans: customary landowners of land leased to BCL and young Bougainvillean mine workers. Regan offers two explanations for the intensity of emotion these grievances generated. Firstly, the Australian colonial officials at the time of exploration and initial establishment of the mine engaged inadequately with the clan lineages who owned the land in the mine lease areas. The second was a failure to increase rent and compensation payments, once the mine was operational, taking into account population growth within these clans over the life of the mine. Referring to Fraser's (2008) work we can identify the former as a claim for recognition and representation and the latter as a claim for redistribution.

Initially working separately towards their own goals, the young Bougainvillean mine workers and customary landowners of the Panguna mine area began to collaborate. During the 1980s they unified around the belief in 'Bougainvilleans' as the equivalent of original owners who should be 'accorded special respect by both BCL and the national government' (Regan, 2010, p. 19). By the mid-1980s a loose coalition was developing between the two groups[10] and the initial claim for recognition transformed into a distributive claim by way of demands for a huge compensation payment from BCL (Regan, 2010, p. 19).

To draw attention to their complaints, Francis Ona, both a landowner and a Bougainville mine worker, rallied colleagues to destroy the company's property. The most damaging attack on BCL property occurred in late November 1988 when electricity pylons at the mine site were blown up, cutting off essential electricity for operations at Panguna. Following these attacks and a number of other violent incidents, the PNG Government sent in police mobile squads (made up of non-Bougainvilleans) to regain control of the area. In the context of existing tensions between Bougainville and PNG, this action resulted in immediate claims of police brutality, and violence escalated quickly. The behaviour of the police is recognised as the 'catalyst for mobilization of a wider secessionist rebellion' (Regan, 2010, p. 20).

In May 1989, the mine closed and has never reopened. Ona continued to gather support from groups outside of the mine lease areas, including criminal gangs and former Bougainvillean members of the Papua New Guinea Defence Forces (PNGDF) (Regan, 2010, p. 21). These groups eventually became known collectively as the Bougainville Revolutionary Army (BRA) under the political leadership of Ona and Sam Kauona as military leader. Support for the activities of the BRA grew over the next year, with some estimates of up to 300 armed and active members in 1990 (Wesley-Smith, 1991, p. 189).

In response to the activities of the BRA and in an attempt to restore mining activities at Panguna, in April 1989 the PNG Government then mobilised the PNGDF. However, this did little to resolve the situation as the PNGDF were also accused of brutality against Bougainvilleans. These actions enhanced community support for the BRA, which eventually found itself in control of Bougainville after a brief ceasefire in 1990.

Support for BRA forces was not universal across Bougainville. Members were often undisciplined and many Bougainvilleans experienced violent victimisation. Others opposed the BRA because they resented the withdrawal of government services available to Bougainvilleans following attacks on government services and the sea and air blockade imposed on Bougainville on 2 May 1990. These Bougainvilleans then formed what became known as the Bougainville Resistance Forces (BRF), which, for the first time, overtly pitted Bougainvilleans against Bougainvilleans, adding new complexities and dimensions to the conflict. Bitter conflict both deepened support for independence, and generated divisions among Bougainvilleans, with the question of independence increasingly elevated as a core issue.

The peace process and the future of mining

From mid-1997, Bougainville made significant progress towards peace building. Following a number of what appeared to be unsuccessful peace efforts, war weariness and a stalemate provided momentum for negotiations on a political settlement between Bougainville and PNG. These negotiations culminated in the 2001 Bougainville Peace Agreement. Key components of the Agreement were:

- autonomy for Bougainville within PNG;
- a referendum on independence for Bougainville deferred for 10–15 years after autonomy began to operate;
- withdrawal of PNG forces from Bougainville and disposal of weapons held by Bougainville factions;
- constitutional entrenchment of the arrangements;
- sequencing of implementation steps to provide incentives to parties to implement what they might otherwise have seen as against their interests[11] (Regan, 2012, pp. 124–5).

At the time of writing, Bougainville is formally recognised as an autonomous region of PNG, and has experienced over 15 years of peace-building activity. The primary focus of these initiatives has been to open spaces of dialogue between Bougainvillean and PNG leaders, as well as reconciliation between Bougainvilleans caught on different sides of the conflict. Although the peace process has generally been viewed as successful (Turner, 2007, p. 93), it did not include important issues relating to resource development, such as a revenue sharing agreement for future mining. There are also concerns that PNG has failed to fulfil all of its funding obligations under the Bougainville Peace Agreement (Oppermann & McKenna, 2013), leading some analysts to conclude, 'Bougainvilleans do not yet have realistic options to choose either autonomy or independence' (Jennings & Claxton, 2013, p. 6).

Despite the centrality of mining to the Bougainville conflict, there has been increasing support for the possibility of reopening the mine. That development is attributable to the belief of many Bougainvilleans that neither autonomy nor independence will be economically viable without a substantial source of revenue, separate from the grants provided by PNG that the current Autonomous Bougainville Government relies upon. The long-held desire among a significant proportion of Bougainvilleans for political independence from PNG therefore continues to frame the mining debate on the island.

West Papua and Indonesia

Geography and early history

West Papua comprises the western half of the island of New Guinea and a number of surrounding islands. It incorporates two provinces of Indonesia, Papua and

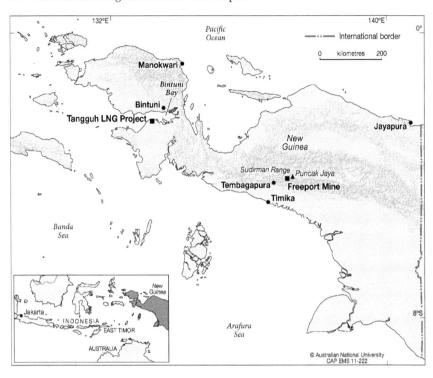

Figure 2.2 Map of West Papua

West Papua (see Figure 2.2). West Papua is 420,000 square km and represents 22 per cent of the Republic of Indonesia's total land area (Garnaut & Manning, 1974, p. 1).

West Papua is located 250 km to the north of Australia, and is Indonesia's easternmost province. Akin to the eastern side of New Guinea (PNG), West Papua contains a diversity of ethnic groups. Yet indigenous Papuans are of Melanesian descent in contrast to the ethnic Malay people who comprise the majority of the Indonesian population[12] (Tebay, 2012, p. 4). From this perspective, the border that was drawn between the western and eastern halves of New Guinea in 1883 'follows neither the island's geography nor traditional cultural patterns of its population' (Garnaut & Manning, 1974, p. 1).

European colonialism in West Papua began earlier than in PNG but was less intense with colonial exploration and administration spreading relatively slowly (Garnaut & Manning, 1974, p. 9; Rutherford, 2012, pp. 50–6; Webster, 2001–2, p. 510). West Papua became the site of an imperial struggle between colonial powers (British, Germans and Dutch) in the eighteenth and nineteenth centuries. As early as 1824, the British agreed that the region would form part of the Dutch East Indies. However, the first successful European settlement occurred some 30 years later with a German missionary settlement on the island of Mansinam offshore of Manokwari. In 1898 Dutch Administration posts had been established at Manokwari and Fak Fak (Garnaut & Manning, 1974), though, like Bougainville, missionaries were more influential (Garnaut & Manning, 1974, p. 10). Mission influence varied according to geographic location with a key difference between highland and coastal communities. However, the region was usually administered from a distance due to the large size of the territory and the rugged terrain (Ploeg, 1999, p. 191). While many communities in the highlands of West Papua had no extensive contact with foreigners until 1963 (Chauvel, 2005, p. 42), coastal groups had substantial contact with the Moluccas prior to European arrival.

The Dutch undertook little commercial activity on West New Guinea until the 1930s. The Netherlands East India Company decided the main value of the region was to act as a barrier to intrusion by other European powers to the Spice Islands in the Moluccas (Bone, 2009, p. 18). While oil had been discovered in Sorong and Bintuni Bay in 1936 and 1939, commercial production did not begin until after the Pacific War (Garnaut & Manning, 1974, p. 10). In 1936, a substantial copper deposit had also been discovered by a Dutch geologist, Jean-Jacques Dozy, working for Shell Oil in the Central Highlands (Ballard, 2002, p. 15). Three years later, Dozy published a report of his discovery of the mountain he named Ertsberg, 'Ore Mountain' (Leith, 2003, p. 1). However, his report lay forgotten at the onset of the Second World War and was not discussed until 1959, when a geologist working for Freeport heard of Dozy's report (Leith, 2003, p. 1).

Following the conclusion of the war in 1945, West Papua was returned to the Dutch. At the same time, Indonesian nationalists made claims for all of the Dutch East Indies to form part of the Republic of Indonesia.[13] Following a four-year conflict, the Dutch eventually agreed at the 1949 Round Table Conference in The Hague to transfer the sovereignty of the Dutch East Indies to the Republic of Indonesia, with the exception of West New Guinea (Verrier, 1976, p. 18).

Ethnicity and nationalism

Conflict in West Papua can be seen to have begun as an international conflict between two states: a dispute between Indonesia and the Netherlands about historical claims over territory (Heidbuchel, 2007, p. 36). From the early 1950s, the Dutch were unwilling to relinquish their control of West Papua as they considered the territory a separate entity from the rest of the Dutch East Indies (Tebay, 2012, p. 4). The Dutch subsequently sought to prepare West Papua for potential independence (Chauvel, 2005, p. 20) through developing 'a sense of West Papuan nationalism which was destined to come into head-on collision with the assertive nationalism of … Indonesia' (Verrier, 1976, p. 18).

West Papuan nationalism was one factor that led to an escalation of conflict 'as Indonesia's President Sukarno realised that Papuan nationalism was a much greater threat to Indonesia's designs than was the continuation of Dutch rule' (Chauvel, 2005, pp. 20–1). However, Papuan leaders were not uniform in their response to international influences. In particular, they disagreed on 'the issue of self-determination and the prospect of an independent state of West Papua'

(Chauvel, 2005, p. 21). According to Ondawame (2010, p. 47), the Papuan community was divided between three factions: pro-Indonesia, pro-Dutch and pro-independence. Nonetheless, it has been argued that even those who were pro-Indonesian believed in Papuan self-determination, as it was thought that Indonesia would grant independence in the near future (Ondawame, 2010, p. 47).

Comparable again to Bougainville, a Papuan identity emerged through comparison with competing ties (Latour, 2005, p. 32), particularly with Indonesians during Dutch colonial rule (Chauvel, 2005, pp. 41–2). In an account of Papuan identity prior to Indonesian integration, Chauvel (2005, p. 42) describes a process of 'dual colonialism' whereby differences between Indonesians and Papuans took root. During the Dutch period, only a handful of the most senior positions in the Administration were held by Dutch officials. In contrast, many of the police, civil servants and military officials of the colonial government were Indonesians (Chauvel, 2005, p. 44). Consequently, Indonesians became the face of Dutch colonialism (Chauvel, 2005, p. 42). Chauvel argues that these colonial interactions had contradictory consequences for Indonesians and Papuans. 'For the Indonesians, the experience contributed to their nationalist sense that Papua was part of Indonesia, while for most Papuans it contributed to a sense of difference' (Chauvel, 2005, p. 43). Specifically, Papuans resented Indonesians for taking away sought after jobs as well as attitudes towards Papuans as 'stupid', 'dirty' and 'curly haired' (Chauvel, 2005, p. 45). This accentuated and politicised racial ideologies that compared Papuans and Malay (Ballard, 2008).

Beyond the differences between 'Papuans' and 'Indonesians', Papuans are extraordinarily diverse with differences in languages and traditions, especially between the peoples of the highlands and the peoples of the coasts and lowlands. There are more than 300 ethno-linguistic groups in West Papua and 257 languages are still spoken in the region (Ondawame, 2010, p. 43). Prior to European contact over half of the Papuan population lived in the highlands, comprising several major and many smaller language groups (Müller, 2009, p. 9). The vast majority of Papuans lived in widely scattered hamlets that had little contact with each other or the outside world (Budiardjo & Liem, 1983, p. 1). Common ancestry was the key unifying feature of West Papua's sovereign small tribal states and anyone not connected by ancestry was considered a foreigner (Hindom cited in Budiardjo & Liem, 1983, p. 1).

While recognising the considerable differences between 'coastal' and 'mountain' groups (neither of which are homogeneous entities themselves), Müller (2009, p. 79) suggests there are also many similarities across West Papua in terms of leadership, marriage obligations and the strong contribution by women to work. Some of the main lifestyle differences relate to subsistence practices (for example, highlanders are agriculturalists and farmers whereas coastal groups are fishermen, hunters and gatherers) and primary food sources (for example, sweet potato for the highlanders and sago for coastal groups) (Müller, 2009, pp. 80–9).

Integration into Indonesia

Papuan identity was further politicised when the region was transferred from the Dutch to Indonesia in 1963 (Mote & Rutherford, 2001, p. 120). After several failed negotiations between the Sukarno government and the Netherlands, an agreement sponsored by the US was signed in 1962 in New York to transfer the sovereignty of Western New Guinea from the Netherlands to Indonesia. Under the terms of the New York Agreement, 'Indonesia was obliged to hold a plebiscite on Papua's future, an "Act of Free Choice",[14] within six years of the transfer of power to Jakarta in 1963' (Wing & King, 2005, p. 1). According to Singh (2008, pp. 96–7), 'as a means of increasing the chance of winning the 1969 Referendum, the Indonesian government ... went out on a political mission to "Indonesianize" the people of West Irian', and Papuan elites who were considered to be pro-Netherlands and pro-Papua came under pressure from the Indonesian security forces. Therefore, in contrast to Dutch policy on education and economic development, which encouraged Papuans to think of themselves as culturally distinct from the rest of the Indonesian archipelago (Chauvel, 2006, p. 181), Indonesia attempted to reformulate the Indonesian nation as a 'cultural polity', replacing competition and conflict with harmony at the expense of diversity (Chauvel, 2006, p. 181). As a result of these conflicting ideologies, Papuans increasingly came to perceive Indonesia as their new coloniser (Singh, 2008, p. 97).

The Act of Free Choice took place in 1969 through a series of regional consultations that were widely believed to be stage-managed by Indonesian intelligence officials (McGibbon, 2006, p. 12; Bertrand, 2014, p. 179; Webster, 2001–2, p. 519). The Indonesian Government hand-picked 1,025 voters from a population of 815,906 to participate in the referendum, all of whom voted unanimously for integration into Indonesia. This was a somewhat implausible result made possible by the repressive security environment surrounding the 'free choice' (McGibbon, 2006, p. 12, Wing & King, 2005, p. 1). Although the UN has subsequently been criticised for going along with the farce of a 'free choice' for Papuans (McGibbon, 2006, p. 13), Indonesian sovereignty over West Papua was henceforth recognised by the international community.

Following the Act of Free Choice, West Papua was declared by the Indonesian Government to be a Military Operation Zone in which freedom of movement was severely restricted and regulated (Wing & King, 2005, p. 1). During Suharto's New Order 'expressions of cultural identity, such as songs sung in local languages, were considered a manifestation of a separatist movement and were punishable by torture and even death' (Wing & King, 2005, p. 1). Despite the devastating effects of Indonesia's security-driven approach to West Papua, it is believed to have been counterproductive, in that it served to strengthen a separate Papuan identity and cement the desire for independence (Chauvel & Bhakti, 2004, pp. 1–2).

One manifestation of this has been the small and poorly armed guerrilla group called the *Organisasi Papua Merdeka* (Free Papua Movement or OPM). The OPM's primary goal is nothing short of full political independence for West Papua (Singh, 2008, p. 127), and although it has never threatened Indonesian control of the province and has divided along different factions (Bertrand, 2014, p. 180), the movement has played an important symbolic role in representing a Papuan identity and associated political aspirations (Chauvel, 2006, p. 181). The OPM launched its first operations against Indonesian forces in

1965. The Indonesian Government's retaliation to these operations extended until 1969.

Papuan resistance to Indonesia has continued via a largely peaceful independence campaign through the creation of representative institutions and the election of formal representatives of the Papuan people (Bertrand, 2014, p. 181; International Crisis Group [ICG], 2002, p. i). Despite incredible cultural heterogeneity on the Papuan side, the demand for *merdeka* (freedom or liberation) has become almost universal among indigenous people of the region (ICG, 2002). Repression of Papuan aspirations for *merdeka* is believed to be somewhat less intense than in the 1960s, but human rights violations including torture,[15] forced disappearances, summary executions and the application of treason and blasphemy laws to limit freedom of expression continue to be reported.[16]

Suharto's New Order and the entry of Freeport

By the time the Act of Free Choice was held in 1969 Indonesian leadership had shifted from Sukarno to Suharto. 'The new President focused on rebuilding the economy, left in tatters by Sukarno, by putting a group of prominent US trained economists in control of economic policy' (McGibbon, 2006, pp. 11–12). Whereas Sukarno's economic approach was inward looking and dominated by state enterprises, the New Order aimed to open the Indonesian economy to foreign aid and investment (Robertson-Snape, 1999, p. 593).

Corruption was endemic in the Indonesian economy under both administrations (Robertson-Snape, 1999, p. 592). Indeed, under Suharto Indonesia held the 'dubious distinction of being perceived as the most corrupt nation in Asia' (Leith, 2003, p. 33). The Indonesian brand of crony capitalist corruption had crucial implications for the economic development of West Papua, for which the Administration received considerable support from the World Bank. As Leith (2003, pp. 33–4) claims:

> one of the greatest services the World Bank did for the Suharto regime was to routinely 'soften' or 'sanitize' its influential country reports on Indonesia … which Jakarta and its Western allies could then use as a first line of defense against the regime's critics.

Such tactics promoted Indonesia to international financial markets without demanding accountability for human rights violations or the squandering of natural resources (Leith, 2003, p. 34). Emphasising Hilson's (2012) call in Chapter 1 to keep in mind why extractive companies are operating in conflict-affected societies before expanding CSR expectations, Suharto's Indonesia provided a short-term environment of incredible freedom for extractive companies to develop operations in West Papua with little regulation. Environmental legislation was sidestepped, civil society silenced and companies shielded from societal demands (Leith, 2003, p. 257).

The first international company to take advantage of the liberal environment created by the Suharto regime was 'Freeport Sulphur'. Freeport signed a Contract of Work, the first of its kind, with the Indonesian government in 1967. The contract gave Freeport mining rights for 30 years within a 250,000 acre concession area of a mine site at Ertsberg. The agreement stipulated that Freeport would be free from land rents and included a three-year 'tax holiday' with no Indonesian equity requirement. The contract essentially designated Freeport as a contractor employed by the Suharto regime (Ballard, 2001, p. 12), and granted the company rights to take over land and impose resettlement of the local indigenous inhabitants of the mine site (Braithwaite *et al.*, 2010a, p. 71).

Freeport commenced mining operations in West Papua on Ertsberg Mountain in 1972 and operated quietly for nearly 20 years (Leith, 2003, pp. 63–4). According to Leith, 'during its life it [the Ertsberg mine] had produced approximately thirty-two million tonnes of copper, gold, and silver and had succeeded in generating on average $300 million of revenue annually for the company'. This made Ertsberg one of the largest above-ground copper mines in the world at the time (Leith, 2003, p. 69).

By the late 1980s, mining at Ertsberg had virtually come to an end. However, this did not signal the withdrawal of Freeport because in 1988 the company discovered a new deposit of gold at Grasberg and the company significantly expanded its Papuan operations. The Grasberg mineral district is located in the Sudirman Mountain Range, about 2.2 km from Ertsberg. It includes open pit and underground mines and contains the world's largest gold reserve (Leith, 2003, pp. 64–5).

Freeport operates on land belonging to the highlander Amungme[17] and the lowland Kamoro[18] peoples, as well as other groups including: the neighbouring Nduga, the Moni, the Ekagi, the Damal, and the Western Dani (Elmslie, 2002, p. 154). When Freeport began to establish campsites in the area, the immediate response of the Amungme was to set up 'crosses of wood that traditionally indicated that trespass beyond the point indicated was not permitted by the owner of the land' (Ballard, 2001, p. 24). However, the 1967 contract did not require Freeport to obtain consent to proceed with the development of the mine. Rather, the Indonesian Government explicitly bestowed upon the company rights to acquire land and resettle the indigenous population with no obligatory consultation or compensation procedures (Smith & Ng, 2002, p. 102).

As will be discussed in the following chapter, this history has led Freeport to become a symbol for Papuans of underlying relations of exploitation (Kirksey, 2012, p. 83). This is reflected in the areas surrounding Freeport's mining operations, 'in which death and the terror of dying are implanted in the landscape and rendered perpetually present for its inhabitants' (Ballard, 2002, p. 13).

BP enters the conflict

Based on the experience of Freeport, BP's entry into West Papua generated significant fear that the Tangguh LNG project would become another 'Freeport'.

On top of the significant security concerns, the denial of customary land rights has been a key criticism in the Bintuni Bay area. The acquisition of the land required for the development of this project as well as the scale of its activities generally, has implicated BP in the complex relationship between West Papua and Indonesia.

The Indonesian Government approved the Tangguh LNG project in 2005 through a production-sharing contract with Indonesia's regulatory body for oil and gas, BPMigas.[19] Financed by several international banks, the facility 'involves the tapping of six fields to extract combined proven reserves of around 14.4 trillion cubic feet of clean gas' (BP, 2015).

Prior to BP's involvement in West Papua, the Atlantic Richfield Company (ARCO) and British Gas conducted exploration activities in the area. Following their discovery of significant natural gas reserves, a consultation and negotiation process took place between ARCO and BPMigas for the acquisition of a 3,200 ha plot for the LNG site, and a 200 ha plot for the resettlement of the Tanah Merah community who occupied the area (BP Berau Limited, 2006, p. xxi). As will be discussed in further detail, landowning clans now contest the fairness of the consent processes under which the land was acquired in 1999 to develop the Tangguh project (JATAM, 2003; Down to Earth, 2005, p. 6). Three clans previously held the traditional land rights to the LNG site: the Wayuri, Soway and Simuna (BP Berau Limited, 2006, p. xxxvi).

Special autonomy

Since the fall of the Suharto regime there have been numerous attempts to decentralise government administrative functions and cede more decision-making authority to regional governments. On 21 November 2001, President Megawati Sukarnoputri enacted a Bill on the subject of 'The Special Autonomy for the Province of Papua'. The key components of The Special Autonomy Law are: the acknowledgement that indigenous Papuans are Melanesians and that substantial mistakes have been made by the state in the past; the establishment of the Papua People's Assembly (MRP); recognition and protection of the rights of the customary community; and the restriction of transmigration (Sumule, 2002, pp. 13–16). There was a mixed reception of Special Autonomy, whereby some Papuans considered autonomy a potential stepping stone to independence, while others regarded it as an Indonesian attempt to buy off West Papua's urban elite (Kirksey, 2012, p. 88). Regardless, implementation of Special Autonomy was slow and incomplete and in 2005 the Papuan Customary Council arranged a ceremony to 'symbolically return' the Special Autonomy Law to Jakarta (Bertrand, 2014, p. 176). Special Autonomy was then officially 'returned' by the Papuan People's Assembly (*Majelis Rakyat Papua* [MRP]) on 18 July 2010 following consultations on the law and its implementation (Bertrand, 2014, p. 192). Dissatisfaction with Special Autonomy was in part driven by recognition that after more than a decade, there remained little accountability for human rights violations (IPAC, 2014, p. 1). With this in mind, reconciliation processes in West Papua can be considered more constrained than those on Bougainville.

Conclusion

This chapter has introduced the background to the Bougainville and West Papua conflicts, particularly highlighting group formation and re-formation. In this analysis, similarities and differences have been identified, the main similarities being the incorporation of small 'traditional' societies into a larger nation-state and the prominent role of natural resources in solidifying these connections. Consideration of the interdependence of extractive companies in broader historical processes reveals how the industry can become enmeshed in a variety of justice claims that extend beyond their business activities. A key example highlighted in this chapter has been the way in which resource extraction has taken place alongside the politicisation of identity and struggles for respect.

Fraser's 'three species of injustice' are identifiable in the Bougainville and West Papua conflicts: economic (such as the inequitable distribution of wealth); cultural (such as repression and racism); and political (such as the exclusion of a majority of Papuans from formal processes to determine West Papua's future). We will see through this book that these justice claims have had particular implications for the way BCL, Freeport and BP have been perceived in Bougainville and West Papua.

Just as the chapter has revealed a 'heterogeneity of justice discourses' (Fraser, 2008, p. 2), the complexity of Bougainvillean and Papuan societies has also been highlighted. In both cases, there have been numerous factions and divisions within groups and a variety of actors, organisations and objects have played a role in stabilising and destabilising these relationships. It has also showed how claims for recognition (for example, as the original owners of the land) can be transformed into claims for redistribution (for example, for compensation). Left unresolved, these injustices can lead to the escalation of violence. This problematises understandings of combatants in resource conflicts as motivated either by greed or by grievance. For example, while rebellion might be triggered by experiences of cultural marginalisation, complaints may be framed to extractive companies as a demand for greater material rewards (probably because material wealth is seen as a primary focus of business). Therefore, reacting to claims for the reallocation of resources may not be able to tackle the underlying issues, which could necessitate an entirely different response.

In the following chapters, eight sites of interdependence between the case study companies and the variety of justice claims at the heart of the Bougainville and West Papua conflicts are explored. At the same time, each chapter provides some texture as to how these interdependencies might be incorporated into an integrated framework for corporate engagement with resource conflict. This narrative begins with an analysis of the colonial logic that drove the beginnings of natural resource exploitation in Bougainville and West Papua. In doing so, it will reveal how extractive companies can deny the social aspects of their projects in different ways, and the implications this has on the dynamics of conflict they operate within. Let us begin this journey by first seeing the social as inevitably historical and for colonised peoples, profoundly colonial in their consciousness.

Notes

1 For a more detailed description, see Oliver (1991), and for analysis of the geology of Bougainville, see Davies (2005).
2 For an analysis of Bougainville in the Second World War, see Nelson (2005).
3 Bougainville's years under the Australian Administration will be discussed in more detail in Chapter 3.
4 Nasioi is a language of south-eastern Bougainville. The pit of the Panguna mine is located on Nasioi land.
5 While most language and cultural groups in Bougainville are matrilineal, men dominate Bougainville's public and political life (Regan, 2010, p. 11). Bougainville's matrilineal societies may therefore be better described as 'matrilineal in social structures but patriarchal in terms of distribution of power' (Regan, 2010, p. 11).
6 Discussed in more detail in Chapter 4.
7 Discussed in more detail in Chapter 3.
8 According to Denoon (2000, p. 15) in 1967 there were approximately 6,700 people earning wages on Bougainville's plantations, 4,000 of whom were from outside the district.
9 According to Oliver (1973, p. 1), the Bougainvilleans are the blackest islanders in the Pacific. For a discussion of why the people of Bougainville look unique, see Friedlaender (2005).
10 Some members were part of both groups, such as Francis Ona.
11 For a comprehensive account of the Bougainville peace process, see Regan (2010, 2012).
12 However, as argued by Lijphart (1996, p. 26), Indonesia also consists of a large number of different ethnic groups, including Papuans on the islands of Eastern Indonesia.
13 For a discussion of the negotiations between the Dutch and Indonesians and arguments put forward by both sides for sovereignty over West Papua, see Lijphart (1966) and Penders (2002).
14 For a detailed analysis of the processes leading up to the Act of Free Choice, see Drooglever (2009).
15 See Hernawan (2013).
16 See U.S. Department of State (2013) and International Coalition for Papua and Franciscans International (2013).
17 The Amung people 'occupy seventeen valleys on the southern slope of the Sudirman range and organize their space according to kinship affiliation and environmental factors' (Cook, 1995, p. 1).
18 For an analysis of how the Kamoro have adapted to major political and economic changes through interaction with outsiders, see Harple (2000).
19 BPMigas has since been dissolved; it is discussed further in Chapter 4.

Bibliography

Ballard, C. 2001. 'Human rights and the mining sector in Indonesia: A baseline study'. London: International Institute for Environment and Development. <http://pubs.iied. org/pdfs/G00929.pdf> [accessed 7 May 2015].

Ballard, C. 2002. 'The signature of terror: Violence, memory and landscape at Freeport', in B. David & M. Wilson (eds.), *Inscribed Landscapes: Marking and Making Place*. Honolulu: University of Hawaii Press, pp. 13–26.

Ballard, C. 2008. '"Oceanic negroes": Early British anthropology of Papuans, 1820–1869', in B. Douglas & C. Ballard (eds.), *Foreign Bodies: Oceania and the Science of Race 1750–1940*. Canberra: ANU Press, pp. 157–202.

Ballard, C. & Banks, G. 2009. 'Between a rock and a hard place: Corporate strategy at the Freeport mine in Papua, 2001–2006', in B. P. Resosudarmo & F. Jotzo (eds.), *Working with Nature against Poverty: Development, Resources and the Environment in Eastern Indonesia*. Singapore: ISEAS Publishing, pp. 147–77.

Bedford, R. & Mamak, A. 1977. *Compensating for Development: The Bougainville Case*. Bougainville Special Publication, no. 2, University of Canterbury, Christchurch.

Bertrand, J. 2014. 'Autonomy and stability: The perils of implementation and "Divide-and-Rule" tactics in Papua, Indonesia', *Nationalism and Ethnic Politics*, vol. 20, no. 2, pp. 174–99.

Bone, R. C. 2009. *The Dynamics of the Western New Guinea Problem*. Singapore: Equinox Publishing.

BP. 2015. 'Tangguh LNG'. <www.bp.com/sectiongenericarticle.do?categoryId=9004779& contentId=7008759> [accessed 8 May 2015].

BP Berau Limited. 2006. 'Indigenous peoples development planning document'. <www. adb.org/sites/default/files/project-document/68965/38919-01-ps-ipdp.pdf> [accessed 8 May 2015].

Braithwaite, J., Braithwaite, V., Cookson, M. & Dunn, L. 2010a. *Anomie and Violence: Non-Truth and Reconciliation in Indonesian Peacebuilding*. Canberra: ANU Press.

Braithwaite, J., Charlesworth, H., Reddy, P. & Dunn, L. 2010b. *Reconciliation and Architectures of Commitment: Sequencing Peace in Bougainville*. Canberra: ANU Press.

Brown, M. J. F. 1974. 'A development consequence: Disposal of mining waste in Bougainville, Papua New Guinea', *Geoforum*, vol. 5, no. 2, pp. 19–27.

Budiardjo, C. & Liem S. L. 1983. *West Papua: The Obliteration of a People*. London: Tapol Campaign.

Chauvel, R. 2005. 'Constructing Papuan nationalism: History, ethnicity, and adaptation'. Washington, DC: East-West Center. <www.eastwestcenter.org/fileadmin/stored/pdfs/ PS014.pdf> [accessed 7 May 2015].

Chauvel, R. 2006. 'Violence and governance in West Papua', in C. A. Coppel (ed.), *Violent Conflicts in Indonesia: Analysis, Representation, Resolution*. Abingdon: Routledge, pp. 180–92.

Chauvel, R. & Bhakti, I. N. 2004. 'The Papua conflict: Jakarta's perceptions and policies'. Washington, DC: East-West Center. <http://scholarspace.manoa.hawaii.edu/bitstream/ handle/10125/3518/PS005.pdf?sequence=1> [accessed 8 May 2015].

Davies, H. L. 2005. 'The geology of Bougainville', in A. J. Regan & H. M. Griffin (eds.), *Bougainville before the Conflict*. Canberra: Pandanus Books, pp. 20–30.

Denoon, D. 2000. *Getting Under the Skin: The Bougainville Copper Agreement and the Creation of the Panguna Mine*. Carlton: Melbourne University Press.

Dorney, S. 2000. *Papua New Guinea: People politics and history since 1975*. Milson Point, NSW: Random House.

Down to Earth. 2005. 'Tangguh – ignoring the reality'. <www.downtoearth-indonesia.org/ story/tangguh-ignoring-reality> [accessed 8 May 2015].

Drooglever, P. 2009. *An Act of Free Choice: Decolonisation and the Right to Self-Determination in West Papua*. Oxford: Oneworld.

Elmslie, J. 2002. *Irian Jaya Under the Gun: Indonesian Economic Development versus West Papuan Nationalism*. Honolulu: University of Hawaii Press.

Escobar, A. 2006. 'Difference and conflict in the struggle over natural resources: A political ecology framework', *Development*, vol. 49, no. 3, pp. 6–13.

Filer, C. 1990. 'The Bougainville rebellion, the mining industry and the process of social disintegration in Papua New Guinea', in R. J. May & M. Spriggs (eds.), *The Bougainville Crisis*. Bathurst: Crawford House Press, pp. 73–112.

Fraser, N. 2008. *Scales of Justice: Reimagining Political Space in a Globalizing World*. Cambridge: Polity Press.

Friedlaender, J. 2005. 'Why do the people of Bougainville look unique? Some conclusions from biological anthropology and genetics', in A. J. Regan & H. M. Griffin (eds.), *Bougainville before the Conflict*. Canberra: Pandanus Books, pp. 57–70.

Garnaut, R. & Manning, C. 1974. *Irian Jaya: The Transformation of a Melanesian Economy*. Canberra: ANU Press.

Griffin, J. 2005. 'Origins of Bougainville's boundaries', in A. J. Regan & H. M. Griffin (eds.), *Bougainville before the Conflict*. Canberra: Pandanus Books, pp. 72–6.

Harple, T. S. 2000. 'Controlling the dragon: An ethno-historical analysis of social engagement among the Kamoro of South-West New Guinea (Indonesian Papua/Irian Jaya)'. PhD Thesis, Australian National University, Canberra.

Heidbuchel, E. 2007. *The West Papua Conflict in Indonesia: Actors, Issues and Approaches*. Wettenberg: Johannes Herrmann J&J-Verlag.

Hernawan, Y. B. 2013. 'From the Theatre of Torture to the Theatre of Peace: The Politics of Torture and Re-imagining Peacebuilding in Papua, Indonesia'. PhD Thesis, Australian National University, Canberra.

Hilson, G. 2012. 'Corporate social responsibility in the extractive industries: Experiences from developing countries', *Resources Policy*, vol. 37, no. 2, pp. 131–7.

Howley, P. 2002. *Breaking Spears and Mending Hearts: Peacemakers and Restorative Justice in Bougainville*. London: Zed Books.

Imbun, B. Y. 2000. 'Mining workers or "opportunist" tribesmen? A tribal workforce in a Papua New Guinea mine', *Oceania*, vol. 71, no. 2, pp. 129–49.

International Coalition for Papua & Franciscans International. 2013. 'Human Rights in West Papua 2013'. <http://humanrightspapua.org/images/docs/HumanRightsPapua2013-ICP.pdf> [accessed 8 May 2015].

International Crisis Group (ICG). 2002. 'Indonesia: Resources and conflict in Papua', *ICG Asia Report*, no. 39. <www.crisisgroup.org/~/media/Files/asia/south-east-asia/indonesia/Indonesia%20Resources%20and%20Conflict%20in%20Papua> [accessed 8 May 2015].

IPAC. 2014. 'OTSUS PLUS: The debate over enhanced Special Autonomy for Papua'. <http://file.understandingconflict.org/file/2013/11/IPAC_Otsus_Plus_The_Debate_over_Enhanced_Special_Autonomy.pdf> [accessed 8 May 2015].

JATAM. 2003. 'Behind the BP Tangguh project propaganda'. <http://wpik.org/Src/286686.html> [accessed 8 May 2015].

Jennings, P. & Claxton, K. 2013. 'A stitch in time: Preserving peace on Bougainville'. Australian Strategic Policy Institute, Special Report. <www.aspi.org.au/publications/special-report-a-stitch-in-time-preserving-peace-on-bougainville/SR59_bougainville.pdf> [accessed 7 May 2015].

Kirksey, E. 2012. *Freedom in Entangled Worlds: West Papua and the Architecture of Global Power*. Durham, NC: Duke University Press.

Latour, B. 2005. *Reassembling the Social: An Introduction to Actor-Network Theory*. Oxford: Oxford University Press.

Leith, D. 2003. *The Politics of Power: Freeport in Suharto's Indonesia*. Honolulu: University of Hawaii Press.

Lijphart, A. 1966. *The Trauma of Decolonization: The Dutch and West New Guinea*. New Haven: Yale University Press.

McGibbon, R. 2006. 'Pitfalls of Papua: Understanding the conflict and its place in Australia–Indonesia relations'. The Lowy Institute for International Policy, 13. <www.lowyinstitute.org/files/pubfiles/McGibbon%2C_Pitfalls_of_Papua.pdf> [accessed 8 May 2015].

Mealey, G. A. 1996. *Grasberg: Mining the Richest and Most Remote Deposit of Copper and Gold in the World, in the Mountains of Irian Jaya, Indonesia*. New Orleans: Freeport-McMoRan Copper & Gold.

Momis, J. L. 2005. 'Shaping leadership through Bougainville indigenous values and Catholic seminary training: A personal journey', in A. J. Regan & H. M. Griffin (eds.), *Bougainville before the Conflict*. Canberra: Pandanus Books, pp. 300–16.

Mote, O. & Rutherford, D. 2001. 'From Irian Jaya to Papua: The limits of primordialism in Indonesia's Troubled East', *Indonesia*, vol. 72, pp. 115–40.

Müller, K. 2009. *Highlands of Papua*. Papua: DW Books.

National Museum of Australia. n.d. '1906: Australia takes control of Papua as an "external territory"'. <www.nma.gov.au/online_features/defining_moments/featured/Papua_New_Guinea> [accessed 19 May 2015].

Nelson, H. 2005. 'Bougainville in World War II', in A. J. Regan & H. M. Griffin (eds.), *Bougainville before the Conflict*. Canberra: Pandanus Books, pp. 168–98.

Ogan, E. 1996. 'Copra came before copper: The Nasioi of Bougainville and plantation colonialism, 1902–1964', *Pacific Studies*, vol. 19, no. 1, pp. 31–51.

Ogan, E. 1999. 'The Bougainville conflict: Perspectives from Nasioi', State Society and Governance in Melanesia Discussion Paper, no. 3. <https://digitalcollections.anu.edu.au/bitstream/1885/41820/3/ssgmogan99-3.pdf> [accessed 8 May 2015].

Ogan, E. 2005. 'An introduction to Bougainville cultures', in A. J. Regan & H. M. Griffin (eds.), *Bougainville before the Conflict*. Canberra: Pandanus Books, pp. 47–76.

Oliver, D. 1973. *Bougainville: A Personal History*. Carlton: Melbourne University Press.

Oliver, D. 1991. *Black Islanders: A Personal Perspective of Bougainville 1937–1991*. South Yarra: Hyland House.

Ondawame, O. 2010. *One People, One Soul: West Papuan Nationalism and the Organisasi Papua Merdeka*. Adelaide: Crawford House Press.

Oppermann, T. & McKenna, K. 2013. 'Sustainability of Bougainville'. State, Society & Governance in Melanesia in Brief, no. 7. <http://ips.cap.anu.edu.au/sites/default/files/SSGM%20IB%202013_7.pdf> [accessed 7 May 2015].

Penders, C. L. M. 2002. *The West New Guinea Debacle: Dutch Decolonisation and Indonesia, 1945–1962*. Honolulu: University of Hawaii Press.

Ploeg, A. 1999. 'Colonial land law in Dutch New Guinea', *Special Issue: Historical Perspectives on West New Guinea*, vol. 34, no. 2, pp. 191–204.

Regan, A. J. 1998. 'Causes and course of the Bougainville conflict', *Journal of Pacific History*, vol. 33, no. 3, pp. 269–85.

Regan, A. J. 2003. 'The Bougainville conflict: Political and economic agendas', in K. Ballentine & J. Sherman (eds.), *The Political Economy of Armed Conflict: Beyond Greed and Grievance*. Boulder, CO: Lynne Rienner, pp. 133–66.

Regan, A. J. 2010. *Light Intervention: Lessons from Bougainville*. Washington, DC: US Institute of Peace Press.

Regan, A. J. 2012. 'Bougainville: Conflict deferred?' in E. Aspinall, R. Jeffrey & A. J. Regan (eds.), *Diminishing Conflicts in Asia and the Pacific: Why Some Subside and Others Don't*. Abingdon: Routledge, pp. 119–36.

Robertson-Snape, F. 1999. 'Corruption, collusion and nepotism in Indonesia', *Third World Quarterly*, vol. 20, no. 3, pp. 589–602.

Rutherford, D. 2012. *Laughing at Leviathan: Sovereignty and Audience in West Papua*. Chicago: University of Chicago Press.

Sack, P. 2005. 'German colonial rule in the Northern Solomons', in A. J. Regan & H. M. Griffin (eds.), *Bougainville before the Conflict*. Canberra: Pandanus Books, pp. 77–107.

Singh, B. 2008. *Papua: Geopolitics and the Quest for Nationhood*. London: Transaction Books.

Smith, A. L. & Ng, A. 2002. 'Papua: Moving beyond internal colonialism?', *New Zealand Journal of Asian Studies*, vol. 4, no. 2, pp. 90–114.

Sumule, A. 2002. 'Protection and empowerment of the rights of indigenous people of Papua (Irian Jaya) over natural resources under Special Autonomy: From legal opportunities to the challenge of implementation'. Resource Management in Asia-Pacific, Working Paper 36. <https://digitalcollections.anu.edu.au/bitstream/1885/40984/3/rmap_wp36.pdf> [accessed 8 May 2015].

Tebay, N. 2012. *Reconciliation & Peace: Interfaith Endeavours for Peace in West Papua*. Goroka: Melanesian Institute.

Turner, M. 2007. 'Autonomous regions and the contribution of international relations to peace and development: Mindanao, Bougainville and Aceh', *Ethnopolitics*, vol. 6, no. 1, pp. 89–103.

U.S. Department of State. 2013. 'Country Reports on Human Rights Practices for 2013'. <www.state.gov/j/drl/rls/hrrpt/humanrightsreport/index.htm#wrapper> [accessed 8 May 2015].

Verrier, J. R. 1976. 'Australia, Papua New Guinea and the West New Guinea question, 1949–1969'. PhD Thesis, Monash University, Melbourne.

Webster, D. 2001–2. '"Already sovereign as a People": A foundational movement in West Papuan nationalism', *Pacific Affairs*, vol. 74, no. 4, pp. 507–28.

Wesley-Smith, T. 1991. 'Papua New Guinea in 1990: A year of crisis', *Asian Survey*, vol. 31, no. 2, pp. 188–95.

Wesley-Smith, T. & Ogan, E. 1992. 'Copper, class, and crisis: Changing relations of production in Bougainville', *The Contemporary Pacific*, vol. 4, no. 2, pp. 245–67.

Wing, J. & King P. 2005. *Genocide in West Papua? The Role of the Indonesian State Apparatus and a Current Needs Assessment of the Papuan People*. Sydney: Centre for Peace and Conflict Studies, University of Sydney.

3   Historical injustice

Introduction

In the literature relating to resources and conflict in Bougainville and West Papua, the starting point is often the historical chain of events leading up to the contemporary conflict scenarios. Historical approaches have been usefully adopted to describe the geographic, social, cultural, economic and environmental contexts of Bougainville and West Papua. They are also employed to elucidate the conditions that have shaped specific local complaints about the manner in which resource exploitation has occurred. These analyses of the past, however, have not always been extended to include, or been integrated into, contemporary debates on the role of business in conflict-prone areas. Rather, the entanglement of resource exploitation with colonisation and decolonisation processes has lurked as a shadow that appears somehow beyond the scope of the responsibilities of business.

This chapter takes a different view, arguing that an acknowledgement of the intertwining of resource companies with colonisation and/or decolonisation processes is a possible starting point to engaging with cultural and political inequalities at the root of resource conflicts. But first it is necessary to consider why these processes are directly relevant to extractive companies. In order to do so, the chapter will explore the ways in which BCL, Freeport and BP have been perceived by some Bougainvilleans and Papuans as implicated in the colonisation and decolonisation of Bougainville (vis-à-vis PNG) and West Papua (vis-à-vis Indonesia). These perceptions are then juxtaposed with the views of corporate executives from the companies involved. The aim of this approach is to identify how and in what ways the companies have attempted to engage and or disengage with these entanglements, as well as the consequences of disengagement.

The chapter begins with a discussion of understandings of colonialism and post-colonialism. This discussion is important for highlighting the links between resource extraction, historical processes and nationalist narratives.

Colonialism, post-colonialism and mining

The concept of 'colonialism' is used in several ways depending on the context. Firstly, colonialism can refer to a moment in time, which is evident in Holmes,

Hughes and Julian's (2012, p. 432) definition as 'a period in history during which a Western nation maintains power over a territory other than its home territory'. In a second usage, colonialism forms a framing device to explain the historical, economic, political and social dynamics of the past, present and future. This use of the term is evident in the characteristics of the 'colonial situation' as defined by Fanon (cited in Barfield, 1997, p. 69). That is: political and legal domination over an alien society; relations of economic and political dependence; a reorientation of the political economy towards imperial economic interests and needs; and institutionalised racial and cultural inequalities. Thirdly, colonialism is sometimes used to describe an administrative structure and set of policies such as a UN mandated territory or trusteeship. In this chapter, the concept of colonialism is used to refer to specific colonial administrative structures established on Bougainville and West Papua (which have included the activities of large corporations), stemming from the economic and civilising missions of the colonial powers.

The case studies of Bougainville and West Papua demonstrate that processes of colonisation are not clear-cut. Relationships between 'coloniser' and 'colonised' are not fixed, but constantly negotiated, renegotiated and sometimes even overthrown. This was evident in the previous chapter where colonialism was seen to retrace group identities. Nor does colonialism simply refer to domination over an 'oriental other'. After experiencing several waves of European colonisation, Bougainvilleans found themselves transformed into an 'internal colony' of the newly decolonised state of PNG. Moreover, the very process of PNG decolonisation signalled just a new phase of colonisation for Bougainville. Both West Papua and Bougainville have experienced multiple layers and stages of colonial domination. What this chapter seeks to do is explore the ways in which resource development has been caught up in these layers. Paradoxically, natural resource wealth has come to symbolise the potential for sustainable self-determination and one of the largest obstacles to political independence.

Colonialism was declared illegitimate by the UN in 1960, which condemned it as 'alien subjugation, domination and exploitation' (cited in Slater, 2004, p. 175). Nonetheless 'there is a general sense throughout much of the developing world that decolonization has not resulted in meaningful economic or political independence' (Barfield, 1997, p. 69). Further, there is wide recognition that the colonial encounter continues to have ongoing impacts on the lives of many.

To explain the continuity of the 'colonial situation', scholars have adopted the term 'post-colonialism'. This term represents an attempt to capture the contemporary problems in developing countries through 'a retrospective reflection on colonialism' (Said, cited in Banerjee & Prasad, 2008, p. 91). Similar to colonialism, therefore, 'post-colonialism' is a concept that is used as a descriptor for a particular historical moment[1] as well as an analytical tool to think about the ongoing impacts of the colonial era. The 'traces of colonialism in the present' (Banerjee, 2000, p. 5) explored in this chapter relate to the pre-specification of the path to 'development' and 'progress' (Banerjee & Prasad, 2008, p. 91) for PNG and Indonesia at the expense of Bougainville and West Papua.[2] The argument presented is that for Bougainville and West Papua, the pathway to development has been characterised by the domination of physical space, reformation of indigenous knowledge systems, and framing of local economic histories from foreign perspectives (Parsons, 2008, p. 102). These expressions of external domination have profoundly conditioned relationships between the states, provinces and extractive companies of the two case studies.

While Bougainville and West Papua are not considered post-colonial contexts, in that they do not yet enjoy political independence from the national governments of PNG and Indonesia, post-colonial theory raises important questions and concerns for the conduct of large-scale resource development in these areas. Of interest for this chapter is the emphasis in post-colonial thought on recognising the connections between the past and the present and the ways in which understandings of the past can determine possibilities for the future. Extractive industries occur amid, and contribute to, the social processes through which groups of people seek to make sense of the past and lay foundations for the future. Moreover, extractive companies do not operate within an a-historical vacuum but form a dynamic component of an ever changing, contested and negotiated 'social', including the 'metaphorical lines of responsibility that mining companies draw around themselves' (Banks, 2006, p. 260).

Many Bougainvilleans and Papuans have drawn on the entry point of resource companies to challenge the 'self-justificatory narratives' (Chakrabarty, 2006, p. 341) of capitalist development in the hands of their central governments. As argued by Chakrabarty (2006, p. 341), history is contradictory, plural and heterogeneous. Challenges to narratives include coercion and political, institutional and symbolic violence that is:

> often dispensed with dreamy-eyed idealism, and it is this violence which plays a decisive role in the establishment of meaning, the creation of truth regimes, in deciding, as it were, whose and which 'universal' wins.
>
> (Chakrabarty, 2006, p. 341)

This chapter seeks to expose some of the corporate and nationalist narratives of resource development and show how these narratives are shaped by the structures of colonialism.

The case studies of Bougainville and West Papua reveal how struggles for self-determination can be informed by collective memory[3] within contexts of power imbalance that defines whose history is spoken, heard and subsequently recognised. As Karagiannis (2004, p. 65) writes, 'the confinement of responsibility to future good intentions and its translation into "global responsibility" are equivalent to forgetting the colonial past'. This 'forgetting', however, is not total. It requires a narrative that exacts a cost on both the designers and recipients. This chapter takes up this point, arguing that community perceptions of extractive companies are conditioned by the past. Resolving these concerns, therefore, may require corporate engagement with perceptions of their business activities as implicated in a variety of historical injustices.

Bougainville

As discussed in the preceding chapter, the Bougainville conflict cannot be understood in isolation from the island's colonial history. Under the Australian Administration, Bougainvillean leaders debated whether to allow their lands to be 'returned' to the Solomon Islands or if they should lobby for secession (Braithwaite *et al.*, 2010b, p. 12). However, the Australian Administration did not countenance either of these options, maintaining that Bougainville was politically a part of PNG and should remain so. The fact that early explorations for alluvial gold in the 1930s indicated the presence of rich natural resources on the island was further motivation for Australia to maintain control of Bougainville (Sirivi & Havini, 2004, p. xvi). When rich deposits of copper ore were later discovered at Panguna in central Bougainville in the 1960s, Australia was eager to find a way of using these resources to finance its withdrawal as administrators of PNG.

BCL as operator of the mine then became closely associated with these processes. This was due to the timing of BCL's entry, the Australian origin of the firm, and the fact that it entered into a legal agreement with the Australian Government via the Territory of New Guinea, rather than with indigenous landowners. As a result, BCL was perceived by many Bougainvilleans interviewed for this study as a symbol of Australian colonialism, and more specifically, as the provider of the financial capacity that cemented their entrapment in an unwanted political relationship with PNG.

The first major agreement on the development of the Panguna resource between BCL and the Territory of New Guinea was reached and then enacted by the Territory's House of Assembly in 1967 (Denoon, 2000, p. 1). Australian civil servants and lawyers for CRA negotiated the agreement without consulting Panguna landowners (Ogan, 1999, p. 5).

Concern about how the Bougainville Copper Agreement (enacted as the *Mining* (Bougainville Copper Agreement) *Ordinance 1967*) was negotiated was a persistent theme in the Bougainville fieldwork. The Agreement will be discussed here as an example of the historical injustices which underpinned the development of the mine. Indeed it was a negotiation that took place against a background of the hegemony of Australian thinking on tax revenue for state building, rather than the protection of individuals or landowning groups.

The marginalisation of landowners in the 1967 Agreement is partly attributable to the Administration's understanding of development as linked to modern 'progress'. This understanding held little room for indigenous perspectives about the significance of land. According to the Bougainville fieldwork data, BCL's operations were symbolic of the cultural, social and economic changes imposed on Bougainville under the Australian Administration. This is not to say, however, that mining on Bougainville was the first encroachment on traditional life. German plantations had been established on the island prior to Australian rule (Ogan, 1996) and more plantations were established thereafter. BCL therefore did not arrive in a completely untouched 'traditional'

society. Yet much of the blame for the disruption of traditional cultural practices brought about through new economic modes of development has been
levelled at BCL.

The Australian Administration

Australia's 1947 mandate over PNG was subject to the obligation that the cultural and education advancement of the peoples of PNG would be assured, and
'an increasingly progressive share in the administrative and other services given
to them, as the territory developed' (Oliver, 1991, p. 78). Indicative of the characteristics of the 'colonial situation' identified by Fanon (cited in Barfield, 1997,
p. 69), this set of ideas shaped the way Bougainvillean societies could operate
through Western understandings of civilisation, education and integration. The
traditional order of Bougainville was essentially in the process of being replaced by
the 'white man's wishes' (Elder, 2005, p. 150). These wishes were largely exercised
though a plantation economy which destroyed long-established Bougainvillean
garden culture and local modes of production (Elder, 2005). Moreover, those who
inhabited alienated land were sidelined. Where minerals existed, colonial law
vested ownership of them with the state. This was a key colonial transformation
that enabled the development of the mine in a manner that contravened the
express wishes of landowners. Land is often a tension in colonial relationships
as it not only provides an incentive for the coloniser to hold on to territory, but
it also highlights the colonial refusal to recognise alternative systems, especially
with regard to land use and control (Banerjee & Prasad, 2008, p. 93).

Conflicting understandings about the right to control land became a crucial
source of dissatisfaction for landowners once the mine began production. In
colonial contexts an administration's development activities are often pursued
within a discourse of 'caretaking' and 'stewardship'. However, these same activities can be just as easily understood within paradigms of 'exploitation'. The fact
that prospecting for mineral resources began to occur during the very early phase
of Australian rule on Bougainville is indicative of the caretaking/exploitation
tension.

Discovering Panguna

The second period of Australian rule is the most important phase for this discussion of BCL's intersection with Bougainville's colonial history. It was during this time that the Australian Government paved the way for BCL to begin
mining activities. As a BCL executive stated, 'Australian colonialism ... was in
our best interests. It got the mine running. It was impressive given the isolated
location' (B2).

During the late 1960s,[4] the Australian Labor Party (ALP) 'broke the bipartisan
tradition and made Papua New Guinea's destiny an issue in Australian politics'
(Denoon, 2000, p. 37). Whitlam advocated the decolonisation of PNG, as he
believed that:

Australians could justify their role in PNG's society and economy only if the indigenes perceived that they themselves were being prepared for participation in all the jobs which were being performed anywhere in PNG.

(Whitlam, 2002)

Following tours of PNG in the 1960s, Whitlam declared that 'the rest of the world will think it anomalous if PNG is not independent by 1970' (Whitlam, 2002). When he was elected leader of the ALP in 1967, Whitlam began establishing the early conditions for an independent PNG, which he believed could be made possible through economic 'development' (Denoon, 2000, p. 36). Several years before Whitlam took over the ALP leadership, a report was released by a 'Territory of Papua and New Guinea geologist, which suggested the existence of a large low grade porphyry copper deposit on Bougainville' (Jackson et al., 1971, p. 1). Following this discovery CRA arrived in Bougainville with a Special Prospecting Authority issued by the Administration to further investigate the resource potential of the site (Denoon, 2000, p. 62).

While a few villagers living near the mining complex welcomed the development and anticipated the material rewards they could reap from it (Oliver, 1973, p. 162), the early exploration period was marked by resistance. Opposition briefly curtailed some of the prospecting activity, making it clear to both CRA prospectors and colonial officers that there was opposition to mining. However, with power to control the land vested in the Administration, CRA and the Australian Government continued negotiations, affording those against the mine little choice in whether or not the project would occur.[5] As a Bougainvillean civil servant explained,

Mr Barnes [the Minister for External Territories to Bougainville in mid-1966] was the Australian minister for external affairs. When there was resistance he flew in by chopper and literally told them [protesting villagers] we will get the mine working whether they [protesting villagers] like it or not.

Meanwhile, CRA considered central Bougainville to be a promising site to extract copper and devised a corporate structure to manage the investment and development, with Bougainville Copper Pty Ltd (BCPL, later BCL) as the operating company. One of the first objectives of BCL was to gain the support of the Australian Government to go ahead with the mine. It did so by appealing directly to the Administration's financial interests in making PNG less fiscally dependent on Australian largesse, and by making a case for the benefits of development for Bougainvilleans.

The 1967 Agreement

On the eve of PNG's independence in 1975, Bougainville attempted to secede (Tonks & Dowling, 1999, p. 11). At this time, the current President of the Autonomous Region of Bougainville, John Momis, lobbied for Bougainville's independence, making his case to the UN Trusteeship Council in New York. According to Whitlam (2002):

> Momis said that Bougainville wished to determine its own destiny and that its 90,000 people were ethnically and culturally part of a separate Solomon Islands group. Olewale [Ebia Olewale, the PNG Minister for Justice] told the Council that if the separatist principle was accepted 'it could result in the creation of 700 potential mini-states in Papua New Guinea'. The Trusteeship Council unanimously extended congratulations to Papua New Guineans on their successful preparations for independence and expressed confidence that the unity of the country would be successfully maintained.

According to Tonks and Dowling (1999, p. 12), it was also an independent PNG Government, rather than Bougainvilleans specifically, that the first Chairman of BCL, Frank Espie, prioritised. Moreover, Espie was overt in stating that he wanted a mining agreement that would be seen as satisfactory for the first Prime Minister of an independent PNG Government (Tonks & Dowling, 1999, p. 12).

Furthermore, Denoon (2000, p. 90), argues that instead of concern for the impacts the project would have on the people of Bougainville, the main issue considered by the company's negotiating team was the protection for the financial backers of the project, because:

> in the end, the project cost about $A423 million. Shareholders invested $130 million, and borrowings amounted to $334 million, of which the twenty-seven banks in the Bank of America syndicate found $110 million.
> (Denoon, 2000, p. 91)

In spite of this, Denoon claims that there were some measures included in the Agreement, which attempted to take into account the welfare of those affected by mining, such as raising education and health facilities to a specific standard (Denoon, 2000, p. 95). However, some of these matters were not outlined in the Agreement itself, but in an exchange of letters between senior officers of the Administration and officials within the company.

BCL was anxious to initiate these kinds of community schemes so that people from the mining-lease areas could benefit from the venture (Tonks & Dowling, 1999, p. 13). BCL also established a Village Relations Department to provide information to affected villagers on compensation, how to establish small businesses and information on crops and livestock. In addition, the Department provided mediation between Bougainvillean and expatriate employees.

While BCL's training and localisation programme reflected industry best practice at the time (Filer & Macintyre, 2006, p. 215), in hindsight no amount of training would be enough to tackle the much deeper concern that Bougainville's land was being exploited to finance an independent PNG. BCL had become a key player in a triangular relationship between the Australian Administration, aspiring leaders of an independent PNG and Bougainvilleans advocating separatism.

Although the blame for the Bougainville Copper Agreement being an unfair deal for Bougainville has largely been levelled at the Australian and PNG governments, interviews conducted for this study reveal a perception of BCL as the face of the social changes ushered in under Australian colonialism, and which continued when the region was incorporated into PNG. In one interview a BCL executive sought to challenge the existence of this perception arguing that:

> BCL was seen as the only way to get attention from the national government. It wasn't a symbol of Australian colonialism – the Bougainvilleans wanted to get at the government, not the commercial entity.

Regardless of whether these perceptions are considered legitimate by corporate executives, they are important to consider as they represent perceptions of the company in a crucial period of Bougainville's history.

North Solomons Provincial Government

The 1970s were characterised by increasing support for secession on Bougainville. Bougainville's emerging leaders began working for change using the colonial system (Momis, 2005, p. 309). A notable example was John Momis' successful run for election to the House of Assembly in 1972. Momis' aim was 'to change the mining policy and to seek the introduction of a decentralised system of government for Papua New Guinea' (Momis, 2005, p. 309). He wanted to give Bougainvilleans 'real self-determination' within the framework of a national constitution (Momis, 2005, p. 309).

In his maiden speech to the House of Assembly, Momis called for the renegotiation of the Bougainville Copper Agreement in order to increase the benefit flows of the mine to Bougainville (Momis, 2005, p. 310). The PNG Government approved this request, along with a commitment to review the Agreement every seven years[6] (Momis, 2005, p. 310). That same year, Prime Minister Somare appointed Momis deputy chairman of the Constitutional Planning Committee (CPC) which was 'charged with responsibility for developing the detailed proposals for Papua New Guinea's independence Constitution' (Momis, 2005, p. 310).

The main goal of the CPC was to develop a constitution that would be 'responsive to the felt needs and aspirations of an emerging Papua New Guinea society' (Momis, 2005, p. 311). One issue of importance to the CPC was the development of a 'constitutionally guaranteed decentralised system of government for the provinces, so as to enable the people to effectively and meaningfully participate in the processes of government and development' (Momis, 2005, p. 312). Their concern was that the centralised system of the Administration would 'only marginalise and alienate the people' (Momis, 2005, p. 312), given the aspirations of some provinces for self-determination and the extraordinary cultural diversity of the region.

Initial proposals made by the CPC were met with disapproval but continued to be debated in 1974 and 1975. In July 1975, Somare pushed for the deletion of a chapter in the Draft Constitution that proposed a provincial government system (Momis, 2005, p. 313). Ghai and Regan (2006, p. 593) claim that the CPC's proposals were rejected on the grounds of unity (of PNG), efficiency and economic rationality.

Following his resignation from the House of Assembly, Momis was appointed leader of a Bougainville team that planned for self-determination. While many were determined to achieve immediate independence, the team received little support from the international community and there were divisions among Bougainvilleans (Momis, 2005, p. 313). On the PNG side, Somare was conscious of the fact that if Bougainville were granted self-determination, other provinces would expect the same (Ghai & Reagan, 2006, p. 593).

In the face of escalating tensions between the Somare government and Bougainville, Momis decided to phone Somare in 1976 to request him to declare a truce and ask the people of Bougainville to negotiate with the National Government (Momis, 2005, p. 314). Both sides eventually agreed to negotiate and in August 1976 an agreement was reached 'on constitutionally entrenched autonomy arrangements for Bougainville' (Ghai & Regan, 2006, p. 593). Bougainville was subsequently able to:

> establish its own provincial government with limited autonomy but with provisions for further devolution of powers and functions to Bougainville. It also provided for transfer to the Bougainville government of the mining royalties payable by Bougainville Copper Ltd (BCL) to the National Government.
>
> (Momis, 2005, p. 314)

While Bougainville got all mining royalties from 1977 (5 per cent to landowners and 95 per cent to NSPG), it was not enough to satisfy those lobbying for greater provincial powers. This was due to the fact that 'the concessions towards autonomy secured by Bougainville had been generalized to other provinces … In the end the constitutional amendment provided for an almost completely uniform system of devolution' (Ghai & Regan, 2006, p. 593). The only exception was the distribution of mining royalties that in practice applied only in Bougainville at the time and 'ensured a unique degree of fiscal independence for the North Solomons Provincial Government (NSPG)' (Ghai & Regan, 2006, p. 594).

Momis claims that this should have given Bougainville what it wanted, but alleges the National Government 'did not really honour its undertaking of further devolution of powers and functions' (2005, p. 315). Ghai and Regan (2006, p. 596) support this claim, arguing that the powers of the NSPG were quite limited. Consequently, the NSPG (suspended in 1990) had limited power to respond to ongoing mining-related grievances, particularly those that related to the politicisation of identity (Ghai & Regan, 2006, p. 596). According to Ghai and Regan (2006, pp. 596–7), 'had the NSPG wielded power over land and mining, and possessed some ability to limit squatting on customary land by outsiders, the situation would probably have developed quite differently'.

Summary

The story of the Panguna copper mine reflects the colonial character of the relationship between PNG and Bougainville that BCL could not be separated from, however distinct the company's staff may have considered themselves to be. It is clear that in the context of Australian decolonisation of PNG, Bougainville experienced the exploitation of the 'periphery' for the benefit of the 'core' (PNG). Having said this, it is worth noting that from the perspective of leaders such as Somare and Whitlam these actions might be viewed as occurring in the interests of 'all the people of PNG'. Further, BCL did attempt to benefit residents of its lease areas. Nonetheless, many Bougainvilleans have perceived the company as a facilitator of the colonial and national government's interests, rather than an organisation committed to responding to the interests and objections of those most directly affected by mining. These historical connections can entrench a particular negative perception of the company, which can constrain future attempts to benefit resource-producing communities.

West Papua

> It is hard to find any problem in Papua not connected to Freeport. It shows how significant it is when one talks about Papua. Any problem with Indonesia is the same as what people accuse Freeport of doing. Some people accuse Indonesia of polluting culture. Freeport is the other side of the same coin of Indonesia – modernisation, social diseases … Put that in context and start to think about CSR and it will be more complex.
>
> (WP1, Papuan NGO worker)

The terms on which West Papua was incorporated into Indonesia is the core grievance expressed by independence activists. Similar to the way that the nature of mining operations in Bougainville were characterised by Australian, then PNG colonial power, West Papua has been described as an 'internal colony' (Smith & Ng, 2002) where 'the core dominates the periphery politically and exploits it materially' (Hechter, 1999, p. 9). A significant proportion of Papuans have contested the coercive nature in which their homeland was incorporated into Indonesia, and most importantly, the treatment of Papuans by the Indonesian Government and security forces since that time.

The incorporation of West Papua into the Republic of Indonesia, as well as its economic underdevelopment relative to the rest of the nation, laid the foundations for its independence movement, including the OPM. West Papua's core objections are political and historical, directly linked to contested processes such as the 'Act of Free Choice'. However, state violence, cultural factors and the emphasis on 'difference' (ethnically, culturally and geographically) have also contributed to keeping 'the demands for autonomy or complete independence alive' (Smith & Ng, 2002, p. 95).

In crucial ways, the American mining company, Freeport-McMoRan Copper & Gold is perceived by Papuans to have been used as a tool by the Indonesian state to exploit West Papua through the political relationships the company shared with the US Government and Suharto's New Order regime; the justification and source of funding the huge mining project provided the Indonesian military and the lack of financial returns to the West Papuan economy. Of significance to the future of Freeport's presence in West Papua, respondents in this study also highlighted Freeport's controversial entry into the province as a key factor constraining progress in the company's long and fraught relationship with Papuan communities. As a Papuan member of the Freeport union for indigenous workers 'Tongoi Papua' stated, 'before the status of Papua, Freeport already made a contract in 1967. That's the problem. That's why until now there is always a problem' (WP24).

The remainder of this chapter explores the history of complex relations between Freeport and those indigenous Papuans who contest the company's operations and seeks to explain the historical injustices that have conditioned Freeport's later attempts in the mid-1990s to establish more valuable relationships with indigenous Papuans.

A contract with the state, not indigenous Papuans

As discussed in Chapter 2, the 1967 contract between the Indonesian Government and Freeport essentially established the company as a contractor working for the regime (Ballard, 2001, p. 12). Mining was to be used as an investment to serve the interests of the company and the state, rather than indigenous Papuans.[7] Freeport was not obliged to participate in local or provincial development programs and no restrictions were placed on the company's environmental practices. Consequently, the company has been strongly resented in West Papua for the relatively small financial returns delivered to the region in comparison with the substantially larger profits flowing to the central government, the Suharto family and the military[8] (Sumule, 2002, p. 9).

Compounding the relationship between economic and cultural injustice, Freeport has also been charged with the destruction of 'sites of considerable traditional significance' (Ballard, 2001, p. 30). The 1967 contract contained an overt disregard for the customary land rights of the Amungme and Kamoro, with the land effectively considered *terra nullius*. As such, Freeport has been perceived as deeply connected to internal colonialism occurring in West Papua at the hands of the Indonesian state. As a Papuan religious leader said:

Since [1967–8] Papuans see the Indonesian government and Freeport working together without the Papuans. The Papuans became outsiders and Indonesia and Freeport became owners. We are living in that situation now. We West Papuans live as outsiders in our own home. In all countries, it is universal. When someone will visit other people they ask if I can come to you. But in this case they haven't. Kamoro and Amungme never invited them to come here.

(WP27)

This experience of marginalisation was enshrined in Article 2 of the 1967 Contract which granted the company rights to resettle people living in the project area but this was not explained to those affected (Mealey, 1996, p. 303). Accusations subsequently emerged that inadequate protection was afforded to the Amungme and Kamoro in the areas of housing, food, health and the protection of their culture (Soares, 2004, p. 121).

The 1967 contract also led to the presence of troops around the mine site because it explicitly required Freeport 'provide for and meet the logistic needs of government officials' (Ballard, 2001, p. 28). Yet beyond this, troops have also been used as a response to protests by the Amungme, giving rise to a landscape of terror surrounding the mine. A significant example of this was an uprising that occurred in 1977 when a small group of OPM fighters, Amungme leaders and Amungme who held employment with Freeport orchestrated an attack on the mine (Ballard, 2002, pp. 15–16). These protests were believed to have been motivated by the presence of the mine and its failure to translate into shared benefits (Ballard, 2002, p. 15). This was in spite of earlier community protests and the signing of an Agreement in 1974 between Freeport, civilian and military government officials and Amungme leaders (Ballard, 2001, p. 24). In this Agreement, Freeport essentially offered to construct 19 buildings and to re-employ Amungme labourers in return for 'community recognition of its rights to the COW area, already legally valid under the 1967 Contract of Work' (Ballard, 2001, p. 24). Attempting to formalise a social licence to operate, the text of the Agreement was read out to the Amungme. However, according to Ballard (2001, p. 24), the Amungme did not fully understand its implications, and most of the leaders still alive insist they signed the Agreement in a context of intimidation by military officers. As the implications of the Agreement became apparent, frustrations escalated (Ballard, 2001, p. 25). During these protests, two policemen were ejected by villagers at the Akimuga village, to which the army responded by strafing the village (Ballard, 2001, p. 25). According to Ballard (2001, p. 25), several days later, the OPM retaliated by attacking Freeport facilities in an attempt to disrupt the ore pipeline. The army again retaliated with force, killing about 30 villagers (Ballard, 2001, p. 25), and 'putting almost the entire community into flight, with many families spending a year or more hiding in the forest' (Ballard, 2002, p. 16). Akin to Bougainville, therefore, attacks on an object of company infrastructure led to an escalation of violence through the use of force by the state's security forces.

The direct connection between mining and the increased presence of Indonesian troops is closely linked to dissatisfaction of local communities about Freeport's mining operations (Ballard, 2001, p. 28). Freeport, therefore, has been viewed as highly complicit in the Indonesian Government's destruction of the indigenous environment for the benefit of the Republic of Indonesia, helping to shape the experience that development is violently enforced from the outside.

A contested entry

Unfortunately, however, association with the exploitation of the remote fringes of an empire for the benefit of a colonial core is not where the negative 'symbolism' of Freeport in the collective memory of West Papua ends. The contract was signed in 1967, two years before Indonesia was officially given sovereignty over West Papua. Indonesia held interim authority over West Papua under the New York Agreement. Indonesia was given Temporary Executive Authority on the condition that a referendum on independence was to be held in 1969. This period was 'seen by many Papuans [as a time in which] the Indonesian Government shouldn't make any major business decisions' (WP45, former Freeport employee).

Yet the reality was that Indonesia was very active in expanding its position in West Papua during this time, 'and so the period of Indonesian interim rule began that, according to the New York Agreement, was intended to familiarize the local population with their new bosses' (Drooglever, 2009, p. 624). According to Drooglever (2009, p. 624), foreign influences were eliminated as much as possible. The Government banned labour unions and political parties that had been established under the Dutch Administration and Indonesian education was introduced. Additionally, an official policy of transmigration was implemented with the aim of demographically integrating West Papua into the rest of Indonesia. As Gietzelt (1989, p. 201) writes:

> The process, 'Indonesianization', is predicated on the assumption that inculcation of the Indonesian world-view through contact with what are considered 'more advanced' and 'civilized' Javanese, will ultimately strengthen national unity and allow greater exploitation of the rich resources in the region.

The fact that the Contract of Work took place before the granting of Indonesian sovereignty means that the role of the company in the relationship between West Papua and Indonesia has been contested. The New York Agreement itself provided ambiguous terms and conditions for what types of activity could occur during the interim period of Indonesian authority. No mention was made about the terms on which the Indonesian Government might enter into major business decisions. Adding to this ambiguity was the fact that, at the time of the Agreement there was no existing Foreign Investment Law in Indonesia (Mealey, 1996, pp. 81–4). Instead, West Papua was viewed by the Indonesian Government as a frontier region to test the potential for foreign investment and Freeport became the first symbol of foreign investor confidence in the Suharto government (Ballard, 2001, p. 23).

Freeport's entry into West Papua can therefore be read as a contest between the contrasting stories that the Indonesian state and separatist Papuans tell about the past, albeit with unequal capacities to make these histories heard. As McEwan (2009) argues, power dynamics are not only economic and political but also deeply cultural. On the one hand, is an American mining company with an interest in supporting and upholding the wishes and interests of the state and capitalist development; and on the other hand, a small indigenous population living on the periphery in a very remote part of the world.

What we learn from these circumstances is why it was so easy for the Indonesian Government to establish contested mining practices. With West Papua viewed as a 'frontier' of development, the territory was ripe for exploitation. Further, as the territory is located in a remote part of the world, activity in the region went largely unnoticed and unmonitored by the international community. At this time, the international community was primarily concerned with communism in Indonesia and favoured modernisation. Consequently, certain activities might have gone unnoticed but others were possibly wilfully ignored.

Freeport and American interests

As the New York Agreement stipulated that Indonesia held authority over West Papua according to the terms and conditions of a UN Temporary Executive Authority, the UN had a responsibility to ensure the referendum was free and fair (Leith, 2003, p. 12). However, they clearly failed in this task (Leith, 2003, p. 12). The contested manner in which the Act of Free Choice took place and the lack of protection of Papuan rights by the international community, ignited suspicions that Freeport was not only a symbol of Indonesian economic exploitation, but also provided a reason for why 'America used its power to support Indonesian integration' (WP22, human rights worker).

The power that Freeport exercised in the US support for West Papua's integration into Indonesia is also highly contested. On the corporate side, the arguments that support Freeport's lack of influence over the integration point to the small size of both the company and the Ertsberg copper mine during the Act of Free Choice process. As a former Freeport employee responded to this suggestion:

> as if Freeport was used as a bargaining factor between the US and Indonesia. It is wrong because it was a small company. It could not be used as a bargaining factor.
>
> (WP45)

This statement does bear truth as it was not until the current Chairman of Freeport-McMoRan Copper & Gold, James R. Moffett, 'went to Papua to see if the company could get anything else that they discovered the real mine: in Grasberg' (WP45, former Freeport employee). It was the development of this later deposit that led to the expansion of the company's operations in West Papua and transformed Freeport into an international mining company. In contrast, it is more likely that the US was motivated in this Cold War context to support the Indonesian Government as much as possible in an effort to reduce the likelihood of Indonesia leaning towards the communist camp.

Despite evidence suggesting that US support for Indonesian rule in West Papua was not motivated by mining interests, there remains a lot of emotion associated with Freeport and its political connections both in Jakarta and in the US, with demands from some Papuans for 'payback from the US' (Waromi, 2010). As Edison Waromi, the President of the West Papuan National Authority commented:

> We West Papuans have a lot of history with the United States … General MacArthur's children might not know their father dropped us two thousand guns to fight the Japanese during World War 2. John Kennedy's children probably don't want to know their father called us 'just 700,000 cannibals' as he artfully bullied the Dutch into relinquishing its colony to the Indonesians. I would of course remind Ellsworth Bunker's children that their father was the architect of the New York Agreement that enslaved us to the Indonesians. And then there's Mr Kissinger and the whole Freeport mine business.
>
> (Waromi, 2010)

More specifically on the 'whole Freeport mine business', those who argue Freeport did have the power to influence the decisions of the US Government highlight two key areas. First, the 1967 contract which is believed to have been a political move on the part of the Suharto regime, 'aimed at exploiting the "unsubtle connection" between letting foreign companies in and securing international support' (Leith, 2003, p. 60). Second, several influential board members of Freeport also had ties to the US Government (such as members of the Rockefeller family and Augustus 'Gus' Long – a former member of President Johnson's Foreign Intelligence Agency).

In regards to the latter, Leith (2003, p. 13) argues that Freeport was particularly attractive to the New Order regime, despite other international companies competing for the same mining contract. By engaging with Freeport, Indonesia may have believed they could simultaneously strengthen US support for their claim on West Papua (Leith, 2003, p. 13). Moreover, through the company's connections with the 'echelons of power in Washington' (Leith, 2003, p. 58), Freeport was seen as a valuable resource to fulfil the regime's needs on more than one level.

Leith (2003, p. 59) further argues that the links between Freeport's board and the US Government meant that the 1967 Agreement also ushered in the interests and influence of the US in West Papua. She believes that this interest was evident in the way:

> Washington was to directly support Freeport's association with the new regime by guaranteeing $60 million worth of loans the company received from U.S. lending agencies that enabled it to proceed with the project.
>
> (Leith, 2003, p. 58)

In spite of the links between Freeport and the US Government, 'the power relationship between the Indonesian state and foreign capital shifted a number of times; between the regime and the company it shifted significantly – in the state's favour' (Leith, 2003, p. 66). This was because Suharto's regime was no longer plagued by the political insecurities that it held in the 1960s and the country was celebrated for its economic growth. Over time, authoritarian rule gave the New Order the power to confidently exploit foreign capital (Leith, 2003, p. 66). However, this power shift would again reside in the hands of the perceived oppressor of indigenous Papuans – the Indonesian state, and more specifically, Suharto and his business allies (ICG, 2002, p. 18).

The power shift in favour of the New Order took place during a time in which Freeport announced the discovery of Grasberg. The new mine required Freeport to sign contracts with the Indonesian Government in 1991 and 1994 which 'effectively gave the company exploration rights for approximately nine million acres and the right to mine any discoveries for a further fifty-year period' (Leith, 2003, p. 64). However, in contrast to the relatively naïve approach of the Indonesian Government during the 1967 contract, Suharto wrote the terms of the new contract with personal interests at stake.[9] The 1991 contract required 'higher payments to the government, restrictive exploration conditions, incorporation in Indonesia, Indonesian equity in the company … together with an unwelcome commitment to build a smelter on Java' (Leith, 2003, p. 66).

The future of corporate community relations in West Papua

Contemporary expectations that Freeport should provide welfare services to Papuans affected by its activities have become so all-encompassing that the company is considered by some to operate as a de facto form of local government (ICG, 2002, p. 18). However, this is a slightly different situation to examples identified in the literature on CSR in Nigeria. Freeport is not only perceived as substituting for the government, but as a colonial authority in and of itself. As one interviewee stated:

> We are in number three of colonisation. First was big country – USA and Dutch. Second was Indonesia. Third is Freeport – new coloniser. Because he is a partner of Indonesia. They come without anything – everything is not legal. Freeport colonise and has everything – modernisation and things for the military to guard. Money to command the police and military. It is a model of a small state. An environment department, same as a minister. Defence minister, security department … Freeport is a new coloniser for us. So we are most victims because under three [colonisers] above us.
>
> (WP30, Papuan activist)

The story of Freeport's role in the incorporation of West Papua into Indonesia provides an important backdrop for thinking about resource conflict in the region. The logic which enabled West Papua's incorporation into Indonesia has shaped the relationship between indigenous Papuans and Freeport and crucially, local perceptions of the company in relation to later efforts to deliver community benefits. This is reflected in the continuation of sabotage, protest, workers' strikes and clashes (discussed in Chapter 7) regarding Freeport's mining activities in West Papua over the years.

It appears unlikely that calls for Freeport to acknowledge their complicity in the contested nature in which West Papua was incorporated into Indonesia will be met. This is partly because the Indonesian Government has so far resisted Papuan demands for an historical review of the Act of Free Choice as well as ongoing dissatisfaction with Special Autonomy.

What about BP?

The same issues about how Papuan history is defined and understood have not escaped BP's Tangguh LNG project. This is despite the fact that some Papuan NGOs and religious leaders who have been involved with consultations facilitated by BP perceive the company more positively than Freeport. BP's community initiatives do not directly set out to support Papuan calls for an historical review of the Act of Free Choice. However, the company has implemented practical strategies, which indicate some sympathy for some of the injustices that Papuans associate with Freeport. For example, BP has put in place a community-based security strategy that aims to reduce the presence of Indonesian security forces around the project, by drawing on local civilians to provide security services (the strengths and limitations of which will be discussed in Chapter 7). Other examples interviewees discussed in relation to BP include a greater respect for indigenous land rights, a commitment to dialogue (see Chapter 6) and proactive attempts to reduce the in-migration of non-indigenous Papuans (see Chapter 9).

Despite these efforts, there is a distinct sense that Papuan trust in BP is far from secure, with considerable fear associated with the presence of the company in the context of the broader collective memory of Freeport and contemporary notions of resource extraction as a new phase of colonialism. As Socratez Sofyan Yoman (2005), President of the Fellowship of Baptist Churches of Papua, stated in a letter addressed to BP:

> What makes you so sure that you can avoid Freeport's mistakes? We know from experience that dogs will always find vomit to eat. Whether you like it or not, wherever there is money, the TNI [*Tentara Nasional Indonesia*, Indonesian military] will be there sooner or later to lap it up. They will create an 'incident', blame the OPM [Free Papua Movement] and then insist that they provide 'protection', at a price, for a 'vital national asset'. We also know from experience that in West Papua ruled by Indonesia, where foreign companies operate, our people eventually become marginalized in our own land.

By conducting business in West Papua under the Indonesian Government, it is difficult to imagine that BP can completely avoid gaming in the complex and contested colonial relationship that exists between the Indonesian state and indigenous Papuans. In many ways, Papuan concerns about BP's extractive activity do not centre exclusively on demands for greater community development or access to resources. Rather, they centre on the previous experience of Freeport, the activities of the Indonesian security forces, state corruption and the cultural, political and economic marginalisation of indigenous Papuans.

It appears from the data collected for this study that the historical incorporation of West Papua into Indonesia is not an injustice that can be remedied with money alone. As the remainder of this book aims to show, Freeport appears to have been unable to resolve Papuan feelings of injustice through the distribution of community resources. While access to wealth is always valued, it is not necessarily able to tackle much deeper grievances about a company's involvement in the historical incorporation of West Papua into Indonesia – a crucial justice claim of West Papua's independence movement.

Conclusion

This chapter argued that the historical processes that led to Bougainville and West Papua's incorporation into PNG and Indonesia provide important contextual information for analyses of resource conflict in these areas. The negative perception of extractive companies in the collective memory of Bougainvilleans and Papuans due to their alleged complicity in the colonial enterprise of the dominant nation-state, has constrained corporate efforts to improve community relations. This negative perception highlights a key finding from the two case studies. That is, the processes and political conditions which lead to the establishment of resource projects can be difficult to dissociate from future possibilities for meaningful relationships between the companies involved and local communities.

In the cases of Bougainville and West Papua, resource development projects have been entwined with historical injustices associated with the political incorporation into PNG and Indonesia, and their economic exploitation for the benefit of these states. Resolving these concerns cannot be easily achieved through the distribution of material resources alone. As Fraser argues (1996, pp. 5, 65), 'neither redistribution alone nor recognition alone can suffice to remedy injustice today … to pose an either/or choice between the politics of redistribution and the politics of recognition is to posit a false antithesis'. Hence a more holistic response might include material benefits, as well as a retrospective engagement with cultural or symbolic recognition, through for example, rewriting the original agreements between states and corporations or participating in local reconciliation ceremonies.

The chapter also advanced our understanding of the contradictory ideas and group formations (Latour, 2005, p. 29) involved in resource conflicts. That is, opposition to resource projects can at once be a claim for a greater share of resource revenues (i.e. a claim for a slice of the economic pie and inclusion in the development process) and at the same time, a defence or reassertion of culture (i.e. resistance to non-customary ways and the rejection of the modes of production – an issue discussed in Chapter 10). The following chapter further explores these tensions through a discussion of divergent understandings and systems of land ownership.

Notes

1 However, the use of the 'post' in 'post-colonialism' is problematic and has been criticised for upholding the 'imperial idea of linear time' (McClintock, 1992, p. 85) which
promotes the misperception 'that colonialism as a historical reality has somehow ended'
(Banerjee, 2000, p. 5).
2 For a discussion of colonial legacies and the under-performance of PNG's economy, see
Auty (1993, pp. 206–19).
3 Collective memory is defined by Teitel (2000, p. 70) as, 'a process of reconstructing the
representation of the past in the light of the present'.
4 During this time, there were changes in ideas about racial inequality back in Australia
where an early land rights movement had emerged, and ignited a debate over land rights
for Indigenous people in Australia.
5 As stated in the previous chapter, there was no political body to represent Bougainvilleans
until the early 1970s (Regan, 2010, p. 13).
6 The BCA should have been reviewed in 1981 and 1988, but Momis alleges this requirement was ignored by the National Government (Momis, 2005, p. 310).
7 The problems associated with the state setting standards on corporate–community
development and the protection of locals will be discussed in Chapter 4.
8 This will be discussed more extensively in Chapter 7.
9 According to the ICG (2002, p. 18), Freeport guaranteed an estimated US$673 million
in loans to Suharto-linked interests between 1991 and 1997.

Bibliography

Auty, R. M. 1993. *Sustaining Development in Mineral Economies: The Resource Curse Thesis*.
London: Routledge.

Ballard, C. 2001. 'Human rights and the mining sector in Indonesia: A baseline study'.
London: International Institute for Environment and Development. <http://pubs.iied.
org/pdfs/G00929.pdf> [accessed 7 May 2015].

Ballard, C. 2002. 'The signature of terror: Violence, memory and landscape at Freeport',
in B. David & M. Wilson (eds.), *Inscribed Landscapes: Marking and Making Place*.
Honolulu: University of Hawaii Press, pp. 13–26.

Banerjee, S. B. 2000. 'Whose land is it anyway? National interest, indigenous stakeholders
and colonial discourses: The case of the Jabiluka mine', *Organization & Environment*,
vol. 13, no. 1, pp. 3–38.

Banerjee, S. B. & Prasad, A. 2008. 'Critical reflections on management and
organizations: A postcolonial perspective', *Critical Perspectives on International Business*,
vol. 4, no. 2/3, pp. 90–8.

Banks, G. 2006. 'Mining, social change and corporate social responsibility: Drawing lines
in the Papua New Guinea mud', in S. Firth (ed.), *Globalisation and Governance in the
Pacific Islands*. Canberra: ANU Press, pp. 259–74.

Barfield, T. (ed.) 1997. *The Dictionary of Anthropology*. Oxford: Blackwell.

Braithwaite, J., Braithwaite, V., Cookson, M. & Dunn, L. 2010a. *Anomie and
Violence: Non-Truth and Reconciliation in Indonesian Peacebuilding*. Canberra: ANU Press.

Braithwaite, J., Charlesworth, H., Reddy, P. & Dunn, L. 2010b, *Reconciliation and
Architectures of Commitment: Sequencing Peace in Bougainville*. Canberra: ANU Press.

Chakrabarty, D. 2006. 'Postcoloniality and the artifice of history', in B. Ashcroft, G.
Griffiths & H. Tiffin (eds.), *The Post-Colonial Studies Reader*. Abingdon: Routledge,
pp. 340–2.

Denoon, D. 2000. *Getting under the Skin: The Bougainville Copper Agreement and the Creation of the Panguna Mine*. Carlton: Melbourne University Press.

Drooglever, P. 2009. *An Act of Free Choice: Decolonisation and the Right to Self-Determination in West Papua*. Oxford: Oneworld.

Elder, P. 2005. 'Between the waitman's wars: 1914–42', in A. J. Regan & H. M. Griffin (eds.), *Bougainville before the Conflict*. Canberra: Pandanus Books, pp. 143–64.

Filer, C. & Macintyre, M. 2006. 'Grass roots and deep holes: Community responses to mining in Melanesia', *The Contemporary Pacific*, vol. 18, no. 2, pp. 215–31.

Fraser, N. 1996. 'Social justice in the age of identity politics: Redistribution, recognition, and participation'. The Tanner Lectures on Human Values, Stanford University, 30 April–2 May. <http://tannerlectures.utah.edu/_documents/a-to-z/f/Fraser98.pdf> [accessed 11 May 2015].

Ghai, Y. & Regan, A. J. 2006. 'Unitary state, devolution, autonomy, secession: State building and nation building in Bougainville, Papua New Guinea', *The Round Table*, vol. 95, no. 386, pp. 589–608.

Gietzelt, D. 1989. 'The Indonesianization of West Papua', *Oceania*, vol. 59, no. 3, pp. 201–21.

Hechter, M. 1999. *Internal Colonialism: The Celtic Fringe in British National Development*. New Brunswick: Transaction Publishers.

Holmes, D., Hughes, K. & Julian, R. (eds.) 2012. *Australian Sociology: A Changing Society*, 3rd edn. Frenchs Forest, NSW: Pearson.

International Crisis Group. 2002. 'Indonesia: Resources and conflict in Papua', ICG Asia Report no. 39. <www.crisisgroup.org/~/media/Files/asia/south-east-asia/indonesia/Indonesia%20Resources%20and%20Conflict%20in%20Papua> [accessed 8 May 2015].

Jackson, Graham, Moore & Partners 1971, *Bougainville Mining Limited: A Fundamental Evaluation*. Sydney: Jackson, Graham, Moore & Partners.

Karagiannis, N. 2004. *Avoiding Responsibility: The Politics and Discourse of European Development Policy*. London: Pluto Press.

Latour, B. 2005. *Reassembling the Social: An Introduction to Actor-Network Theory*. Oxford: Oxford University Press.

Leith, D. 2003. *The Politics of Power: Freeport in Suharto's Indonesia*. Honolulu: University of Hawaii Press.

McClintock, A. 1992. 'The angel of progress: Pitfalls of the term "post-colonialism"', *Social Text*, vol. 31/32, pp. 84–98.

McEwan, C. 2009, *Postcolonialism and Development*. Abingdon: Routledge.

Mealey, G. A. 1996. *Grasberg: Mining the Richest and Most Remote Deposit of Copper and Gold in the World, in the Mountains of Irian Jaya, Indonesia*. New Orleans: Freeport-McMoRan Copper & Gold.

Momis, J. L. 2005. 'Shaping leadership through Bougainville indigenous values and Catholic seminary training: A personal journey', in A. J. Regan & H. M. Griffin (eds.), *Bougainville before the Conflict*. Canberra: Pandanus Books, pp. 300–16.

O'Faircheallaigh, C. 1984. *Mining and Development*. Beckenham: Croom Helm.

Ogan, E. 1996. 'Copra came before copper: The Nasioi of Bougainville and plantation colonialism, 1902–1964', *Pacific Studies*, vol. 19, no. 1, pp. 31–51.

Ogan, E. 1999. 'The Bougainville conflict: Perspectives from Nasioi'. State Society and Governance in Melanesia Discussion Paper, no. 3. <https://digitalcollections.anu.edu.au/bitstream/1885/41820/3/ssgmogan99-3.pdf> [accessed 8 May 2015].

Oliver, D. 1973. *Bougainville: A Personal History*. Carlton: Melbourne University Press.

Oliver, D. 1991. *Black Islanders: A Personal Perspective of Bougainville 1937–1991*. South Yarra: Hyland House.

Parsons, R. 2008. 'We are all stakeholders now: The influence of western discourses of "community engagement" in an Australian Aboriginal community', *Critical Perspectives on International Business*, vol. 4, no. 2/3, pp. 99–126.

PT Freeport Indonesia. 2006. *Grasberg: 2006 Tour Companion*. Grasberg: PT Freeport Indonesia.

Regan, A. J. 2003. 'The Bougainville conflict: Political and economic agendas', in K. Ballentine & J. Sherman (eds.), *The Political Economy of Armed Conflict: Beyond Greed and Grievance*. Boulder, CO: Lynne Rienner, pp. 133–66.

Regan, A. J. 2010. *Light Intervention: Lessons from Bougainville*. Washington, DC: US Institute of Peace Press.

Robertson-Snape, F. 1999. 'Corruption, collusion and nepotism in Indonesia', *Third World Quality*, vol. 20, no. 3, pp. 589–602.

Sirivi, J. T. & Havini, M. T. (eds.) 2004. *As Mothers of the Land: The Birth of the Bougainville Women for Peace and Freedom*. Canberra: Pandanus Books.

Slater, D. 2004. *Geopolitics and the Post-Colonial: Rethinking North–South Relations*. Oxford: Blackwell.

Smith, A. L. & Ng, A. 2002. 'Papua: Moving beyond internal colonialism?', *New Zealand Journal of Asian Studies*, vol. 4, no. 2, pp. 90–114.

Soares, A. D. J. 2004. 'The impact of corporate strategy on community dynamics: A case study of the Freeport mining company in West Papua, Indonesia', *International Journal on Minority and Group Rights*, vol. 11, pp. 115–42.

Sumule, A. 2002. 'Protection and empowerment of the rights of indigenous people of Papua (Irian Jaya) over natural resources under Special Autonomy: From legal opportunities to the challenge of implementation'. Resource Management in Asia-Pacific, Working Paper 36. <https://digitalcollections.anu.edu.au/bitstream/1885/40984/3/rmap_wp36.pdf> [accessed 8 May 2015].

Teitel, R. 2000. *Transitional Justice*. Oxford: Oxford University Press.

Tonks, G. R. & Dowling, P. J. 1999. 'Bougainville copper: A case analysis in international management', University of Tasmania, School of Management Working Paper Series, vol. 99-08, pp. 1–32.

Waromi, E. 2010. 'WPNA: West Papuans want payback for the US'. <http://westpapuamedia.info/2010/09/22/wpna-west-papuans-want-payback-from-the-us/> [accessed 4 May 2015].

Whitlam, G. E. 2002. 'Hindsight: A workshop for participants in the *Decolonisation of Papua New Guinea*'. The Australian National University, Canberra. <https://digitalcollections.anu.edu.au/bitstream/1885/41971/2/hindsight.pdf> [accessed 8 May 2015].

Yoman, S. S. 2005. 'After a silence of two and a half months, BP has replied (or rather not replied) to a passionate let'. <www.minesandcommunities.org/article.php?a=4947&highlight=bp,tangguh> [accessed 4 May 2015].

4 State law and customary land ownership

Introduction

One of the more important observations in Chapter 3 was the historically inadequate protection afforded to the rights of Bougainvilleans and Papuans by their respective central governments, and their marginalisation in important decisions relating to resource development. The second site of interdependence discussed in this chapter is the involvement of the three companies in conflicts between state ownership rights and rights governed by 'customary law'.

State ownership of high-value natural resources prompts a consideration of the state's role in complementing CSR in peace building. The state's 'control' of natural resources highlights the limited capacity of Interdependent Engagement to resolve conflicts over natural resources when, albeit for different reasons, the state itself fails to protect the rights of the peoples from the areas in which the resources are extracted. Through an analysis of the state's control of natural resources in Bougainville and West Papua, this chapter argues that corporate responsiveness to the terms of access to land defined by the host state does not guarantee the legitimacy or fairness of a resource project. Thus, while corporate agreement to abide by host state regulations should generally be encouraged, the case studies highlight the need to be conscious of the ways in which state law itself can at times deny 'political voice to those who are cast outside the universe of those who "count"' (Fraser, 2008, p. 147).

State capacity, however, is not static (Dauvergne, 1997, p. 2). Nor are power relations entirely asymmetric. Decolonisation has produced a 'duality of states', characterised by 'their unmistakable strengths in penetrating societies and their surprising weaknesses in effecting goal-oriented social changes' (Migdal, 1988, p. 9). PNG and Indonesia are often positioned on opposite ends of a 'spectrum of capabilities' (Migdal, 1988, p. 4). While PNG is portrayed as a 'weak' state (Macintyre, 2008, p. 190), noted for its 'resilient largely self-regulating village-based societies, and police forces with limited reach, resources, and popular legitimacy' (Dinnen *et al.*, 2006, p. 87), 'most scholars of Indonesia see a strong, or at least a medium-strong state, especially in terms of policy formulation and control over nonstate organisations' (Dauvergne, 1997, p. 1). Power relations between states and landowners also change over time, particularly alongside the development of new forums for landowners to challenge national statutes, such as the establishment of the Indonesian Constitutional Court discussed later in this chapter. States therefore, are not monolithic (Dauvergne, 1997, p. 2) and different 'bits of state' pull in divergent directions on various issues according to priorities and interests. In a seemingly strong state like Indonesia, for example, state control can at times be undermined by elite attitudes, poor policies, institutional resources and patron–client links among state officials and resource operators (Dauvergne, 1997, p. 1).

Accepting that host states have different capabilities at different times and across different sectors (Dauvergne, 1997, p. 2), they are nevertheless ultimately responsible for the promotion of peaceful natural resource development. Having said this, it is also important to recognise that corporations have a role to play in ensuring that rights are not unjustly compromised in the pursuit of national economic development. This is not necessarily an unrealistic expectation. In some contexts, extractive companies can have greater presence, organisational capacity and resources than government authorities, such as in rural and remote areas and conflict-affected societies. In addition, extractive companies can hold a greater commitment to global rights regimes in comparison to local states. Put another way, rights are better protected when respect for rights is a plural accomplishment of networked governance (Braithwaite *et al.*, 2012), when many actors (the UN, states, corporations, courts, NGOs) each seek to cover the weaknesses of the other with their own strengths in terms of rights responsiveness.

The role of the state in complementing Interdependent Engagement in peace building

The responsibilities of host states in the promotion of responsible business practices have received increasing interest alongside the debate over the responsibilities of business in zones of conflict. A prominent example is the UN Secretary General on Business and Human Rights, John Ruggie's delineation of the 'responsibilities of states' in the 'Protect, Respect and Remedy Framework'. According to Ruggie (2008, p. 10) host states have a responsibility to reinforce the steps companies take themselves to respect the rights of citizens. This includes: the strengthening of market pressures on companies to respect rights such as mandatory CSR reporting; the development of policies, rules and practices to determine corporate liability and punishment; the promotion of conflict-sensitive business practices; and to advise corporations on human rights risks (Ruggie, 2008, pp. 10–14). While Ruggie recognises that host states find it difficult to strengthen social and environmental standards due to fear of foreign investor challenge (Ruggie, 2008, p. 11), he does not explore states' responsibility to balance the protection of minority rights with the pursuit of national economic development, nor the issue of state capacity in areas of 'limited statehood' (Risse, 2011).

The possibility that states might need assistance in balancing minority rights with national development is highlighted by Ballentine and Haufler (2009, p. 5) who argue that, 'in an ideal world, sovereign states would be willing and able to manage peacefully their internal conflicts and husband their economic assets for the collective well-being of their citizens'. However, at times, 'companies may be undercut not just by less scrupulous companies, but by host governments unconcerned or unable to address issues of corruption, criminality and conflict' (International Institute for Sustainable Development and ICUN – The World Conservation Union, 2006). Conflict-sensitive business cannot take place in the absence of the state's assistance (Ballentine & Haufler, 2009, p. 6), through, for example, security sector reform, transparency, good governance and the protection of human rights. Thus, complementing the focus of this book on the interdependence between business activity and the societies in which they operate, 'whether positive or negative, the behaviour of companies is not simply a function of their own corporate cultures, but also and fundamentally a function of the broader playing field in which they operate' (Ballentine & Haufler, 2009, p. 31). As a result of the interplay between corporate activity and broader political activity, there are limits to what corporations can achieve in the pursuit of social and environmental responsibility without collaboration with national, provincial and local authorities. This is especially true in cases where there is a history of political and economic inequality in the construction of post-colonial states, as in PNG and Indonesia.

This chapter discusses a key avenue through which states can fail to assist corporations to protect the rights of landowners: the overruling of the customary ownership of natural resources. State control of land can at times establish extractive companies as accountable to the laws of nation-states, or to local authorities, who can lack capacity or be plagued by corruption and elite politics (Timmer, 2005). This means that state authorities often wield the power to determine the formal legal responsibilities of large extractive companies, even if affected communities perceive these institutions as 'an alien external force' (Boege & Franks, 2011, p. 7).

Regulations determined by the state include: the use of security to protect the resource project and supporting infrastructure, revenue sharing frameworks, as well as environmental management processes. In this way, the power to control land, people and resources can establish the state as an influential audience and regulator of extractive projects. This can be problematic in situations where the state's mandate to negotiate on behalf of affected communities is contested. Drawing on the ideas of Fraser (2008, p. 147), resource projects can be considered under these circumstances to form broader processes of 'misframing', whereby 'the partitioning of political space blocks some who are poor or despised from challenging the forces that oppress them'.

This is not to say, however, that state power to 'control' land is as absolute in practice as it is in theory and may require a more nuanced analysis of representation than is offered by Fraser (2008, p. 145). This is something that has been recognised in analyses of mineral developments in PNG. Analysts such as Filer (1997, p. 165) have documented the emergence of an 'ideology of landownership' through which 'Papua New Guineans (or "Melanesians") have been learning to think of themselves as people who are distinguished from other nations or races by their singular physical and emotional relationship to "the land" which all of them possess'. Moreover, 97 per cent of land in PNG is held under customary tenure. In practice this means that while the state owns the minerals and is entitled to the returns from mineral development, it must compensate customary land-holders.

Corporations are not always able to gain access to the resources they need, and even when access is granted, operations can still be disrupted (Wesley-Smith, 1990, pp. 11–12). The primacy of the state–company alliance is not 'fixed' and constantly changes over time. An example of this can again be drawn from PNG, where following the Bougainville uprising, greater efforts have been made by successive national governments and extractive companies 'to be more responsive to local people and their economic circumstances' (Macintyre, 2007, p. 50). Measures include landowner equity in the PNG minerals sector (Banks, 2003) and the Government's establishment of 'Development Forums' (Filer, 2008). Corporate responsiveness to the state and to landowner issues is vexed, gradually giving rise to new assemblages and formations of relationships.

Nonetheless, a common experience of resource development globally is the state's need to balance national development with the social and environmental costs to resource-producing areas. While corporations do not have the authority to recognise customary ownership and are obliged to abide by the demands of the host state, they do have important opportunities to protect the rights of minority groups. This might be achieved through adding checks and balances to state laws that are considered detrimental to minority rights and through improved community consultation processes (Hilson, 2012, p. 66). Therefore, corporations may have the ability to engage with and to recognise landowning community grievances, which might otherwise be constrained or denied by 'bits of state'. Consequently, corporations may encounter important opportunities to challenge state and local authorities on social and environmental concerns.

Another caveat, however, is that just as state-based regulatory regimes can be detrimental to the rights of certain groups (i.e. customary landowners), customary/traditional regimes can be detrimental to others. For example, Macintyre (2007) argues that if an extractive company were to engage with a community of landowners through customary modes of authority, the legal rights of young adult men and women are likely to be adversely affected or neglected. Drawing on the example of Bougainville, Macintyre (2007, p. 56) refers to the complexity of customary land tenure processes 'which meant that a woman and her kin could never "lose" land' without complex ritual exchanges. However, as a consequence of those same customary land tenure systems, women were excluded from having a political voice and felt betrayed years later when they realised 'their male relatives agreed to the use or destruction of land that they can never regain' (Macintyre, 2007, p. 56). Macintyre (2007, p. 56) writes:

> While many concede that, at that time, women were reluctant to attend meetings or speak out, they argue that, based on previous experience of the impacts of mining on subsistence and on the lives of women and children,

responsible miners should have ignored the appeal to custom and proceeded according to the national laws and to the United Nations Convention for the Elimination of Discrimination against Women.

This negative appraisal of subsurface rights governed by customary law in contrast to national or international norms echoes Latour's (2005) critique of conceptualising the social as a fixed state of affairs. As he writes:

> When we say that 'something is social' or 'has a social dimension', we mobilize one set of features that, so to speak, march in step together, even though it might be composed of radically different types of entities.
>
> (Latour, 2005, p. 43)

Thus, the question of 'who is included, and who is excluded, from the circle of those entitled to participate within them' (Fraser, 2008, p. 147) operates at different scales and incorporates processes that may simultaneously advantage some while disadvantaging others.

Two conflicting ingredients that shape representation in Bougainville and West Papua are exogenous legal systems and landowner rights governed by customary law. As we will see, however, this is not an unproblematic binary and can be difficult terrain for an extractive company to navigate.

Decolonisation and land ownership

State ownership of subsurface resources in Bougainville and West Papua stems from the decolonisation processes of PNG and Indonesia. Reflective of broader political trends in the twentieth century, newly independent states tended to focus on proclaiming national sovereignty through the institutionalisation of Western European legal systems. This led to the subordination of 'customary' land tenure systems and 'traditional' forms of authority that were often seen as an impediment to modernisation and nation building (Boege & Franks, 2011, p. 6; Kyed & Buur, 2006, p. 1).

Landscapes which 'combine elements of the introduced Western models of governance and elements stemming from local indigenous traditions' (Boege et al., 2008, p. iii), are referred to by some analysts as hybrid political orders. Despite efforts to subordinate custom, indigenous social structures have continued to inform 'the everyday social reality of large parts of the population in developing countries even today, particularly in rural and remote peripheral areas' (Boege et al., 2008, p. 4). The continued importance of 'customary law' in some decolonised societies has resulted in significant contests between landowners and states over the legitimacy of ownership, the appropriate use of land, and entitlements to the benefits it creates. Conflicting perspectives on land ownership can result in significant volatility in regions with a distinct ethnic identity to that of the majority of the national population, or which are geographically distant from the central government. The logic of the state is to maximise resource wealth for the benefit of all peoples of the nation. However, landowners do not always believe the state has the legitimacy to control their land, nor do they adhere to the logic that the resources extracted should be used to fund the development of the nation as a whole.

In saying this, however, it is important to recall that customary law is also a product of the colonial encounter. It simply did not exist until 'the introduction of a sphere of political activity from which it had to be differentiated' (Demian, 2003, p. 100). Rather than conceptualise 'custom' and 'law' as two separate entities that might be combined, they may be better conceived as two resources drawn on at different junctures, with varying degrees of accessibility and influence (Demian, 2003).

The following section explores some of the tensions between state ownership and customary law in Bougainville and West Papua, and the consequences these can have on corporate–community relations.

Bougainville

> BCL and PNG government suppressed our traditional beliefs and system … if they entered [according to] our traditional ways, we wouldn't have [had] the crisis.
>
> (B20, Bougainvillean ABG Government
> Department CEO)

Conflicting perceptions regarding the ownership of minerals extracted from the site of the Bougainville copper mine can be traced to the first company prospectors who reported the large Panguna valley as 'loosely owned and socially inconsequential' (Oliver, 1973, p. 162). This understanding misrepresented the complexity of landownership on Bougainville where there is no such thing as 'wholly free' or unowned land on the island (Oliver, 1973, p. 162). Oliver (1973, p. 162) argues that the company personnel could be forgiven for this misunderstanding but not the Australian Administration because, by the time of exploration, the Administration should have 'gained more insight into the complexities and imponderables of indigenous landownership'.

In contrast to the shared tenets of land ownership of customary tenure, the Territory's 1928 Mining Ordinance stipulated that company prospectors did not require the permission of indigenous owners, and specified that all royalties would go to the Administration for the benefit of the Territory as a whole (Oliver, 1973, p. 163). This was 'considered by some Bougainvilleans to be insanely alien, or transparently deceitful' (Oliver, 1973, p. 164). For the Nagovisi of southern Bougainville for instance, there are procedures relating to access to land even among the lineage. As Mitchell (1976, p. 28) writes, 'full title to permanent property is only infrequently vested in any individual and even more rarely in a male, which could only happen in a case where a lineage had no surviving women'. Therefore, while men may refer to land as 'theirs', 'they could never have the right to alienate the valuables nor use the land for anything except temporary food gardens' (Mitchell, 1976, p. 28). Similarly, Nash writes that 'people may allow others temporary use of their land for food production but not in order to produce wealth' (Nash, 1984, p. 107). While for the Nasioi, Ogan (1971, p. 84) writes:

> merely to talk of 'owning land' is to obscure important aspects of the situation. One is better advised to employ such terms as 'primary', 'subsidiary' and 'derivative rights' … with the qualification that even this terminology may lead to oversimplification.

Divergent perspectives on land ownership had important implications for representation in decision-making relating to the mine, such as was reflected in the NSPG's lack of control over land and mineral policy. As a Bougainvillean member of the ABG reflected, 'BCL said we cannot talk to you. You go and talk to the government and then they will talk to me' (B20, Bougainvillean ABG Department CEO/landowner).

Legal rights for landowners

The exclusion of Bougainvilleans in the Bougainville Copper Agreement is most evident of the marginalisation of landowners in important decisions relating to the production of the mine. Their exclusion from the 1967 Agreement meant that landowning lineages did not have an opportunity to define the obligations with which BCL should comply. Consequently, BCL was only held legally accountable to the state's limited terms of access to land, affording no legal protection to the indigenous landowners.

A particular resentment of Bougainvilleans towards the state was the limited mining revenue and infrastructure that filtered back to the province. As a direct consequence of the state's ownership of subsurface minerals, the Panguna mine provided a major source of national income, with BCL contributing 16 per cent of PNG's internally generated income and 44 per cent of its exports between 1972 and 1991 (Thompson, 1991). The problem for Bougainville, however, was that very little of this income was channelled back to the island where there was a view that 'the roads were not even bitumen and BCL only built roads for where they operated' (BOU11, Bougainvillean civil servant). This bitterness was compounded by the fact that the PNG Government itself was a significant shareholder in the Panguna mine. Consequently, the state held a financial interest in maximising the profit of the mine, while also wielding the power to decide what social and environmental damage would be an acceptable trade-off for these profits[1] (Thompson, 1991, p. 76). Thus, while it was understood that 'BCL were willing to listen [to Bougainville's concerns] but not the national government' (B11, Bougainvillean civil servant), there was only so much that the company could achieve without the cooperation of the state.

The state's role in complementing Interdependent Engagement in this situation could be to ensure that greater benefits are returned to those affected by the resource project than to citizens elsewhere. As discussed in Chapter 3, one example of where the state could have worked towards this was in rene-gotiations of the Bougainville Copper Agreement in 1974. There was also a 'failed' renegotiation in 1981 when the NSPG sought to increase its share of revenue from Panguna and to participate in further mining (Wesley-Smith, 1992, p. 95). Eager to conduct further exploration in the province, BCL was open to this increase as it had a 'pragmatic need to keep on good terms with the provincial government' (Wesley-Smith, 1992, p. 95). Yet in pre-negotiation between the NSPG and PNG, the PNG side rejected what the NSPG pro-posed based on a 'perceived need to protect the privileged position of large foreign enterprises, whose tax contributions help sustain the state bureaucracy' (Wesley-Smith, 1992, p. 101). The failed renegotiation in 1981 demonstrated to Bougainvilleans the unwillingness of the state to tackle the much bigger problem of Bougainville's land being destroyed for the economic development of PNG, with little financial or other benefit to Bougainville. In hindsight, it might have been better to use the renegotiation process to make significant changes in the management and control of the mine, and to channel funds into restoring the social and environmental harms on locally negotiated terms. As we will see in the following chapter, however, local control over revenue streams can be as destructive socially and environmentally as state and corpor-ate control.

West Papua

Although customary land tenure in West Papua is arguably more tightly con-strained than in PNG today, the complexities associated with customary and state law has to a large degree been mirrored by Papuan attitudes to the Indonesian state. Papuans continue to say that when they go to Jakarta and see all the huge office buildings they begin to understand where the money made from Papuan mines has gone. As will be discussed further, however, decentralisation in Indonesia has shifted power relations between the state and landowners, with the consequence that local communities are now competing against 'neighbour-ing groups and their elites who also claim natural resources and compensation' (Timmer, 2005, p. 12).

   Indonesian law has historically overridden customary land tenure in the gov-ernance of mining, oil and gas in West Papua. In recent years, however, the Indonesian Government has begun making efforts to ensure greater social and environmental standards for resource companies through state law. Indonesia became the first country to oblige CSR (Rosser & Edwin, 2010) following the adoption of the 2007 Indonesian Corporate Law No. 40 as well as the 2007 Indonesian Investment Law No. 25 (Waagstein, 2011, p. 455). These laws deliver on the view that the social responsibilities of business will be strength-ened as a legal obligation and not just left to the goodwill of corporations alone. Even though obliging CSR might be a suitable option in theory, there are two key limitations to this approach. Firstly, mandatory CSR does not afford greater recognition of customary land rights. Second, mandatory CSR further entrenches the distributive paradigm of CSR that this book argues is insufficient for the meaningful resolution of local grievances.

Customary land tenure in West Papua

As was discussed in relation to Bougainville, the Papuan experience of resource exploitation has been intricately linked to state control of land. The land in question in the West Papua case holds particular spiritual and cultural significance (see Chapter 10). When Freeport arrived in West Papua, the Amungme and Kamoro were living rich subsistence lifestyles where their land had both economic and spiritual significance. Land was regarded simultaneously as a source of food, a shelter in time of tribal war and a place to communicate with ancestral spirits (Tebay, 2005, p. 11). According to Abrash and Kennedy (2002, p. 64), the mountain on which the Grasberg mine was developed holds particular spiritual significance in Amungme cosmology, which depicts the mountain 'as the sacred head of their mother and its rivers are her milk. To the Amungme, Freeport is digging out her heart.' The permanent alienation of this landscape into the hands of Indonesia has thus not only contradicted land cultivation practices, but has deeply offended the unique Amungme spiritual ties to the mountain.

Land for the Amungme and Kamoro groups is normally inherited through patrilineal lineages (Cook, 1995, p. 214), which cannot be leased, purchased or sold (Muller, 2004, p. 21). If a claim is made to use the land of another lineage, the claimant would require the agreement of all lineage elders, but this would be done in the spirit of generosity and reciprocity, rather than economic gain (Cook, 1995, pp. 218–20). Further, Amungme land can never be taken from a person against their will (Cook, 1995, p. 225). For the Kamoro, traditional rules relating to land ownership are not clear-cut and they cannot be accurately and comprehensively expressed (Harple, 2000, p. 168, Banks, 2009, p. 50). However, disposal rights are inalienable and only those who are descendants of the first to settle (according to myth) can claim disposal rights over a certain area (Pouwer, 1970, p. 27).

Indonesian law during the 1960s did in fact recognise customary land rights. However, customary law holds a weak position in the governance of natural resources due to two clauses in the Indonesian Constitution. Article 33, Clause 2, states that: 'branches of production which are important for the state and which affect the life of most of the people shall be controlled by the state' (cited in Sumule, 2002, p. 6), while Clause 3 stipulates that: 'land and water and the natural riches therein shall be controlled by the state and shall be made use of for the greatest welfare of the people' (cited in Sumule, 2002, p. 6). What this means in practice is that 'should valuable resources be found on their traditional lands or should the state determine that it requires their land, then such land automatically becomes *tanah negara* (state-owned land)' (Leith, 2003, p. 109).

While it is still recognised that natural resources should be governed under the powers of the state for the welfare of the population, this has been challenged on numerous occasions through the Indonesian Constitutional Court. For example, BPMigas (Indonesia's oil and gas regulator) was dissolved in 2012 due to a number of scrapped articles of the 2001 Oil and Gas Law. The Court ruled that BPMigas no longer held the 'control and power over the country's resources as a regulatory and monitoring body, so it was not able to directly run oil and gas businesses and instead relied on private companies to run the businesses' (Primanita et al., 2012). A further significant example was a 2013 (MK35/2012) ruling that customary forests no longer be categorised as 'state forests' but as 'forests subject to rights' (Down to Earth, 2014). This means that customary forests are now 'formally subject to the traditional rights of communities who rely upon those resources' (Butt, 2014, p. 71).

In addition, a strategy the Indonesian government has deployed to weaken Papuan independence movements has been to allocate a higher level of funding per capita to West Papua than to other Indonesian provinces. Yet critics argue that this is:

> far less than the revenue generated by the region's natural resources. In particular, much of the revenue from the hugely profitable Freeport mine in Mimika district went straight to the central government, fuelling tensions between Jayapura and Jakarta.
>
> (Resosudarmo et al., 2014, p. 43)

In saying this, however, Jakarta is not the sole target of landowner criticism as both 'central and local governments have been involved in a power struggle over Papua' (Jamin et al., 2014, p. 367). While Special Autonomy is perceived to have failed to enhance the protection of Papuan rights,[2] it does enable local governments to issue licences for investors wanting to do business in mining and palm oil, and has given West Papua wider authority in contrast other provinces of Indonesia (Jamin et al., 2014, p. 369). Nevertheless, there has been considerable disappointment in local powers to effectively manage the higher share of mining revenue since the implementation of Special Autonomy (Timmer, 2005, pp. 5–6; Resosudarmo et al., 2014, p. 442). Under the Papuan Special Autonomy Law, 80 per cent of revenue from forestry, fisheries and mining, and 70 per cent from oil and gas exploration are returned to West Papua. Yet detractors contend that this revenue has 'mainly benefited the residents of Jayapura, where most of the money has been spent' (Resosudarmo et al., 2014, p. 442). Moreover, there are concerns that decentralisation through Special Autonomy has been an attempt by Jakarta to 'divide and rule' the Papuans (Timmer, 2005, p. 6). For example, Megawati Sukarnoputi's 2003 decision to create two new provinces in Papua, three new regencies and one municipality has been criticised for the lack of consultation with provincial authorities (Timmer, 2005, p. 11). According to Timmer (2005, p. 12) one effect of this decision on state–company–landowner relations has been that:

The expectations of monetary flows that resource development projects might bring, and the related competing claims over land and resources, pose problems for local people who no longer know whom to raise their voices with outside companies and the government.

(Timmer, 2005, p. 12)

In this context, the Indonesian state is seen by Papuans as neither holding the legitimacy to negotiate with resource companies on their behalf, nor demonstrating sensitivity to their culture and spiritual ties to the land. However, dissatisfaction with Papuan elites and divisions within communities mean that the situation cannot be characterised as a 'united Papuan cause that is frustrated by Indonesia' (Timmer, 2005, p. 13). As Resosudarmo *et al.* (2014, p. 442) argue, the 'process of subdivision of districts into ever smaller administrative units (*pemekaran*) has also created conflict between competing elites over the spoils of governments'. Therefore, what most Papuans have in common is the experience of development programmes and democratisation efforts dogged by unfulfilled promises and failures (Timmer, 2005, p. 13).

Legal rights for landowners

There is no denying the importance of legal protection to landowners in formal agreements between states and corporations. However, the fact that the legal basis of these agreements can contradict the cultural significance of land results in contested understandings of the results of these negotiations. Affording landowners greater property rights alone is not necessarily sufficient to guarantee their protection in the process of resource extraction.

This has been most evident in accusations put forward by three landowning clans residing in the vicinity of BP's Tangguh LNG project. The landowners argue that the handover of their land was involuntary despite signing a written agreement relinquishing their customary land rights for the development of the LNG site (Down to Earth, 2005, p. 8).

Prior to BP's involvement in the Tangguh project, ARCO and British Gas were involved in exploration activities in Bintuni Bay. Following the discovery of significant natural gas reserves, a consultation and negotiation process took place between ARCO and BPMigas for the acquisition of land (BP Berau Limited, 2006, p. xxi). Reinforcing the complexities of attaining and maintaining consent (Macintyre, 2007), ARCO has since been accused of being given access to the customary lands of three landowning communities, the Wayuri, Soway and Simuna, without their approval (JATAM, 2003; Down to Earth, 2005, p. 6).

In BP's resettlement planning document (BP Berau Limited, 2006), the company defends ARCO's acquisition of land, arguing that 'from the outset the project recognised indigenous or *adat* communities with special connections to land and resources'. As suggested earlier, recognition of traditional rights in Indonesia has historically held little significance, as these customary land rights can be overridden by the state. However, it is now a requirement in Indonesian law that land is obtained in consultation with the customary landowners and the establishment of appropriate methods of compensation (BP Berau Limited, 2006, p. 46).

The Wayuri, Soway and Simuna communities do not deny that representatives signed the agreement that relinquished their land rights; however, they do dispute the terms of the agreement. The clans' core objection is that according to Indonesian law, once these traditional rights are extinguished, they are irretrievable. The landowning groups claim that in signing the agreement they believed land rights would be relinquished for the life of the gas project, not for ever. However, as BP states, 'the law makes it clear that a traditional land right that has been relinquished cannot be revived or reclaimed by heirs' (BP Berau Limited, 2006, p. 45).

As an appendage to BP's resettlement planning document (BP Berau Limited, 2006), the company included the minutes of the Agreement between PERTAMINA/ARCO and representatives of the landowners, dated 20 May and 19 July 1999. The Minutes documented that the:

> landowners irrevocably relinquish the rights to the land, and their *hak ulayat* (indigenous land rights) will become forever null and void. The status of the land is released to the State, so that the Government shall grant the title to the land to PERTAMINA.[3]
>
> (BP Berau Limited, 2006, p. 265)

The minutes were signed by representatives of all three clans and witnessed by members of the Manokwari local government. Five years later, the three landowning clans released a statement addressed to BPMigas claiming that:

> the process whereby the Soway, Wayuri and Simuna relinquished land to Pertamina was not legally valid because it did not reflect whatsoever the value we place on land as a source of livelihoods which had been handed down to us through the generations.
>
> (quoted in Down to Earth, 2005, p. 6)

The contested nature of the PERTAMINA/ARCO agreement raises important questions about processes of consent, in particular how much information the landowners were given, the language in which the information was provided and how much pressure was placed on the landowners to sign the documents. Beyond issues of consent, further research may also consider questions regarding the potential inability of internal community decision-making processes and shifting alliances between different segments of the community and various NGOs. However, the fundamental issue raised by the landowners is that the Agreement does not align with the significance of land in their lives. While ARCO and the Indonesian Government might not have acquired the land in violation of Indonesian land laws, in the eyes of the clans the status of the land remains contested.

The West Papua case study demonstrates that even when states enact new laws in an attempt to promote legal certainty, they can also increase uncertainty for the social licence to operate for extractive companies in contexts where land ownership is contested. Moreover, intergenerational views on legitimacy and the justness of earlier agreements may vary over time.[4] This can lead to significant implications for the sustainability of extractive operations. For example, the conflict that ensued in Bougainville led to the cessation of mining activities altogether. One social issue that BP must now manage is that the Soway, Wayuri and Simuna clans will continue to claim the invalidity of the acquisition of their land from which the company profits significantly.

Since the core complaint of these landowners is related to the permanent alienation of their land, a distributive CSR paradigm may not be adequate to resolve this conflict. While further research into these complaints is needed, representatives of these particular landowning clans[5] do not appear to be seeking greater levels of compensation or more community development projects. Rather, as the signatory landowners argue:

> the community development projects and plans about new settlement and proposed community fund are part of BP's social commitment as set out in the Environmental Impact Assessment. They are nothing to do with the issue of the status of land that we are demanding.
>
> (Down to Earth, 2005, p. 6)

Unless BP and the Indonesian Government work hard to tackle the underlying issues associated with the status of land, it is possible that no revenue or community development package is likely to be considered sufficient recompense by the three protesting clans. Indeed, demands for changes to state law to return the legal ownership of the land to the traditional owners fall within the remit of governments, not corporations. However, a voluntary approach to CSR opens an opportunity for BP to contribute to peaceful development in West Papua. It may be possible for BP to use its financial and political influence to lobby Jakarta for greater recognition not only of traditional landowning rights, but also the importance of land to the cultural identity of Papuans. In this way, voluntary CSR could be used to promote status equality, feeding into the resolution of justice claims for recognition as articulated by Fraser (2008). As is demonstrated in the Papuan case, such claims for recognition can hold equal, in some cases more, weight in the peaceful resolution of local resentments of resource extraction.

One practical step that BP has mentioned it is willing to take in the pursuit of Papuan claims for recognition is to approach the Government to reverse the irrevocability of *hak ulayat* and to return these rights to the landowners once the Tangguh project has been completed (BP Berau Limited, 2006, p. 69). A potential risk associated with greater corporate involvement in state decision-making, however, is that it could lead to the emergence of what Kapferer (2005, p. 291) calls the 'corporate state', whereby state forms and practices become modelled after corporate-organisational and management ideals. Nevertheless, the history of resource development in West Papua indicates that if BP does not handle this conflict successfully, its corporate image will become increasingly enmeshed in, and tarnished by broader Papuan strug-gles for *merdeka*.

Resource politics as money politics

> Indonesia doesn't see us as real Indonesian citizens. They just use us for what they need in Jakarta.
>
> (WP29, religious leader)

Comparable to Bougainville, the state's ownership and control of West Papua's natural resources has been further complicated by the fact that parts of the Indonesian Government draw significant financial profit from the Freeport and BP projects. Consequently, the state and its security forces have a strong interest in maximising the profits of the two resource projects.

During the period 1991–2000 Freeport paid an average of US$180 mil-lion in taxes and revenues to the Indonesian government each year, making it Indonesia's largest taxpayer (Tebay, 2005, p. 19). In regard to BP, early estimates suggest that the Indonesian Government will earn nearly US$9 billion from the Tangguh LNG project from 2006–30, of which US$3.6 billon will go to West Papua (Tebay, 2005, p. 19).

On the face of it, $3.6 billion to the province of West Papua and $9 billion for the whole nation might not appear inequitable. As discussed above, how-ever, there have been significant problems in ensuring that these resources trickle down to local communities due to concerns related to local capacity of govern-ment. Therefore, it appears from the data collected for this study that Indonesia has attempted to give Papuans a greater share of revenues, without simultan-eously engaging with broader disputes over the recognition of customary land and the social and environmental problems caused by resource development.

Conclusion

This chapter has argued that as a result of the state's ownership of natural resources in Bougainville and West Papua, BCL, Freeport and BP are perceived by participants in this research as implicated in power relationships between states, local authorities and landowners. In this way, extractive companies may be seen by local communities as acting to endorse or entrench the denial of cus-tomary land tenure. Evident here is the complexity of defining the 'social'. While the social is 'imagined to be a limited specific domain' (Latour, 2005, p. 8) it might more accurately be conceptualised as a fluid, complex and heterogeneous web of associations.

Inadequate engagement or recognition of this complexity in relation to land has been a core objection of both the Bougainville and West Papua independence movements. Although the state is ultimately responsible for promoting peaceful development, it has been argued that corporations can, where possible, work to promote minority rights in the pursuit of national economic development. As the

Bougainville and West Papua cases illustrate, without this level of engagement there is a risk that the companies will become caught up with broader political struggles against the nation-state. It also increases the risk that resource projects will be shut down altogether.

An important observation in this chapter was that the state's control of natural resources often results in the inequitable distribution of resource wealth. In the following chapter, regional inequality in Bougainville and West Papua will be explored more extensively. It will be argued that even though a logical solution to this issue may appear to centre on providing landowners a greater share of mining royalties, these funds can distort relationships and create new internal divisions over access to wealth.

Notes

1 The issue of contests over resource wealth will be discussed in more detail in the next chapter, but it is raised here in order to illustrate how local interests can often be compromised by state equity in resource projects.
2 The implementation of Special Autonomy was 'slow due to the lack of capacity of legislators and that the establishment of the *Majelis Rakyat Papua* (MRP) or Papuan People's Assembly did not receive support from Jakarta' (Timmer, 2005, p. 6).
3 PERTAMINA is the Indonesian state oil company, which previously held the regulatory function of Indonesia's oil and gas Industry prior to BPMigas.
4 Discussed more extensively in the following chapter.
5 By no means should this be considered representative of all landowners.

Bibliography

Abrash, A. & Kennedy, D. 2002. 'Repressive mining in West Papua', in G. Evans, J. Goodman & N. Lansbury (eds.), *Moving Mountains: Communities Confront Mining & Globalisation*. London: Zed Books, pp. 59–72.

Ballentine, K. & Haufler, V. 2009. *'Enabling economies of peace'*. New York: United Nations. <www.unglobalcompact.org/docs/issues_doc/Peace_and_Business/Enabling_Economies_2009.pdf> [accessed 8 May 2015].

Banks, G. 2003. 'Landowner equity in Papua New Guinea's minerals sector: Review and policy issues', *Natural Resources Forum*, vol. 27, no. 3, pp. 223–34.

Banks, G. 2009. 'Activities of TNCs in extractive industries in Asia and the Pacific: Implications for development', *Transnational Corporations*, vol. 18, no. 11, pp. 43–60.

Boege, V. & Franks, D. M. 2011. 'Reopening and developing mines in post-conflict settings: The challenges of company–community relations', in P. Lujala & S. A. Rustad (eds.), *High-Value Natural Resources and Post-Conflict Peacebuilding*. Peacebuilding and Natural Resources, vol. 1. London: Earthscan, pp. 87–120.

Boege, V., Brown, M. A., Clements, K. P. & Nolan, A. 2008., 'States emerging from hybrid political orders: Pacific experiences'. Brisbane: *The Australian Centre for Peace and Conflict Studies Occasional Paper Series*, no. 11. <http://espace.uq.edu.au/eserv/UQ:164904/Occasional_Paper_No_11__Online_final.pdf> [accessed 8 May 2015].

BP Berau Limited. 2006. 'Indigenous peoples development planning document'. <www.adb.org/sites/default/files/project-document/68965/38919-01-ps-ipdp.pdf> [accessed 8 May 2015].

Braithwaite, J., Charlesworth, H. & Soares, A. 2012. *Networked Governance of Freedom and Tyranny*. Canberra: ANU Press.

Butt, S. 2014. 'Traditional land rights before the Indonesian Constitutional Court', *Law Environment and Development Journal*, vol. 10, no. 1. <www.lead-journal.org/content/14057.pdf> [accessed 8 May 2015].

Cook, C. D. 1995. 'The Amung way: The subsistence strategies, the knowledge and the dilemma of the Tsinga Valley people in Irian Jaya, Indonesia'. PhD Thesis, University of Hawaii, Manoa.

Dauvergne, P. 1997. 'Weak states and the environment in Indonesia and the Solomon Islands'. Resource Management in Asia-Pacific, Working Paper 10. <https://ccep.crawford.anu.edu.au/rmap/pdf/Wpapers/rmap_wp10.pdf> [accessed 8 May 2015].

Demian, M. 2003. 'Custom in the courtroom, law in the village: legal transformations in Papua New Guinea', *Journal of the Royal Anthropological Institute*, vol. 9, no. 1, pp. 97–115.

Dinnen, S., Mcleod, A. & Peake, G. 2006, 'Police-building in weak states: Australian approaches in Papua New Guinea and Solomon Islands', *Civil Wars*, vol. 8, no. 2, pp. 87–108.

Down to Earth. 2005. 'Tangguh – ignoring the reality'. <www.downtoearth-indonesia.org/story/tangguh-ignoring-reality> [accessed 8 May 2015].

Down to Earth. 2014. 'Forestry Ministry reluctant to relinquish control over forests'. <www.downtoearth-indonesia.org/id/node/1105#_edn1> [accessed 8 May 2015].

Filer, C. 1997. 'Compensation, rent and power in Papua New Guinea', in S. Toft (ed.), *Compensation for Resource Development in Papua New Guinea*. Canberra & Boroko: National Centre for Development Studies and Resource Management in Asia-Pacific Project (Australian National University) and Law Reform Commission (Papua New Guinea).

Filer, C. 2008. 'Development forum in Papua New Guinea: Upsides and downsides', *Journal of Energy & Natural Resources Law*, vol. 26, pp. 120–50.

Fraser, N. 2008. *Scales of Justice: Reimagining Political Space in a Globalizing World*. Cambridge: Polity Press.

Harple, T. S. 2000. 'Controlling the dragon: An ethno-historical analysis of social engagement among the Kamoro of South-West New Guinea (Indonesian Papua/Irian Jaya)'. PhD Thesis, The Australian National University, Canberra.

Hilson, G. 2012. 'Corporate Social Responsibility in the extractive industries: Experiences from developing countries', *Resources Policy*, vol. 37, no. 2, pp. 131–7.

International Institute for Sustainable Development & ICUN – The World Conservation Union. 2006. Promoting Conflict-sensitive business: fostering responsible business in fragile states. <www.iisd.org/pdf/2005/tas_objective_5.pdf> [accessed 8 May 2015].

Jamin, M., Nurjaya, I. N., Ridwan, M. & Safa'at, R. 2014. 'Shifting politics of law in the recognition of customary court in Papua following the enactment of Special Autonomy Act', *The US-China Law Review*, vol. 11, no. 4, pp. 367–88.

JATAM. 2003, 'Behind the BP Tangguh project propaganda'. <http://wpik.org/Src/286686.html> [accessed 8 May 2015].

Kapferer, B. 2005. 'New formations of power, the oligarchic-corporate state, and anthropological ideological discourse', *Anthropological Theory*, vol. 5, no. 3, pp. 285–99.

Kyed, H. M. & Buur, L. 2006. 'Recognition and democratisation: "New roles" for traditional leaders in Sub-Saharan Africa', Danish Institute for International Studies, Working Paper no. 2006/11. <www.isn.ethz.ch/Digital-Library/Publications/Detail/?lang=en&id=16739> [accessed 8 May 2015].

Latour, B. 2005. *Reassembling the Social: An Introduction to Actor-Network Theory.* Oxford: Oxford University Press.

Leith, D. 2003. *The Politics of Power: Freeport in Suharto's Indonesia.* Honolulu: University of Hawaii Press.

Macintyre, M. 2007. 'Informed consent and mining projects: A view from Papua New Guinea', *Pacific Affairs*, vol. 80, no. 1, pp. 49–65.

Macintyre, M. 2008. 'Police and thieves, gunmen and drunks: Problems with men and problems with society in Papua New Guinea', *Australian Journal of Anthropology*, vol. 19, no. 2, pp. 179–93.

Migdal, J. S. 1988. *Strong Societies and Weak States: State-Society Relations and State Capabilities in the Third World.* Princeton: Princeton University Press.

Mitchell, D. D. 1976. *Land and Agriculture in Nagovisi.* Boroko: Institute of Applied Social and Economic Research.

Muller, K. 2004. 'Background texts for the Amungme book'. <http://papuaweb.org/dlib/tema/amungme/muller/> [accessed 23 July 2015].

Nash, J. 1984. 'Women, work and change in Nagovisi', in D. O'Brien & S.W. Tiffany (eds.), *Rethinking Women's Roles: Perspectives from the Pacific.* Berkeley: University of California Press, pp. 94–119.

Ogan, E. 1971. 'Nasioi land tenure: An extended case study', *Oceania*, vol. 42, no. 2, pp. 81–93.

Oliver, D. 1973. *Bougainville: A Personal History.* Carlton: Melbourne University Press.

Pouwer, J. 1970. 'Mimika land tenure', *New Guinea Research Bulletin*, no. 38, pp. 24–33.

Primanita, A., Sihite, E. & Daslani, P. 2012. 'Constitutional Court invalidates BPMigas', *Jakarta Globe.* <http://thejakartaglobe.beritasatu.com/archive/constitutional-court-invalidates-bpmigas/> [accessed 4 May 2015].

Resosudarmo, B. P., Mollet, J. A., Raya, U. R. & Kiwai, H. 2014. 'Development in Papua after special autonomy', in H. Hill (eds.), *Regional Dynamics in a Decentralized Indonesia.* Singapore: ISEAS Publishing, pp. 433–59.

Risse, T (ed.) 2011. *Governance without a State? Policies and Politics in Areas of Limited Statehood.* New York: Columbia University Press.

Rosser, A. & Edwin, D. 2010. 'The politics of corporate social responsibility in Indonesia', *The Pacific Review*, vol. 23, no. 1, pp. 1–22.

Ruggie, J. 2008. 'Promotion and protection of all human rights, civil, political, economic, social and cultural rights, including the right to development'. Human Rights Council, Eighth Session, Agenda item 3. <http://198.170.85.29/Ruggie-report-7-Apr-2008.pdf> [accessed 8 May 2015].

Sumule, A. 2002. 'Protection and empowerment of the rights of indigenous people of Papua (Irian Jaya) over natural resources under Special Autonomy: From legal opportunities to the challenge of implementation', Resource Management in Asia-Pacific, Working Paper 36. <https://digitalcollections.anu.edu.au/bitstream/1885/40984/3/rmap_wp36.pdf> [accessed 8 May 2015].

Tebay, N. 2005. 'West Papua: The struggle for peace with justice'. London: Catholic Institute for International Relations. <www.west-papua.nl/Publiciteit/struggle%20for%20peace.pdf> [accessed 8 May 2015].

Thompson, H. 1991. 'The economic causes of the Bougainville crisis', *Resources Policy*, March, pp. 69–84.

Timmer, J. 2005. 'Decentralisation and elite politics in Papua'. State, Society and Governance in Melanesia Discussion Paper, no. 6. <https://digitalcollections.anu.edu.au/bitstream/1885/43227/2/05_06_dp_timmer.pdf> [accessed 8 May 2015].

Waagstein, R. W. 2011. 'The mandatory corporate social responsibility in Indonesia: Problems and implications', *Journal of Business Ethics*, vol. 98, no. 3, pp. 455–66.

Wesley-Smith, T. 1990. 'The politics of access: Mining companies, the state, and landowners in Papua New Guinea', *Political Science*, vol. 42, no. 2, pp. 1–19.

Wesley-Smith, T. 1992. 'The non-review of the Bougainville Copper Agreement', in M. Spriggs & D. Denoon (eds.), *The Bougainville Crisis 1991 Update*. Political and Social Change Monograph 16. Bathurst: Crawford House Press.

5 Hierarchies of revenue and compensation

Introduction

Chapter 4 highlighted several concerns associated with the perceived inequitable distribution of resource wealth in favour of the central governments of PNG and Indonesia, over the resource-producing regions of Bougainville and West Papua. However, akin to power relations surrounding extractive projects, inequity in the distribution of resource revenues is not isolated to a core–periphery conflict between rebel groups and national governments. Instead, contests over resource wealth (encompassing resource rents, occupation fees and compensation) can occur across multiple scales and at various stages throughout the life of an extractive project. This chapter introduces a third site of interdependence, revenue distribution. It does this through an analysis of the contests that have arisen at the national, provincial and local levels in Bougainville and West Papua. The problem exposed is that addressing these tensions can be more complex than simply giving resource-producing regions a greater share of wealth, either through formal revenue sharing formulas or compensation payments. Rather, the potential to avoid conflict could be contingent on how these payments interact with a broader range of dynamics, such as communication problems and experiences of 'relative deprivation'.

Wealth sharing is important because it aims to ensure all stakeholders benefit from a resource project. Claims for access to economic benefits, however, are not just about money. They can also be used to express a variety of other political and environmental concerns and may even indicate that no amount of material wealth will be enough to satisfy opposition to a particular development. The stakes for all parties are high because if revenue distribution is perceived to be unfair or unjust, production can be threatened.

This is not to suggest, however, that extractive companies are always to blame for such divisions and contests. Revenue sharing is inherently inequitable, particularly when it comes to compensation. Some individuals and groups are likely (and arguably, rightly) to receive more benefits than others, according to the damages experienced. The argument of this chapter, however, is that these contests can give rise to conflict when they compound other problems such as communication weaknesses, misunderstandings and jealousies.

Due to resource constraints, this chapter will not discuss every aspect that could be considered in relation to the case studies. Rather, the chapter aims to draw out the most salient points that have emerged from the fieldwork conducted, and subsequently woven into the arguments of this book. It is important to reiterate that the Bougainville data include the perspectives of those looking back over more than two decades to consider the distribution of wealth generated through the Panguna mine, as well as the socio-economic impacts these benefits have had. It is possible that there are inaccuracies in these narratives, or that they have been selectively recalled. Yet these are the stories that continue to be told and they offer important insights into how large extractive projects can reconfigure social relationships through the economic benefits they generate.

The chapter uses the lens of hierarchies of revenue and compensation to further develop the broader argument of this book as a whole, that distributing material resources to local communities is not necessarily sufficient to resolve local grievances and contests over extractive projects. Quite the contrary, material resources have the potential to ignite, prolong and exacerbate conflict. This problematises CSR strategies that rely on redistribution, and calls for a closer engagement with the interconnectedness of an extractive project with broader processes of social change.

Revenue sharing frameworks, compensation and peace building

Revenue sharing and compensation regimes are notoriously difficult and are unlikely to be supported by all (Filer, 1997, p. 156). As discussed in the preceding chapter, this is something which has been recognised in PNG and the notion of an 'ideology of landownership' (Filer, 1997). According to Filer, this ideology colours the status of 'landowners' who have '*only* become landowners over the course of the last 10 years' (Filer, 1997, p. 162). Filer (1997, p. 158) argues that as a result of this ideology, compensation payments are not necessarily determined through economic principle. Rather, they 'constitute one possible and widely variable element in the negotiation of specific social and political relationships' (Filer, 1997, p. 158).

This has been noted in accounts of the Lihir Gold Mine in PNG, where landowners are believed to have sought to manipulate social networks in order to gain and limit access to the economic benefits the mine generates (Bainton, 2009, p. 19). Landowners do this by keeping traditional networks and exchange obligations from view and by asserting distinct ethnic identities (Bainton, 2009, p. 19). In 'cutting short' these social ties, Bainton (2009, p. 19) contends that Lihirians have sought to redefine 'the "rationales of ownership" and the boundaries of exclusion, coupled with a re-categorisation of non-Lihirians in ways that ideologically shift notions of sociality, obligation and reciprocity'.

In spite of the conflicts that have emerged as a result of these kinds of 'manipulations', the emerging literature on post-conflict resource management has tended to focus on the impacts of wealth sharing at the national level. This is in contrast to the changes that can occur within provinces and between landowners themselves. Thus, while important arguments have been put forward with regard to the inclusion of revenue sharing frameworks into broader peace building efforts (Le Billon, 2008), less attention has been paid to how extractive companies might navigate the socio-economic impacts of revenue distribution at levels 'below the state'.

For example, as part of a three-tiered framework for the management of resource revenues in post-conflict environments, Le Billon puts forward proposals to enable 'resource revenues to consolidate a transition to peace' (2008, p. 1). The first proposals focus on 'extraction management', covering issues such as recovering looted wealth, post-conflict contractual reappraisal, as well as commitments to facilitate domestic entrepreneurship and employment (2008, p. 1). The second set of proposals refers to resource wealth distribution, such as direct disbursement to populations and the creation of 'special funds'. The final set of proposals concern the governance of natural resources, such as collaborative initiatives that bring together government, companies and civil society on issues related to extractive industries (2008, p. 1).

In setting out this three-tiered framework, Le Billon identifies two key challenges of post-conflict revenue management: how to address resource-related identity politics; and how to ensure revenues contribute to a sustainable and diversified economy (2008, p. 7). To address these issues, Le Billion advocates either direct disbursement of revenues to the population or some kind of 'hybrid scheme'. A hybrid scheme involves direct distribution of part of the revenue to the population, while 'the other part is retained by the government for public investment and social expenditure' (Le Billon, 2008, p. ii). Le Billon argues in favour of direct payments because they can send 'a signal to the population that resources are owned by the people, not by the government or the parties that control it' (2008, p. 9). Direct cash payments may also have trickle-down effects towards poverty alleviation and disaster recovery. Importantly, Le Billon also suggests that a sense ownership of the resources among the population can contribute to a sense of 'national identity and common destiny' (2008, p. 9).

While it is true that resource ownership could harness energy toward a common goal, the experience of Bougainville also suggests that direct payments can solidify minority identities and reinforce group differences. Further, while there are connections between resource revenue distribution and identity politics, disputes over access and control of resources are rarely caused by a single issue. As we have already seen, large-scale extractive industries in Bougainville and West Papua has been marked by what Rustad and Binningsbø (2012, p. 534) refer to as horizontal inequality, 'where some groups (ethnic, religious, geographical, etc.) think that others are receiving more than they are, or groups in natural resource-rich areas expect to get a bigger share of the resource revenues than they realistically can get'. The escalation of conflict in Bougainville and West Papua, however, is not solely attributable to the inequitable distribution of benefits between the central governments of PNG and Indonesia and the two resource-producing areas. Instead, over the life of the three resource projects, tensions have emerged between groups at different scales, sowing the seeds for conflict.

One example of the evolving nature of such tensions is when competition for access to benefits alters previously harmonious relationships between original inhabitants and 'economic migrants' who arrive in search of opportunities (Bainton, 2009, p. 23). Existing policy frameworks for the responsible management of natural resources have a tendency to sideline these factors and focus predominantly on the core–periphery relationship. A possible explanation for this is the emphasis on state capacity in the natural resource conflict literature, rather than the way in which resource development can reconfigure social networks, such as through: the redefinition of the terms of inclusion and exclusion (Bainton, 2009); the denial of access to funds to women (Kirsch, 2001, p. 155); and challenges to the legitimacy of the state to control resource-related wealth (Bainton, 2009, p. 19).

These changes have crucial implications on landowner compensation, narrowly defined as money given to compensate loss or injury, or for requisitioned property (Shorter Oxford English Dictionary, 2002, p. 467). While this may appear straightforward, people often hold divergent understandings of what compensation is as well as who should receive it and how much it should amount to (Filer et al., 2000, p. 1). Further, as discussed above, the real determinant of who receives compensation from mining companies does not necessarily reflect any intrinsic value to what is lost or damaged. As Filer, Henton and Jackson write: 'it follows that the proper compensation recipients are those who could stop operations, and the proper amount of compensation is the lowest amount which they will accept as the price of not doing this' (2000, p. 3).

This has important flow-on effects on other relationships involved in an extractive site, such as the authority of the state that is undermined when it is 'unable to prevent landowners from exercising veto power over resource developers' (Kirsch, 2001, p. 156). Further, resonant of Fraser's (2008, p. 16) understanding of justice as participatory parity, the ambiguous character of compensation can establish an experience of 'relative deprivation' within and between communities, potentially leading to misunderstandings and heightening jealousies.

The remainder of this chapter fleshes out some of these experiences in Bougainville and West Papua and illustrates how they have been linked to conflict. It explains how the distribution of wealth in Bougainville and West Papua has played into important changes in relationships between individuals, groups and local environments (Filer, 1990, p. 190).

Bougainville

The Australian Administration determined the first compensation procedures for the Panguna mine under the 1963 Prospecting Authority and the 1928 Mining Ordinance (Bedford & Mamak 1977, p. 3). Under this legislation, compensation payments related to damaged trees, gardens and other personal property destroyed by the company prospectors (Connell, 1991, p. 61; Bedford & Mamak, 1977, p. 7). Once the Administration and the company decided to go ahead with the mine, more formal procedures for the delineation of mining leases were required, which 'could not be issued by the Administration under the terms of the existing Ordinance' (Bedford & Mamak, 1977, p. 13). While the 1966 amendments encompassed occupation fees and compensation, the overall objective of these amendments was not to increase benefits for landowners but to provide a legal basis for the company to continue its exploration activities (Bedford & Mamak, 1977, pp. 9–13). Subsequently, in 1966 the Australian Government amended its 1928 Mining Ordinance to grant the company three leases that included: the port mine access road; the special mining lease; and the tailings area around the Kawerong-Jaba river system. The 1966 amendment incorporated the following provisions for compensation:

- damage to surface and improvements;
- loss of surface rights and access;
- consequential damage;
- formalisation of procedures through the Mining Warden;
- payment of occupation fees for 5 per cent of unimproved value (Quodling, 1991, p. 47).

Concerned about the inadequacy of the financial benefits that would flow to Bougainville under these amendments, Bougainville's House of Assembly member, Paul Lapun, lobbied the Australian Administration in June 1966 to obtain a better deal for landowners. One of Lapun's concerns was that Bougainvilleans were only entitled to 'a minimum occupation fee of $1 per acre per annum to landowners affected by prospecting or mining activity' (O'Faircheallaigh, 1984, p. 220). Lapun proposed that in addition to occupation fees, 5 per cent of the royalties payable to the Government should be paid to landowners (Bedford & Mamak, 1977, p. 13).

Lapun warned the House of Assembly that if the people were dissatisfied with the revenue sharing formula, trouble could arise and that the company would be welcomed if the landowners were given a share of the potential benefits (O'Faircheallaigh, 1984, p. 221). Concerned that a concession to landowners would give rise to consistently higher demands, Australian officials rejected this suggestion (Griffin, 2005, p. 293). Furthermore, the Administration persistently argued 'that the owners of the ground would be adequately compensated through the payment of the proposed occupation fee: the royalties in contrast belong to the country and will be used to promote development throughout Papua New Guinea' (Bedford & Mamak, 1977, p. 14).

Lapun's Mining Bill was defeated twice in the House of Assembly before he eventually convinced some members of the Administration in November 1966 that a share of royalties would satisfy his constituents and that some payments would be required to guarantee access to land (O'Faircheallaigh, 1984, p. 221; Bedford & Mamak, 1977, p. 11).

In spite of Lapun's victory, the concession 'did little to improve the situation on Bougainville, where conflict between the local people and CRA continued. In fact, many villagers refused to accept the payments due to them lest their acceptance to be interpreted as indicating their willingness to alienate their land' (O'Faircheallaigh, 1984, p. 221). Lapun was also criticised by some Bougainvilleans for requesting a smaller share for landowners and for Bougainville as a whole than originally anticipated (Bedford & Mamak, 1977, p. 15).

One problem for Lapun was that some landowners did not accept the mining company's presence, or the spreading of its activities. Villagers most directly affected by exploration activity such as those from Guava and Kokorei simply wanted the company to go away. This was reflected in the shutdown of three out of ten drills by August 1966 due to disputes over land access (Bedford & Mamak, 1977, p. 11). Bedford and Mamak (1977, p. 8) attributed this antagonism to antipathy toward the Australian Administration, whose representatives held the 'extremely difficult task of explaining and justifying an Australian-derived law relating to ownership of sub-subsurface minerals to a people who had totally different conceptions of rights accruing from land ownership'. Moreover, as there was no individual or representative body at this time, which had the authority to represent all landowners, Lapun was in the impossible yet common position of trying to represent both those who welcomed the mine, and those who wanted to terminate any future mining.

Company prospectors, however, did not always know about opposition to their activities. With the commencement of drilling activities, prospectors mainly used helicopters to travel between isolated sites and the coastal port town of Kieta (Bedford & Mamak, 1977, p. 9). Travelling by air meant company personnel failed to notice the '*i-tabu*' signs erected by villagers living in close proximity to drilling sites, which were intended to deny entry to strangers (Bedford & Mamak, 1977, p. 9). Failure to acknowledge the signs was seen by villagers as obvious disregard for their wishes (Bedford & Mamak, 1977, p. 9).

The earliest discussions regarding the distribution of wealth from the Panguna mine were therefore conditioned by the colonial experience and deeply entwined with conflicting views over Bougainville's future. The increased fiscal benefits for Bougainvilleans negotiated by Lapun under the 1966 amendments did little to alleviate the concerns of those dissatisfied with the company's presence, with hostilities waxing and waning over the following years. Adding to the complexity was that neither the company nor the Administration was able to inform landowners what the 5 per cent royalty share would actually mean in cash terms until mining commenced (Bedford & Mamak, 1977, pp. 16–17).

The construction and production period

Despite continued opposition by some landowners to the mine, the Australian Government signed the Bougainville Copper Agreement a year after Lapun's amendments (Cooper, 1991, p. 58). It was during this period that the company made some crucial decisions that have subsequently been criticised as major mistakes that could have been avoided if the advice of officials 'on the ground' had been followed (O'Faircheallaigh, 1984, p. 222). As O'Faircheallaigh (1984, p. 222) writes, 'CRA and the Administration could have done considerably more to try and understand the character of the local people, and to act in a way designed to minimise their resentment and allay their fears.' In particular, it is believed that CRA and Australian officials showed little appreciation for the importance of land to Bougainvilleans, as reflected in the small yearly payment landowners received for land that would be permanently lost to them (O'Faircheallaigh, 1984, p. 222). Procedures used to designate usage rights then became a factor contributing to conflict (Braithwaite et al., 2010b, p. 16), as neither the company nor the Administration took:

> into account the traditional hierarchy of land rights that served a different mode of production. Thus, villagers who had subsidiary claims under traditional tenure systems received much less than those who were regarded, however correctly, as primary right holders.
>
> (Wesley-Smith & Ogan, 1992, p. 256)

According to O'Faircheallaigh (1984, p. 223), one of the reasons[1] this was problematic was because:

> numerous individuals other than the current occupier might hold an interest (or potential interest) in any one piece of land. A cash payment might satisfy the occupier, but it offered nothing to other interested individuals who held rights for purposes such as hunting and food gathering.

Moreover, it has only recently been established that it was the Land Titles Commission 'that made final decisions on all matters for each of the more than 800 customary-owned blocks', including applications 'for replacements to be appointed for '"customary heads" who had died' (Office of the Principal Legal Adviser, 2014). This included the appointment of persons 'from a different clan from the original "customary head"', such as in cases where 'an original male "customary head" wanted his own child to replace him' (Office of the Principal Legal Adviser, 2014). This has important implications for the distribution of outstanding 1990 rent and compensation payments discussed in Chapter 10.

In spite of criticisms directed at BCL, former CEO, Paul Quodling (1991, p. 46), defends the company's early revenue distribution policies on the basis that 'there was little in the way of precedents throughout developing countries and virtually none within the Melanesian landownership culture'. While it is true that the Panguna mine was a unique project in the history of PNG, the question of whether previous business experience in Melanesia would have resulted in a deal more conducive to peace in Bougainville is open to speculation. Critics blame the company and Administration for refusing to listen to those who had the most direct experience with locals in the years preceding the Bougainville Copper Agreement (O'Faircheallaigh, 1984, p. 224). As Bedford and Mamak (1977, p. 54) write:

fears of civil disobedience or protracted court action (and associated bad publicity) did more to prompt settlement of disputes with landowners than any genuine desire to understand their problems and complaints.

Despite the contested nature of mining on Bougainville, the construction of the mine commenced, leading to dramatic and sudden social and environmental changes. Alongside these changes, landowners began claiming compensation for a diverse range of damages. For example, during the period 1969–80, compensation was made available to landowners for crops, resettlement, nuisance, land occupation, pollution (of rivers and fish) and loss of bushland (Connell, 1991, pp. 61–2). BCL was also required to build approximately 200 houses for relocated villagers from 1969–1989, along with providing 1,000 gallon water tanks and external toilets; weekly rations for six months plus one third of same for another six months; payment for damage to previous improvements (buildings and crops); A\$50 for severance of land from other land and another \$50 for loss of hunting tracks and footpaths; and A\$200 for loss of traditional lifestyle (Filer *et al.*, 2000, p. 69).

Instead of the positive benefits Le Billion (2008) associates with direct payments, this method proved problematic in Bougainville (Filer *et al.*, 2000, p. 103). A large proportion of these payments were used for short-term ends (Connell, 1991, p. 63; Quodling, 1991, p. 52), and landowners considered 'one-off' arrangements to be an inadequate form of compensation for the loss of cash crops that would have generated income throughout the period of the mine's operation (Connell, 1991, p. 63). There was also confusion on the island about the nature and capital value of these payments, and some Bougainvilleans without land in the mining-lease areas argued that BCL had in fact paid too much for cash crops as many owners still had access to their plantations (Bedford & Mamak, 1977, p. 38). As a result, there came to be a

> widely held belief on Bougainville that very large sums are being paid annually to people living near the mine. On the other hand, others claim that those Bougainvilleans in the lease areas are receiving virtually nothing in the way of compensation.
>
> (Bedford & Mamak, 1977, p. 3)

These conflicting perceptions continue today and are reflected in the Bougainville interview data collected for this study. For example, a Bougainvillean civil servant said:

> landowners were paid like the dole in Australia. They had everything they wanted. They became lazy. We regarded them as wealthy.
>
> (B36)

On the other hand, a former Bougainvillean employee of BCL stated:

> landowners were not benefiting too much. The national government was benefiting. The rate was too low to the locals who own the land.
>
> (B22, former BCL employee)

As the number of compensation claims began to rise, BCL established a Village Relations Department in 1970 'for the primary purpose of processing compensation claims through the Mining Warden's Court, and then avoiding the Warden completely' (Filer et al., 2000, p. 79). This was because of 'an inevitable similarity of many claims, coupled with a growing willingness to accept cash compensation on the basis of a set schedule of rates, rendered the court hearing procedure rather superfluous' (Bedford & Mamak, 1977, p. 33).

In spite of the increased acceptance of compensation rates, concerns about wealth distribution continued. One concern was that despite BCL having paid the required royalties on exports from 1972, landowners in the special mining lease had not received their share by the end of 1974, leading to tensions between the NSPG and the Government in Port Moresby (Bedford & Mamak, 1977, p. 55). Ongoing tensions were attributable to the fact 'that by its very nature [BCL's] purpose will always be in conflict with the cultural environment in which they are operating' and 'it is impossible to resolve this conflict simply through compensation payments' (Bedford & Mamak, 1977, p. 55).

Nevertheless, some form of compensation was required and expected and distribution procedures continued to evolve throughout the mine's operation. In 1980, BCL entered into a new compensation package with landowners (Filer et al., 2000, p. 42). The Agreement covered the Special Mining Lease, Port Mine Access Road Lease, and the three Tailings Leases (Filer et al., 2000, p. 43). The Agreement contained the names of 12 men who were listed as representatives of the PLA, but only four of these men actually signed it (Filer et al., 2000, p. 43). A notable innovation of the 1980 Agreement was the establishment of the 'Road Mining Tailings Leases Trust Fund' (RMTLTF) 'as the recipient of the social inconvenience compensation' (Filer et al., 2000, p. 43). Its purpose was to generate a source of revenue for landowners once the mine ceased operation (Connell, 1991, p. 65) as well as to discourage new types of compensation claims in the future (Filer et al., 2000, p. 44). The package included: an annual payment of K20,000 for disruptions to the Guava Access Road; a commitment by BCL to rectify the 'dusty conditions' along the Panguna–Jaba Road; and an expectation that trustees of the RMTLTF would

> use a portion of the social inconvenience compensation to deal with two particular 'social problems', namely:
>
> - the problem of the mentally disturbed people in the Leases; and
> - the loss and damage suffered by individuals in the Birempa area.
>
> [However,] the agreement provides no further details of the nature or extent of these problems.
>
> (Filer et al., 2000, p. 44)

Trustees of the RMTLTF included 12 titleholders responsible for investing money paid into the Trust for the benefit of future generations as well as to spend the income from these investments for the benefit of the wider community (Filer, 1990, p. 13). However, as Filer (1990, p. 13) notes:

> for reasons which are not entirely clear, formal membership of the Trust was never extended to the whole body of titleholders, while effective control of the funds soon passed into the hands of what appeared to be a self-perpetuating band of local businessmen, part of that class of Bougainvilleans who have apparently grown fat from eating at the table of the mining company.

Thus although the RMTLTF was seen as a logical response to tensions between Bougainvilleans over unequal development; it too gradually became a source of antagonism, with conflict developing between the RMTLTF executive and other landowners (Thompson, 1991, p. 82). Landowners held two concerns about the Fund. First, although the RMTLTF was additional to existing royalty and compensation regimes, it was perceived to 'divert' revenue (Connell, 1991, p. 64) for social inconvenience to the Fund, instead of direct payments being made to landowners and family heads (Filer *et al.*, 2000, p. 103). Second, and as a consequence, some landowners did not enjoy immediate benefits, as the Fund was set up to provide investment on behalf of future generations. As a Bougainvillean landowner explained:

> The money was being paid into the RMTLTF ... the money was not being paid directly to the landowners ... We asked, 'why isn't the RMTLTF setting up benefits for what BCL was paying into their accounts?' There was an expectation that anything to do with disruption to landowners should have been paid direct to the beneficiaries.
>
> (B20, ABG Department CEO/landowner)

Greed or grievance?

Various analysts of the Bougainville conflict have applied the greed and grievance debate to consider how competition for economic benefits contributed to violence. These scholars (Regan, 2003; Banks, 2005; Filer, 1990) share the view that the landowners were not motivated by greed. Regan (2003, p. 134) writes that:

> although grievances about the distribution of mine revenue were central to the origins of the conflict, the conflict was not primarily about rebel access to the wealth of the mine, nor did that wealth provide funding needed to make the rebellion more viable and thereby continue its presence.

Further, Banks (2005, p. 187) argues that although there were calls for money, 'this was less a call for a greater share of resource rents and more a statement that no amount of money would satisfy their grievances'. As such, the dominant thesis in the literature on Bougainville is that although some individuals might well have been motivated by greed, it was not the dominant driver. Instead, as Regan argues:

> local grievances about the impact of mining operations and the way its revenues were allocated fed into a long-standing sense of cultural and political exclusion felt by Bougainvilleans precipitating armed conflict.
>
> (Regan, 2003, p. 134)

As the greed and grievance framework has been considered to offer a limited lens through which to consider the nature of the conflict in Bougainville, scholars such as Filer (1990) and Banks (2005) have built on this framework by including a cultural analysis of the distribution of resource wealth. Banks (2005, p. 188) argues that the greed vs. grievance polarity limits our understanding of Melanesian resource conflicts, which might 'be more accurately mapped around notions of identity: individual, group and region'. Similarly, Filer (1990, p. 190) suggests that resource conflicts in PNG are not primarily about greed or grievance but are 'more centrally about the changes that occur in relationships between individuals, groups, and local environments'.

Banks and Filer thus consider the distribution of resource wealth as a single factor that generates a broader reconfiguration of local space. Mirroring Latour's (2005, p. 1) theory of the social, the local community is not 'a stabilized set of affairs'. Rather, the Bougainville data indicate that competition over access to economic benefits contributed to a three-layered hierarchy of contests.

National level contest – Bougainville

The first contest is created at the national level between PNG and Bougainville and stems from the inequitable amount of wealth channelled back to Bougainville compared with the central government. As discussed earlier, this unequal distribution exacerbated strong feelings of resentment that Bougainville's land was being exploited for the development of other provinces of PNG. As a Bougainvillean women's leader stated:

> the national government was looking to develop other provinces. I don't know why they did it. I was always talking about roads … they were never built like they were in Rabaul. They are important for access to services. Women are still carrying 'veggies' on their back.
>
> (B33)

Provincial level contest – Bougainville

The second contest was created at the provincial level with tensions evolving between landowners from the mining-lease area and Bougainvilleans more broadly. The key driver of this contest was the perceived lack of development for Bougainville as a whole, in contrast to the landowners. While the impact of resource extraction was most intense and visible for the directly affected local landowners, the impacts of the mining project were not limited to people from BCL's mining-lease areas. One Bougainvillean women's leader from another part of Bougainville expressed it this way. The compensation regime

> benefited only the surroundings [of the mine]. It didn't benefit us. That's when the problem started. Big damage was done on the outside too.
>
> > (B26, women's leader/religious leader)

While this is true of the 'big ticket' items such as a hospital that was built in Arawa, the NSPG, however, did channel mining revenue into rural development projects (O'Faircheallaigh, 1984, pp. 267–8).

Local level contest – Bougainville

The third contest took place at the local level between landowners themselves. Young landowners complained that it was the older generation of 'title-holders' that received the rents and compensation, and that there was no increase in these payments to give shares to young adults who came of age after the mine was established (Regan, 2010, pp. 18–19). There was also generational disagreement about how mining-related grievances should be communicated to BCL management, and in relation to the operation of the RMTLTF. As a Bougainvillean former employee of BCL stated:

> the Trust Fund was managed by the landowners. That broke the conflict with old and young.
>
> > (B6, Bougainvillean civil servant/former employee of BCL)

Intergenerational disputes evolved among Bougainvillean landowners as there was a perception that the older generation were reaping the financial rewards of the mine, at the expense of the young. According to two informants, this problem emerged when landowners stopped sharing the compensation payments equitably amongst themselves:

> they [the old PLA] would only get the compensation they were entitled to from the Bougainville Copper Agreement but there were accusations that they weren't giving that money out.
>
> > (B1, BCL executive)

> the problem was that they weren't sharing with families, only certain members of the family.
>
> > (B12, Bougainvillean peacemaker)

West Papua

Freeport

While inequalities in the Bougainville Copper Agreement can be identified, Freeport's Contract of Work with the Indonesian Government was even more problematic (Braithwaite *et al.*, 2010b, p. 71). Unlike BCL, which was required to compensate landowners, Freeport was not required to pay any compensation to the Amungme and Kamoro people (Leith 2003, p. 61). Rather, the 1967 contract was mainly concerned with encouraging foreign investment in Indonesia (Rifai-Hasan, 2009, p. 132). With the discovery of Grasberg, Freeport entered new contracts with the Indonesian government in 1991 and 1994; however, these too required no compensation requirements of the company to the landowners for the loss of land (Rifai-Hasan, 2009, p. 132). While the extension of the 1991 contract was less favourable to Freeport as it required the company to pay royalties at a tax rate of 45 per cent, West Papua has benefited little from these taxes (Rifai-Hasan, 2009, pp. 132–4).

As a result of international and local protests in the mid-1990s, Freeport has since adopted a more committed approach to environmental and social responsibility by undertaking a number of social investment projects (Rifai-Hasan, 2009, p. 129). These efforts have blurred the boundaries between wealth sharing and social investment projects, and the voluntary and legal characterisations of CSR. While some of these projects have been 'viewed as ineffective, inappropriate, and paternalistic by the traditional landowners ... what Freeport was doing was beyond what was legally required, both under Indonesian law and within the Freeport contract' (Rifai-Hasan, 2009, p. 134).

This form of engagement has been established in two different programmes: the 'Land Rights Trust Fund' and the 'Freeport Partnership Fund for Community Development'. The first of these programmes emerged out of an agreement between Freeport and the Amungme in what is referred to as the 1974 January Agreement. Responding to requests from the Amungme representatives for 'dialogue', the company pledged to construct community facilities such as schools, clinics and markets in exchange for their approval of mining activities (Abrash, 2001). According to Mealey (1996, pp. 303–4), six chiefs affixed their thumbprints to a document sealing the exchange of land under the terms set out in the 1974 January Agreement. However, according to several reports (ICG, 2002; Abrash, 2001), the affected villagers 'did not find out until 1995 that, according to state records, they had ceded a million hectares of land for development' (ICG, 2002, pp. 17–18).

Freeport considered the January Agreement a victory for *hak ulayat* in Indonesia as 'subsequent to that agreement the Government of Indonesia formally recognized the right to compensation for *hak ulayat* land rights' (Freeport-McMoRan, n.d.). According to Freeport, 'compensation in the form of recognition (*rekognisi*) is paid to communities for a release of *hak ulayat* rights, as *hak ulayat* is a communal property right. Such payments are made in the form of mutually agreed projects or programs benefiting the community' (Freeport-McMoRan, n.d.). The extent to which these payments have been mutually agreed, however, is contested. As a Papuan Human Rights worker stated:

> Freeport had done something considered compensation for land but the local community view is that this is not compensation – it's just decided by Freeport themselves – no discussion.
>
> (WP22, human rights worker)

From Freeport's perspective, however, the company has implemented two multi-year programmes in the form of *rekognisi*, which were developed and formalised in a Memorandum of Understanding with impacted communities. These programmes:

> have provided millions of dollars of infrastructure, social and economic development projects including housing, school buildings and student dormitories, medical clinics, places of worship, community buildings, roads, bridges, water tanks, electrical power, motorboats, sports facilities and feasibility studies for business opportunities.
>
> (Freeport-McMoRan, n.d.)

The company also claims that additional land rights trust funds were created in 2001 for the Amungme and Kamoro tribes for which Freeport contributed $51.9 million in 2013 (Freeport-McMoRan, n.d.).

In 1996, Freeport also created the Freeport Partnership Fund for Community Development, which became known as the One Per Cent Trust Fund. The Fund represented a commitment by Freeport to distribute 1 per cent of its annual gross revenue annually over each of the next ten years (Leith, 2003, p. 105). According to Freeport, $600 million was contributed through the Fund from 1996–2013 in four main programme areas: health, education, economic development, culture and religion (Freeport-McMoRan, n.d.). While the fund is the largest socio-economic development programme in West Papua, it has been criticised for representing a small fraction of Freeport's profits (Rifai-Hasan, 2009, p. 136).

The One Per Cent Trust Fund is distributed by the Amungme and Kamoro Community Development Organization (LPMAK), and was originally intended to favour those displaced as a consequence of mining (Rifai-Hasan, 2009, p. 136). However, the establishment of the Fund was controversial. As Soares (2004, p. 136) writes, 'before the disbursement of the One Percent Trust Fund, Freeport encouraged the indigenous communities to establish "NGOs" [to represent each of the seven tribes] in order to administer disbursements from the Trust Fund'. According to Ballard and Banks (2009), the Indonesian security forces hijacked this process and appropriated a portion of the funds under the guise of assisting the equitable distribution of the Fund to the indigenous communities. The authors say the Indonesian security forces did this by insisting that:

the fund be disbursed among all of the neighbouring ethnic groups, the so-called 'seven suku [tribes]'. By putting forward their own clients as leaders of these groups, individual security units were able to siphon off the lion's share of the benefits earmarked for the indigenous communities.

(Ballard & Banks, 2009, p. 167)

Competition over access to benefits through the Fund then became linked to violence when a clash erupted between the Amungme and the Dani (one of the seven tribes), in which 11 people were killed (Soares, 2004, p. 136). Following these clashes and due to a number of other social problems associated with the Fund, the Amungme tribal council (*Lembaga Adat Masyarakat Amungme*, LEMASA) eventually refused to accept money from the Fund at all. The reason, Abrash (2001) argues, is that the Fund was considered a bribe on the part of Freeport for its 'social license to operate'. As one LEMASA representative stated, 'with the help of God we shall never [succumb] to the offer of bribes, intimidation or [be] dishonestly induced into accepting PT Freeport Indonesia's "Settlement Agreement"' (anonymous cited in Abrash, 2001). This characterisation was also reflected in my fieldwork observations, where Papuans described the Fund as 'blood money'. As a Papuan activist stated:

> Local people pressured the company and [Freeport] decided to give one per cent of profit and was announced to the world as compensation to local people. But [it] was blood compensation. If they really wanted to do it, why didn't they do it from the beginning?
>
> (WP5)

Despite the many issues associated with the Fund, Freeport continued the initiative, with some estimates that by the end of 2000, $66.1 million had been committed (Leith, 2003, p. 105). Specific contributions included two hospitals, support for public health programmes, schools, community facilities, housing, scholarships and business opportunities (Riafai-Hasan, 2009, p. 136).

The procedure for distributing allocations from the Fund involves LEMASA and the Kamoro tribal council (*Lembaga Musyawarah Adat Suku Kamoro*, LEMASKO) submitting proposals for services to LPMAK. The LPMAK board then decides which projects will receive funding. One criticism from within these organisations is that while LPMAK is ostensibly independent from Freeport, the company has significant control over the allocation of projects that get funded. As a representative of one of these organisations stated:

> I agree that the money be given to LPMAK but not if Freeport is controlling the money. Just leave LPMAK independent and we will arrange it … so people can say LPMAK is not a department of Freeport but is independent.
>
> (WP26)

It is believed, however, that it has been Freeport's plan for Papuans to assume 'increasing responsibility toward self-governance in the management and spending of these funds' (Sethi *et al.*, 2011, p. 5). Yet this intention has been tarnished by concerns that the leaders of these indigenous organisations have been distributing money for unplanned and ineffective projects (Rifai-Hasan, 2009, p. 136).

Moreover, audits of LPMAK projects have revealed problems relating to programme management, safety and hygiene and poor management and leadership of educational programmes (Sethi *et al.*, 2011, p. 12). These outcomes have been attributed to the absence of 'even rudimentary experience in managing financial resources, operations and people' (Sethi *et al.*, 2011, p. 12). As a consequence, Freeport has been advised to 'expand the role of professionals in advising the LPMAK on program objectives, budgeting, spending on medical care, and public health initiatives' (Sethi *et al.*, 2011, p. 18). While the company has acknowledged this need, Freeport argues that 'the LPMAK is a community-owned and -led organization, and funding allocations must be based in community input' (Sethi *et al.*, 2011, p. 18).

BP

The initial compensation procedures for the Tangguh LNG project were quite different to those developed by Freeport. In the 1990s ARCO and British Gas conducted exploration activities, which resulted in the felling of sago, nipa palms and small trees (BP Berau Limited, 2006, p. 54). BP says that the companies agreed to pay compensation for these damages in the form of a single lump sum payment of approximately AUD$7,800 to the affected communities that were distributed among clans by a village leader (BP Berau Limited, 2006, p. 61).

Once the location for the Tangguh project had been decided, more extensive negotiations took place regarding the appropriate form of compensation. According to BP (BP Berau Limited, 2006, pp. 55–6), several meetings were then held between the companies, the resettlement affected communities, community advisers and the government to negotiate the compensation procedures. BP was particularly concerned about the possible social problems that could result from a sudden injection of large amounts of money. The company states:

> it became clear that a compensation package comprising cash and in-kind benefits would be the most effective way of addressing the complex social and cultural issues associated with the land tenure and use rights affected by the Project.
>
> (BP Berau Limited, 2006, pp. 55–6)

In terms of the cash payment, it was agreed that BP would award a lower rate of cash compensation to that stipulated under the Decree of the Bupati of Manokwari No. 213 of 1997 which had guided negotiations for compensation between locals and logging companies in the area. According to the Manokwari Decree, compensation was calculated at IDRP30–50/m². In contrast, it was decided that IDRP15m² (US$$0.0015/m²) would be awarded to the landowning clans in the vicinity of the Tangguh project. This would be in conjunction with 'in-kind' benefits such as new houses, clean water and community facilities (BP Berau Limited, 2006, p. 57).

However, a number of Indonesian NGOs have issued a letter to BP disputing the claim that the compensation was an agreed amount, and suggest that the indigenous landowners continue to be unsatisfied with the compensation arrangements established in 1999 (WALHI, JATAM & KAU, 2005). Therefore, similar to Freeport's 1974 January Agreement, while leaders of the landowning clans in the 1999 Agreement signed documents 'agreeing' to the exchange, the outcome of the negotiations has since been challenged.

An important difference between Freeport and BP was that in order to gain the financial lending necessary for the development of Tangguh, BP was required to follow international regulations regarding indigenous people and involuntary resettlement. In response, a publicly available resettlement planning document (BP Berau Limited, 2006) was developed for the Tangguh project according to the World Bank Group's Operational Directive 4.30 and the Asian Development Bank's policy on involuntary resettlement. The resettlement planning document outlines the compensation procedures for lost assets and income; assistance for relocation; the provision of appropriate housing, land and infrastructure comparable to what the relocated villagers would have without the project; as well as the impacts of resettlement (Asian Development Bank, 2015). The logic underlying the resettlement planning process is to achieve at least the same level of well-being for resettled households as would have been in place if resettlement had not occurred (BP Berau Limited, 2006, p. xxii).

Once the project's exploration phase was complete, it was decided that the optimal site for the Tangguh LNG plant was the southern shore of Bintuni Bay in an area occupied by the Tanah Merah village[2] (BP Berau Limited, 2006, p. xxii). Following the consultation agreements for the exchange of this land, BP established a marine safety exclusion zone and detailed agreements regarding entitlements for resettlement.

Significant problems arose, however, when BP began building houses and new facilities for the relocated households. Conflict and jealousies emerged as a result of BP's allocation of housing, health and infrastructure to villages affected by the development of the LNG plant on the south shore of the Bintuni Bay area. This distribution did not take into account that the gas extracted by BP is partly drawn from a reservoir under the north shore. Communities from the north shore have since lobbied BP for a share of profits associated with the project.

The Bintuni Bay area of the Tangguh project comprises a number of villages scattered along the northern and southern shores of the bay, with Babo (on the south shore) and Aranday (on the north shore) the closest towns to the project site (TIAP, 2002, p. 7). The total budget allocated for the resettled villages from 1999–2009 according to BP, was US$31,126,451, with compensation representing 70.8 per cent (BP Berau Limited, 2006, p. xxiv).

The allocation of these funds and their distribution is documented in an 'entitlement matrix' incorporating the holders of the *hak ulayat* (the Soway, Wayuri and Simuna clans), types of loss (land, marine resources, houses, gardens, forests, community facilities, cultural sites, livelihood and income) and entitlement. The entitlements provided by BP include both cash payments for land, the establishment of a development foundation of US$2 million for the three landowning clans, as well as material objects such as motors for fishing boats, meeting halls and traditional food packages (BP Berau Limited, 2006, pp. xxiv–xxxiii).

The differences between Freeport and BP in regard to compensation are indicative of the 30-year time lapse between the establishment of the two projects, and the more comprehensive regulatory guidelines that resource companies must now adhere to in order to guarantee financial lending. This is evident in the more rigorous public reporting of BP's compensation procedures in comparison to the scarcity of detail on Freeport's. As will be discussed further, however, the new regulatory environment has not guaranteed the avoidance of conflict over BP's compensation. Aside from security, competition and jealousy over the distribution of compensation has been one of the most difficult issues BP has faced in the establishment and maintenance of their operations at Tangguh. In this way, similar to BCL in Bougainville, Freeport and BP's distribution of compensation and revenue in Papua can be seen to have led to the creation of new internal contests.

National level contest – West Papua

The Indonesian Government has received a greater share of revenue from the Freeport project than Papuans. While some Freeport employees proudly claim that 'Freeport is the only company in Indonesia brave enough to give one per cent annually' (WP6 PT Freeport Indonesia employee), this 1 per cent does not amount to much in comparison to Freeport's contributions to Indonesia (Braithwaite *et al.*, 2010a, p. 73). According to Freeport, for the period 1996–2004 the company's total contribution to the Fund was $152 million. However, the direct benefits to Indonesia (through dividends, taxes and royalties) amounted to more than $8 billion (PT Freeport Indonesia, 2008, p. 39). As a result, many Papuans want to see either the closure of Freeport's mining activities or at least a significant increase in the profits to be returned to landowners and to Papuans more broadly.

As discussed in the previous chapter, Indonesia has gradually adopted a more decentralised system of government with significant implications for fiscal balancing between the central and regional governments (Resosudarmo, 2005, p. 4). The Special Autonomy Law has important ramifications for both the Freeport and BP projects. This is evident in the focus of the Autonomy package on recognition that West Papua's natural resources have not been used in a way that has improved the living standards of Papuan natives, or respected their basic rights (BP Berau Limited, 2006, p. 24).

According to the Tangguh Independent Advisory Panel (TIAP) (2011, p. 33), Special Autonomy transfers of BP's revenues have been channelled directly to the province of West Papua since 2008. Yet despite these large cash infusions, in 2011 West Papua province had the highest poverty rate in Indonesia (36.8 per cent), only slightly above Papua province (34.8 per cent) (TIAP, 2011, p. 33). Further, and as discussed previously, the political status of the Special Autonomy package has been rendered uncertain. Some also hold the view that most of these funds will be diverted back to corrupt pockets in Jakarta and will never actually reach West Papua (WP47, Indonesian religious leader).

Provincial level contest – West Papua

The revenue sharing formula set out in the Special Autonomy package has led to the creation of provincial tensions following Megawati's decision to divide Papua into three new provinces: Papua, Central Papua and West Papua. The new divisions meant that the wealth derived from the Tangguh project would only flow to 'West Papua province' and not to West Papua as a whole. As Budiardjo (2004) stated in a letter addressed to BP:

> specifically, the contest of West Papua will mean that the Tangguh revenues will now flow largely to Western Irian Jaya [West Papua] and not to Papua Province as a whole, thus exacerbating the potential for horizontal conflict and economic inequity.

While the risk of conflict associated with the contests led President Susilio Bambang Yudhoyono to impose a moratorium on the creation of new provinces (TIAP, 2011, p. 10), the national legislature enacted a law in 2008 that recognises the separation of Papua into two provinces: Papua and West Papua.[3]

Local level contest – West Papua

One of the most critical contests that Freeport and BP's compensation resources have created is at the local level between landowners and/or villagers living in the vicinity of the project areas. As stated above, Freeport's One Per Cent Trust Fund led to a clash in 1997, which was linked to the deaths of 11 people. While the Fund was considered a landmark at the time, in many ways there have been more critics of the Fund then there have been supporters. This was reflected during my own West Papua fieldwork where I encountered many community leaders critical of Freeport's distribution of large amounts of money. As will be discussed more extensively in Chapter 8, this has led to the creation of entirely new social problems such as substance abuse. As a Papuan religious leader stated:

> they need church programmes and socio-economic programmes to teach people how to use money. A problem for the church is the impact of the money – alcohol and HIV/AIDS.
>
> (WP2)

The distribution of funds among the Amungme and Kamoro groups also appears to remain contentious despite the administrative changes that Freeport has made through the establishment of LPMAK.

However, in trying to verify the compensation sharing formula, it also became clear that there is a lot of confusion within the community as to how the money is being distributed. As a representative from one of these organisations stated:

> I don't understand the contribution of money we have from the one per cent compensation. We don't know how much money consists from one per cent.
> (WP26)

In regard to BP, it could be said that the company was conscious of the potential negative impacts associated with the distribution of the One Per Cent Trust Fund. This is evident in BP's attempt to avoid the sudden insertion of large amounts of money, and instead to channel these funds into community development and infrastructure projects. Despite these efforts, conflict has arisen between the north and south shore villages of the Bintuni Bay area. Although this tension did not escalate into violence, it has nonetheless been one of the biggest problems that BP has had to manage during the life of the Tangguh project.

Conclusion

This chapter argued that BCL, Freeport and BP's revenue and compensation procedures have played into numerous contests within their host societies. It was argued that these tensions have primarily emerged through the creation of hierarchies of revenue and compensation at the national, provincial and local levels.

In Bougainville, the contest at the national level was exacerbated by the unequal distribution of mining revenues in favour of the central government. At the provincial level tensions evolved between Bougainvilleans in general and landowners as a result of miscommunication and misunderstandings. While at the local level a contest was created between landowners themselves as a result of intergenerational disputes over access to BCL's compensation payments.

Akin to Bougainville, contests at the national level in West Papua stemmed from the unequal distribution of mining and gas revenues in favour of the central government. At the provincial level, grievances were also directed towards the central government due to the perceived lack of development in West Papua more broadly. While at the local level, the distribution of compensation though the Tangguh LNG project created new tensions between north and south shore villagers who were not equally compensated despite comparable *adat* claims to the gas resources.

While there is evidence to support Collier and Hoeffler's (2005) emphasis on 'greed' through the Indonesian military capturing Freeport's resources to run a protection racket, the two conflicts are characteristic of a different kind of resource curse to what is discussed in this scholarship. Bougainville and West Papua's opposition movements did not capture BCL, Freeport and BP's resource projects to use them to buy weapons. Rather, it was a curse of the resources not being used to build, but to divide. This highlights the fragility and dynamism of the interactions that circulate alongside natural resource development.

A common theme identified in this chapter with regard to both the Bougainville and West Papua cases has been the problems associated with communication between the companies and local communities, particularly in terms of transparency around the distribution of resource wealth. The next chapter explores how inadequate dialogue between companies and communities can exacerbate experiences of political, cultural and economic marginalisation.

Notes

1 For a discussion of other complexities involved, see Regan (2007).
2 According to BP, the Tanah Merah village community comprised 127 households, which were required to relocate to two locations west of the village, namely the new villages of Tanah Merah and Onar Baru (BP Berau Limited, 2006, p. 6). Construction of the new settlements commenced in 2002 with the Tanah Merah community having been relocated in 2004.
3 According to one Indonesian informant, however, 'the legality of the province of West Papua remains unclear. The main reason is that in 2003 the Constitutional Court already annulled Law No. 45 of 1999 that creates two new provinces (Irian Jaya Tengah and Irian Jaya Barat) and four districts (Sorong, Mimika, Paniai, and Puncak Jaya) as it contradicted the 1945 Constitution. Therefore, all related regulations including Presidential Decree No. 1 of 2003 that enacted Law 45/1999 are deemed invalid. But the reality shows that the province remains in existence. Eventually President SBY [Yudhoyono] issued a Government Regulation No. 1 of 2008 to provide a legal basis for West Papua province. This law gives the same status of "Special Autonomy" to the province of West Papua' (WP47).

Bibliography

Abrash, A. 2001. 'The Amungme, Kamoro & Freeport: How indigenous Papuans have resisted the world's largest gold and copper mine', *Cultural Survival*, vol. 25, no. 1., <www.culturalsurvival.org/ourpublications/csq/article/the-amungme-kamoro-freeport-how-indigenous-papuans-have-resisted-worlds-> [accessed 11 May 2015].

Applied Geology Associates (AGA). 1989. *Environmental, Socio-Economic and Public Health Review of Bougainville Copper Mine, Panguna*. Christchurch: Applied Geology Associates.

Asian Development Bank. 2015. 'Involuntary resettlement'. <www.adb.org/Resettlement/default.asp> [accessed 11 May 2015].

Bainton, N. A. 2009. 'Keeping the network out of view: Mining, distinctions and exclusion in Melanesia', *Oceania*, vol. 79, no. 1, pp. 18–33.

Ballard, C. & Banks, G. 2009. 'Between a rock and a hard place: Corporate strategy at the Freeport mine in Papua, 2001–2006', in B. P. Resosudarmo & F. Jotzo (eds.), *Working with Nature against Poverty: Development, Resources and the Environment in Eastern Indonesia*. Singapore: ISEAS Publishing, pp. 147–77.

Banks, G. 2005. 'Linking resources and conflict the Melanesian way', *Pacific Economic Bulletin*, vol. 20, no. 1, pp. 185–91.

Bedford, R. & Mamak, A. 1977. *Compensating for Development: The Bougainville Case*. Bougainville Special Publication no. 2. Christchurch: University of Canterbury.

BP Berau Limited. 2006. 'Indigenous peoples development planning document'.<www. adb.org/sites/default/files/project-document/68965/38919-01-ps-ipdp.pdf> [accessed 8 May 2015].

Braithwaite, J., Braithwaite, V. Cookson, M. & Dunn, L. 2010a. *Anomie and Violence: Non-Truth and Reconciliation in Indonesian Peacebuilding*. Canberra: ANU Press.

Braithwaite, J., Charlesworth, H., Reddy, P. & Dunn, L. 2010b. *Reconciliation and Architectures of Commitment: Sequencing Peace in Bougainville*. Canberra: ANU Press

Budiardjo, C. 2004. 'Letter to Lord Browne of Madingley'. <www.minesandcommunities. org/article.php?a=720> [accessed 11 May 2015].

Collier, P. & Hoeffler, A. 2005. 'Resource rents, governance, and conflict', *Journal of Conflict Resolution*, vol. 49, n. 4, pp. 625–33.

Connell, J. 1991. 'Compensation and conflict: The Bougainville copper mine, Papua New Guinea', in J. Connell & R. Howitt (eds.), *Mining and Indigenous Peoples in Australasia*. Sydney: Sydney University Press, pp. 54–75.

Cooper, N. 1991. 'Bougainville reconsidered: The role of moral re-armament in the Rorovana land crisis of 1969', *Journal of Pacific History*, vol. 26, no. 1, pp. 57–73.

Filer, C. 1990. 'The Bougainville rebellion, the mining industry and the process of social disintegration in Papua New Guinea', in R. J. May & M. Spriggs (eds.), *The Bougainville Crisis*. Bathurst: Crawford House Press, pp. 73–112.

Filer, C. 1997. 'Compensation, rent and power in Papua New Guinea', in S. Toft (ed.), *Compensation for Resource Development in Papua New Guinea*. Canberra and Boroko: National Centre for Development Studies and Resource Management in Asia-Pacific Project (Australian National University) and Law Reform Commission (Papua New Guinea).

Filer, C., Hinton, D. & Jackson, R. 2000. *Landowner Compensation in Papua New Guinea's Mining and Petroleum Sectors*. Port Moresby: PNG Chamber of Mines and Petroleum.

Fraser, N. 2008. *Scales of Justice: Reimagining Political Space in a Globalizing World*. Cambridge: Polity Press.

Freeport-McMoRan. n.d. 'Indonesia'. <www.fcx.com/sd/community/land_indo.htm> [accessed 11 May 2015].

Griffin, J. 2005. 'Movements towards secession 1964–76', in A. J. Regan & H. M. Griffin (eds.), *Bougainville before the Conflict*. Canberra: Pandanus Books, pp. 291–9.

International Crisis Group. 2002. 'Indonesia: Resources and conflict in Papua', ICG Asia Report, no. 39. <www.crisisgroup.org/~/media/Files/asia/south-east-asia/indonesia/ Indonesia%20Resources%20and%20Conflict%20in%20Papua> [accessed 8 May 2015].

Kirsch, S. 2001. 'Property effects: Social networks and compensation claims in Melanesia', *Social Anthropology*, vol. 9, no. 2, pp. 147–63.

Latour, B. 2005. *Reassembling the Social: An Introduction to Actor-Network Theory*. Oxford: Oxford University Press.

Le Billon, P. 2008. 'Resources for peace? Managing revenues from extractive industries in post-conflict environments'. Political Economy Research Institute, Working Paper Series, no. 167. <http://scholarworks.umass.edu/cgi/viewcontent. cgi?article=1138&context=peri_workingpapers> [accessed 11 May 2015].

Leith, D. 2003. *The Politics of Power: Freeport in Suharto's Indonesia*. Honolulu: University of Hawaii Press.

Mealey, G. A. 1996. *Grasberg: Mining the Richest and Most Remote Deposit of Copper and Gold in the World, in the Mountains of Irian Jaya, Indonesia*. New Orleans: Freeport-McMoRan Copper & Gold.

O'Faircheallaigh, C. 1984. *Mining and Development*. Beckenham: Croom Helm.

Office of the Principal Legal Adviser. 2014. 'Appointing "customary heads" of landowning groups in the Panguna mine lease areas for the purpose of receiving and distributing land rent & compensation'. Autonomous Bougainville Government, Buka. Unpublished document.

PT Freeport Indonesia. 2008. 'Core values: 2008 working toward sustainable development report'. <www.fcx.com/sd/pdfs/WTSD_2008.pdf> [accessed 11 May 2015].

Quodling, P. 1991. *Bougainville: The Mine and the People*. St Leonards: Centre for Independent Studies.

Regan, A. J. 2003. 'The Bougainville conflict: Political and economic agendas', in K. Ballentine & J. Sherman (eds.), *The Political Economy of Armed Conflict: Beyond Greed and Grievance*. Boulder, CO: Lynne Rienner, pp. 133–66.

Regan, A. J. 2007. 'Development and conflict: The struggle for self-determination in Bougainville', in M. A. Brown (ed.), *Security and Development in the Pacific Islands: Social Resilience in Emerging States*. Boulder, CO: Lynne Rienner, pp. 89–110.

Regan, A. J. 2010. *Light Intervention: Lessons from Bougainville*. Washington, DC: US Institute of Peace Press.

Resosudarmo, B. P. 2005. 'Introduction', in B. P. Resosudarmo (ed.), *The Politics and Economics of Indonesia's Natural Resources*. Singapore: ISEAS, pp. 1–10.

Rifai-Hasan, P. A. 2009. 'Development, power, and the mining industry in Papua: A study of Freeport Indonesia', *Journal of Business Ethics*, vol. 89, no. 2, pp. 129–43.

Rustad, S. A. & Binningsbø, H. M. 2012. A price worth fighting for? Natural resources and conflict recurrence, *Journal of Peace Research*, vol. 49, no. 4, pp. 531–46.

Sethi, S. P., Lowry, D. B., Veral, E. A., Shapiro, H. J. & Emelianova, O. 2011. 'Freeport-McMoRan Copper & Gold, Inc.: An innovative voluntary code of conduct to protect human rights, create employment opportunities, and economic development of the indigenous people', *Journal of Business Ethics*, vol. 103, no. 1, pp. 1–30.

Shorter Oxford English Dictionary. 2002. *Shorter Oxford English Dictionary on Historical Principles*, 5th edn., vol. 1: A–M. Oxford: Oxford University Press.

Soares, A. D. J. 2004. 'The impact of corporate strategy on community dynamics: A case study of the Freeport mining company in West Papua, Indonesia', *International Journal on Minority and Group Rights*, vol. 11, pp. 115–42.

Tangguh Independent Advisory Panel (TIAP). 2002. 'First report on Tangguh LNG project'. <www.bp.com/content/dam/bp-country/en_id/Documents/TIAPReport/2002%20 TIAP%20First%20Report.pdf> [accessed 11 May 2015].

Tangguh Independent Advisory Panel (TIAP). 2011. 'First report on operations phase of the Tangguh LNG project'. <www.bp.com/content/dam/bp-country/en_id/Documents/ TIAPReport/2011%20TIAP%20First%20Report%20on%20Operations%20Phase. pdf> [accessed 11 May 2015].

Thompson, H. 1991. 'The economic causes of the Bougainville crisis', *Resources Policy*, March, pp. 69–84.

WALHI, JATAM, & KAU. 2005. 'Tangguh LNG project-Papua-Indonesia'. <www. forum-adb.org/inner.php?sec=13&ref=extras&id=21> [accessed 11 May 2015].

Wesley-Smith, T. & Ogan, E. 1992. 'Copper, class, and crisis: Changing relations of production in Bougainville', *The Contemporary Pacific*, vol. 4, no. 2, pp. 245–67.

6   Preventive peace dialogue

Introduction

This chapter discusses the efforts made by BCL, Freeport and BP to initiate dialogue with local communities. The fourth site of interdependence identified between the companies and the root causes of conflict in Bougainville and West Papua, therefore, is representation.

The chapter opens with a discussion of the concept of 'stakeholder dialogue'. Scholars and companies use this concept to refer to processes of communication between large corporations and local communities. The effectiveness of stakeholder dialogue as a tool for promoting peaceful development in Bougainville and West Papua will then be analysed. It will be argued that although stakeholder dialogue as a mechanism to facilitate peaceful development is a good idea in theory, the case studies reveal that it is complex to achieve in practice. This is because its success appears to be contingent on the level of progress made on a variety of other justice claims.

Stakeholder dialogue

'Stakeholder dialogue' is a business practice that emphasises consultation as the baseline for good corporate governance (Unerman & Bennett, 2004, p. 685). The concept was popularised in the mid-1990s and was implemented by NGOs such as the World Wildlife Fund, closely followed by individual companies such as Body Shop. Stakeholder dialogue was later adopted by coalitions of companies including the World Business Council for Sustainable Development (WBCSD) (Kaptein & van Tulder, 2002, p. 208). The WBCSD describes stakeholder dialogue as 'a powerful catalyst for change. It promotes greater transparency, information sharing and inspires society to work together' (WBCSD, n.d., p. 2). In recent years, the concept has been so widely accepted in both academic and business circles that it has been acclaimed as 'a cornerstone of corporate social, environmental, economic and ethical governance' (Unerman & Bennett, 2004, p. 685).

Stakeholder dialogue is underpinned by a commitment between corporations and society to better understand the challenges and pressures facing each other

(Burchell & Cook, 2008, p. 44). This commitment is made manifest through principles of 'openness' and a willingness to consider alternative viewpoints (Burchell & Cook, 2008, p. 36). In the context of the extractives industry, the goal of stakeholder dialogue could be described as a commitment on the part of corporate management to see the resource project through the eyes of the local community, and for the local community to see the project through the eyes of corporate management.

What constitutes 'dialogue' in stakeholder dialogue discourse is somewhat loosely defined but can include: information dissemination, conferences, reports, training and consultation, as well as more structured forums between companies and NGOs (Burchell & Cook, 2008, p. 157). However, since the 1990s, there has been an increasing acceptance on the part of business that there is a need to move beyond information dissemination to respond to the concerns that stakeholders define for themselves (Burchell & Cook, 2008, p. 167). Subsequently there is recognition of the need for firms to go further than simply publishing documents about the company's priorities to proactively engage with the priorities of locals.

The process of achieving effective and meaningful stakeholder dialogue is difficult and complex. Pedersen (2006, p. 138) identifies five characteristics of effective stakeholder dialogue: inclusion, openness, tolerance, empowerment and transparency. Pedersen argues, 'as a participatory ideal, the stakeholder dialogue should include the important groups and individuals who affect and/or are affected by the decision or the issue in question'. In the case of the extractives sector this could include: landowners, NGOs, women's leaders, religious organisations, the state, military and police. However, corporations hold the power and capacity to decide who is included and who is not (Kapelus, 2002, pp. 290–1). These decisions are fraught as the inclusion of one group can involve the corresponding exclusion of another (Mena et al., 2010, p. 167). The potential for conflict to arise in such situations is extremely high and is evident in the cases of Bougainville and West Papua.

An important question to be raised of stakeholder dialogue rests on how the goals of 'inclusion, openness, empowerment and transparency' between companies and stakeholders can be achieved in the context of resource projects, in which some of these groups are subject to considerable cultural, political and economic marginalisation. This question takes in broader considerations than just how companies might accurately and justly identify stakeholders. The argument presented in this chapter is that there appears to be a gap between the ideals of stakeholder dialogue in theory and what might be required to achieve it in practice.

The crux of the argument put forward in this chapter is that 'understanding' between parties and 'empowerment' of local communities appears unlikely to manifest in the absence of broader commitments by the company to make progress on justice outcomes in other areas or alongside particular dialogues about the nature of the company's operations. This feeds into a broader vision for a reconfiguration of CSR to be discussed in detail in Chapter 11. The proposed reconfiguration includes preventive peace dialogue on the social, political and

environmental terms of access to land through ongoing and collaborative negotiations between a range of stakeholders on the full range of justice claims that
the resource project feeds into. Although, as reflected in the Bougainville and
West Papua case studies, this is far easier to express than it is to put in place in
the complex social environments that extractive industries engender in conflict
and post-conflict societies.

The emphasis on representation in Interdependent Engagement is wider than
that generally encompassed by the discourse of stakeholder dialogue. This is
because it highlights the importance of not just the creation of a 'safe space' for
locals to communicate their concerns to company representatives, but also the
potential for resource companies to initiate dialogue on the institutional changes
required for these concerns to be perceived as adequately recognised.

Bougainville

While 'stakeholder dialogue' had not been articulated into a formal set of principles or techniques in the days of the preparation for and operation of the
Panguna mine, there is evidence to suggest that BCL did recognise the value of
dialogue. For example, BCL appointed Village Relations officers who undertook
the specific task of conveying the grievances of Bougainvilleans to BCL management. Despite these appointments, communication problems became one of
the crucial issues the company faced leading up to the conflict (Vernon, 2005,
p. 258).

Communication was a particular problem for BCL because although the
technique it used was not named 'stakeholder dialogue' it was based on similar principles and, as a result, shared the same apparent limitations. Specifically,
the Bougainville fieldwork data suggest that BCL did not recognise that progress needed to be made on the cultural, political and economic marginalisation
felt by a significant proportion of Bougainvilleans at the hands of the Australian
Administration, the PNG Government and the company itself, before meaningful dialogue could occur. Unawareness of this was compounded by differences
between Bougainvillean and Australian culture, and the ways in which they
might impact on processes of dialogue and communication.

Colonialism, language and racism

The earliest constraint for BCL in establishing a positive relationship with landowners and the people from villages surrounding its mining-lease areas was the
colonial logic that drove the development of the mine. The development of the
mine exacerbated a 'long-standing sense of cultural and political exclusion felt
by Bougainvilleans' (Regan, 2003, p. 55). So from the outset putting in place
Pedersen's (2006, p. 138) precondition of 'inclusion' for effective stakeholder dialogue was highly problematic.

While not unique to Bougainville, there were specificities in the relationship
between Bougainvilleans and BCL, which added greater complexity, such as language diversity. The company found it difficult to effectively inform locals of the

expected social and environmental impacts of the mine. Former CEO of BCL, Don Vernon claims that during the early stages of the mine's development there were approximately 20 distinct language groups present in Bougainville, none of which was dominant (Vernon, 2005, p. 263). The company initially relied on colonial officers for interpretation, before choosing to use Pidgin[1] (Vernon, 2005, p. 263). Two of BCL's first community programmes were sponsorship of Pidgin language training for expatriate staff (Vernon, 2005, p. 263), and an employee orientation programme that included education about Australian and Bougainvillean social conventions (Robinson cited in Tonks & Dowling, 1999, p. 13).

In addition to being a strategy to improve communication between expatriate employees and Bougainvilleans, the Pidgin language training and employee orientation programme were also aimed at achieving 'tolerance, acceptance and understanding' between the company employees and locals. BCL believed that encouraging communication between expatriates and Bougainvilleans would introduce new ideas to the community (Bougainville Copper Limited, BCL Environment and Community Relations Division, n.d.) and would reduce the risk of racist behaviour by Australian staff. According to a current executive of BCL the company's efforts in this regard were:

> a form of self-regulation. The big stick was how expensive it was to ship people out if they did anything wrong that was likely to cause any disruption to the mine. Employees had to undergo psychological tests on racism for example. It did not always work but the precaution was there.
>
> (B1, BCL executive)

Some Bougainvilleans believe that in fact there was racism displayed by BCL employees, and that it demonstrated the ineffectiveness of BCL's efforts to achieve effective dialogue. For example, Momis stated in a letter addressed to a former CEO of BCL that 'so many of your employees are racist, openly contemptuous of us, just as the kiaps were' (Quodling, 1991, p. 92). Momis' reference to racism highlights the connection between the effectiveness of stakeholder dialogue and progress made in dealing with deeper sources of injustice, namely, Bougainville's colonial history. This deeper issue remained salient regardless of whether racism was experienced widely, or whether it was expressed 'on the odd occasion' by a minority of individuals. Racism in the colonial context is intertwined with broader feelings of subjugation on the part of the colonised (Bougainvilleans), and the perceived sense of superiority of the colonisers (Australians). As a Nasioi landowner stated:

> racism was not a major issue, but the people were illiterate and the people who came in were educated. It was a sudden impact on the people from the primitive to the modern.
>
> (B29, Nasioi landowner)

This quote demonstrates that achieving 'tolerance, acceptance and understanding' is not only constrained by language and incidents of racism, but also by the company's history and association with broader experiences of colonialism and associated relationships of dependency.

For language programmes and dialogue on the social and environmental impacts of the mine to achieve its intended aims, it's possible that BCL would have needed to first recognise and engage with issues associated with the company's involvement in historical injustices. Teaching hundreds of employees Pidgin would have required considerable effort on the part of BCL; however, considering the exclusion of Bougainvilleans from the Bougainville Copper Agreement, it is not difficult to see how, for many, these efforts were met with suspicion, perceived as disingenuous and ultimately proved ineffectual.

Perceptions of BCL's effort

Discrepancies between the mechanisms BCL thought appropriate to establish dialogue with Bougainvilleans and the expectations of affected communities continued throughout the life of the mine. Because the mine affected such a large area of Bougainville, local villages were affected in very different ways. One of the biggest criticisms of BCL's Village Relations Department was that its staff primarily engaged with villagers in the immediate vicinity of the mine. As a Bougainvillean former employee of BCL claims:

> BCL provided avenues to bring our complaints but liaison officers could have really gone out, not only the places around BCL. There was a liaison officer. Liaison officers were Bougainvillean or Papua New Guinean but they failed to go to the villages. Or if they did, they could have done better.
>
> (B27, former BCL employee/women's leader)

Moreover, the inability to find a sustainable solution to the complex and long-running relationship between Bougainvilleans and the PNG Government meant that landowners felt excluded from the project at times and became increasingly frustrated by the lack of response to their complaints. Bougainvillean suggestions on how progress could have been made on this issue give one insight as to an alternative approach to dialogue that might have been more effective:

> what BCL should have done is sit with the landowners and discuss a resolution. Then approach the PNG Government. This would not have been rejected by the landowners. It's our culture. We contribute ideas to the discussion. Share grievances and decide on steps. We could have ended it that way.
>
> (B20, ABG Department CEO/landowner)

If BCL had engaged with the landowners in this way, participants in this research suggest the company may have been able to demonstrate that they were willing to learn more about the landowners' experiences of the impacts of the mine.

This strategy may also have recognised the concerns held by Bougainvilleans that the PNG Government was failing to represent and protect their interests in the pursuit of national economic development. Yet the Bougainville fieldwork data suggest that BCL did not believe that any of the criticisms outlined above reflected a lack of initiative or failure on their part. Rather, the company's management believed that their lack of understanding about landowners' concerns was attributable to 'cultural problems' associated with hiring Bougainvilleans in the company's Village Relations Department.

Village Relations and the 'wantok system'

> Management weren't getting the true picture from the community because of the rivalry between clans. If we had known this at the time, the conflict could have been very different.
>
> (B1, current executive of BCL)

It has been argued by BCL executives that the problems in BCL's Village Relations Department were the result of a clash between two systems: 'clan loyalty' and 'bureaucratic neutrality'. The 'wantok system', a Melanesian form of social responsibility (Lea, 1993, p. 91) became a problem for BCL when it appointed Bougainvilleans to work in the company's Village Relations Department and in senior management positions. These employees were hired to voice the concerns of Bougainvilleans generally, but they were 'subject to local loyalties and politics and thus under suspicion that they favoured some groups more than others' (Vernon, 2005, p. 264).

According to Lea (1993, pp. 91–2), 'wantokism' 'has its roots in the traditional pre-eminence of community values over individual preferences' and sets out 'the mutual duties and responsibilities, which exist between those individuals who share the same language'. *Wantoks* (from one 'talk' or language) 'were expected to help one another with food, lodging and employment' (Levine, 1999, p. 170). The system requires that *wantoks* share the benefits and advantages that they acquire (Lea, 1993, p. 91) with networks of friends, neighbours and acquaintances, and is essentially an egalitarian way for the community to take care of one another.

Local loyalties became a problem for BCL because *wantok* obligations meant Bougainvillean Village Relations officers were required to maintain responsibility to their own clans rather than relevant landowners or to Bougainvilleans generally. As a consequence, BCL claims that it was not getting a clear picture of community problems because of personal rivalries. A current executive of BCL claims:

> this complexity was the reason we had no Bougainvilleans on the BCL board. [A senior Bougainvillean] would just tell BCL community opinions from his own clan – not the experiences of other clans. [Francis] Ona wanted to get rid of him for this reason.
>
> (B1, current BCL executive)

Discontent with BCL's Village Relations Department staff was reportedly so high that some landowners called for the replacement of the non-landowning Bougainvilleans with expatriates to avoid bias (Filer, 1990, p. 7).

The assertion by BCL, however, that the problems with Village Relations officers were linked to the *wantok* system is contested. As a Bougainvillean who once worked for BCL as a welfare officer claimed, 'it was just an attitude problem of the people who worked in Village Relations' (B33) rather than any structural limitations of the *wantok* system. The former welfare officer went on to say:

> it was run by [one of the landowners]. They didn't understand their role ... and it was the very place that people took their grievances. They were not kind characters. They were the kind of characters to make a situation diffuse ... Why couldn't he speak in his language to his own people? BCL were always willing. It was just these people that were problematic. Why couldn't they feel for the landowners?
>
> (B33)

Other Bougainvilleans interviewed for this study believe the communication problem was more symbolic of a lack of initiative on the part of BCL, rather than any inherent limitations of the *wantok* system in being able to represent the interests of others. The CEO of an ABG Department claimed:

> People have to be called together. We have clan connections. One will go and talk to that side and bring the parties together. It's our culture.
>
> (B20, ABG Department CEO/landowner)

These kinds of discrepancies between the views of BCL and those of Bougainvilleans bring us to the heart of the complex relationship between foreign multinationals and the life worlds of host communities. As a current executive of BCL argued:

> there is no magic bullet to deal with this complexity. Every place is different and there is always a lack of understanding. It is always a problem because we are not them ... even when we employed the best anthropologists like [Douglas] Oliver, we still had this problem.
>
> (B1, current executive of BCL)

The method of employing anthropologists as a way to overcome this complexity is limited because no one, no matter how deep their understanding of the behaviour of any one group can be expected to accurately predict how that group will behave in future radically changed circumstances. As Latour (2005, p. 28) argues, 'relating to one group or another is an on-going process made up of uncertain, fragile, controversial and ever-shifting ties'.

Generational disputes

The need for long-term dialogue with various groups in the community became most evident in Bougainville when a generational dispute erupted within the PLA. From 1981 a new generation of landowners became increasingly frustrated both with BCL's response to several long-standing disputes, and the perceived complacency of the older landowners (Wesley-Smith, 1991, p. 188). In 1987 a separate group, the NPLA formed under the leadership of Francis Ona's cousin, Perpetua Serero. According to a Bougainvillean landowner who was a part of the NPLA:

> BCL and national government, they didn't do anything about this one. There was a meeting called. Landowners went but two executives didn't turn up. First roadblock started then.
>
> (B24, chief/landowner)

The BCL executives chose not to turn up to the meeting according to Tanis, because 'the management of BCL refused to recognise the NPLA, and maintained its links with the long-established PLA, representing the older generation' (Tanis, 2005, p. 463). A current executive of BCL supports this claim, stating that:

> the so-called NPLA approached the company and asked for an unrealistic sum of money – but Paul Quodling [CEO of BCL at the time] said no.
>
> (B1, current executive of BCL)

Although most agree that the demands being put forward by the NPLA were unrealistic, including K10 billion in compensation, there is a popular perception on Bougainville that if BCL and the PNG Government had at least negotiated with them, it is possible that the conflict would not have erupted in the way that it did. As a Bougainvillean former employee of BCL claimed:

> At one stage we heard about the K10 billion claim. After that, the crisis started. No answer to [the] claim. Obviously there was some communication weakness. There might have been a different outcome.
>
> (B34, former BCL employee)

Contrary to the perspective of BCL executives, therefore, the communication problems the company faced was not just born out of the complexity of Bougainvillean culture and social structures. Miscommunication between the company and landowners also appears to have emerged through a lack of initiative on the part of BCL to engage with broader sources of injustice, especially feelings of exclusion, subjugation and the heterogeneity of local communities.

One strategy that has evolved in the PNG context in an attempt to minimise the social impacts of mining is what Filer (1990, p. 18) refers to as the 'package/

forum concept'. The concept is based on the assumption 'that it is possible to control the actual or potential opposition of local landowners to other mining projects by adjusting the size and contents of their compensation "package" through a form of consultation'. Filer (1990, p. 19) describes the forum/package concept as 'both a way of controlling the relationship between mining companies and local interest groups (landowners, communities, provincial governments) and a way of trying to maintain the principles of long-term benefit and "regional equality" at a national level, against the special pleadings of these local interest groups'. Filer (1990, p. 22) argues that one problem with the forum concept is that '"deals" done with one generation of landowners, or their leaders, will be repudiated by the next generation, regardless of the manner in which these deals are negotiated'.

This takes us back to the problem of inherent inequality in the distribution of compensation discussed in the previous chapter. While 'deals' of some kind must be made, Filer (1990, p. 22) questions whether stakeholder dialogue would generate a different outcome, stating that: 'attempts to reform or expand the process of consultation will not make much difference, in the long run, to the perceived validity of agreements between landowners, mining companies and government agencies'. One possible explanation for this is that the involvement of local leaders in agreements with mining companies can over time undermine their leadership, leaving them unable to settle disputes between generations and factions within the community (an example of this will be provided in Chapter 10).

West Papua

Unlike BCL in Bougainville, Freeport and BP's activities in West Papua have extended beyond the 1990s to include an era in which the business community has more explicitly adopted concepts of stakeholder dialogue. As a result, both Freeport and BP have operated under heightened international pressure to establish open relationships with landowners, community organisations and NGOs. Despite this new set of processes and expectations, Freeport has struggled to establish effective communication as reflected in (1) the secrecy in which the company has operated, (2) the climate of fear associated with the militarisation of the Freeport area and (3) divisions in the local community over access to Freeport's community funds. In contrast, BP is believed to have been somewhat more successful in establishing effective communication with Papuans prior to the construction of the Tangguh project and the establishment of the Tangguh Independent Advisory Panel (TIAP). However, it too has been criticised for failing to represent all stakeholders in its dialogue initiatives.

Freeport

> So far what we feel is that Freeport doesn't think Papuans exist … Papuans are like stones or useless.
>
> (WP5, Papuan peace activist)

Unlike BCL, which tried to engage with the local population in the early stages of business development, Freeport did not do so in earnest until the mid-1990s. Indeed the literature (Leith, 2003; Rifai-Hasan, 2009) suggests, and my interviews confirm, that in the initial phases of mining operations, Freeport initiated few measures to engage with landowners that were any-where near as developed or proactive as BCL's language programmes or Village Relations Department.

Freeport-McMoRan Copper & Gold, based in Phoenix, Arizona, is notori-ous for the closed nature in which it conducts its business activities. The com-pany is well known for denying access to researchers and human rights groups for the purpose of conducting social and environmental evaluations of the pro-ject site.[2] Freeport's lack of transparency has been compounded by the fact that Indonesia continues to keep West Papua largely hidden from the outside world. This occurs through the routine denial of permission to visit the territory by foreign journalists[3] and the eviction of humanitarian organisations, including the International Commission of the Red Cross, Cordaid and Peace Brigades International (Matsuno et al., 2011).

In spite of this secrecy, Freeport has been involved in a number of international business initiatives designed to promote dialogue on responsible business conduct. For example, the President of Freeport-McMoRan is also the current Chairman of the International Council on Metals and Mining, a CEO driven initiative, which aims to strengthen business performance on 'sustainable development'.[4] Freeport has also publicly expressed a commitment to stakeholder dialogue indi-cating a desire to work 'to improve mutual understanding and respect to enable the local people to achieve their aspirations and to continue harmonious rela-tionships' (PT Freeport Indonesia, 2006, p. 10).

Notwithstanding Freeport's verbal public commitment to stakeholder dia-logue, this has not necessarily translated into a positive perception of Freeport by many Papuans. This might be considered to stem from three key factors. First, as discussed in Chapter 5, the primary stakeholder that Freeport has been responsive to historically is the Indonesian Government, rather than Papuan communities. As a result, Freeport has been perceived by indigenous Papuans as working to further the interests of the Indonesian Government in relation to ongoing tensions between the 'core' and the 'periphery'. Second, as discussed earlier, Freeport's community initiatives have tended to take the form of reactive measures to combat violence in the Contract of Work area, rather than proactive efforts to engage with affected communities. Finally, and similar again to Bougainville, there have been problems in communica-tion due to cultural differences between the company and local stakeholders. Moreover while Freeport has been relatively successful in communicating a commitment to stakeholder dialogue to its *shareholders*, it has not been per-ceived to translate this verbal commitment into action on the ground in West Papua.

As outlined in Chapter 5, one of Freeport's earliest commitments to establish-ing a 'partnership' with Papuans was motivated by riots that had broken out in

Freeport's concession area. This reactive measure took the form of financial distributions from the One Per Cent Trust Fund. One criticism of this Fund is that it was doled out without first understanding or engaging with the complexities of Papuan culture and social structures. Leith (2003, p. 89) argues that Freeport failed to understand that the communities most directly affected by its mining operations, the Amungme and Kamoro, hold different expectations of the company and tend to employ quite different communication styles.

This accusation however, is not reflected in Freeport's public communication associated with its Trust Funds and in statements outlined in Memoranda of Understanding (MoUs). In Freeport's 2006 *Underlying Values* report, the company states:

> We also continually strive to learn more about the Papuan people, their histories, culture and changing circumstances, to build more constructive relationships and to enhance our outreach efforts. Most important is our commitment to extend respect to indigenous Papuans and their cultures and to engage with them in an ongoing dialogue on issues of mutual interest.
>
> (2006, p. 9)

It must also be acknowledged that Freeport has undertaken various forms of 'cultural recognition', through: exhibitions, the promotion of traditional dance, food, art and the sponsoring of studies of the Amungme and Kamoro people.[5] In addition, Freeport has entered into formal MoUs with Amungme and Kamoro community organisations, such as the 2000 MoU signed by representatives of the Amungme and Kamoro tribal councils and Freeport, which led to the establishment of an 'MOU Forum'. According to Freeport (2006, p. 10):

> The MOU Forum meets regularly to discuss issues related to implementation of the 2000 Memorandum of Understanding. This continual dialogue has led to further agreements and mutually beneficial projects and has instilled a sense of partnership and community between us and our Papuan neighbors aligning our shared interests in a sustainable and more promising future.

Critics of this initiative argue, however, that it offers nothing tangible in response to public health, land tenure and environmental protection (Abrash & Kennedy, 2002, p. 72), and while the MoU boosted Freeport's stock rating, community representatives continue to criticise Freeport's stance towards the Amungme and Kamoro (Abrash & Kennedy, 2002, p. 73).

2011 worker strikes

While labour issues and landowner issues are not the same, Freeport's alleged failure to 'enable the local people to achieve their aspirations and to continue harmonious relationships' (PT Freeport Indonesia, 2006, p. 10) became highly visible in July 2011 when approximately 8,000 Freeport workers[6] at the Grasberg mine went on strike. The strikers sought a pay increase from US$1.50 per hour to US$3 per hour to make the wages of Grasberg workers comparable to Freeport employees in other parts of the world (where wages range from $15 to $30 per hour). Freeport management called on the employees to return to work, stating that, 'the company sees there is no legitimate justification for any form of strike' (Sirait cited in Wanda, 2011).

Following a week-long protest, the company and the workers union failed to come to an agreement, which resulted in the union initiating a one-month strike. In response, Freeport reportedly offered a 10 per cent pay rise in the coming year and another 10 per cent for the following year (Chatterjee & Rondonuwu, 2011). Unsatisfied with this offer, the workers continued to lobby for higher wages. Following more failed negotiations and a decline in Freeport's operating capacity, 114 armed police reportedly arrived in the mining area in addition to the 600 paramilitary troops already present (Workers at Freeport, 2011). Freeport was then accused of enflaming an already volatile situation by issuing the striking workers with a 'No work, No pay' note, claiming the company was not legally obliged to pay those who chose to take part in the strike (Rusmana, 2011).

Unable to resolve the strike and coax the employees back to work, Freeport began replacing the striking workers with new labour. The strikers set up protests against Freeport's attempt to transport the replacement workers into the mining area, which escalated into a violent clash with police. News outlets reported that in response to being pelted with stones, the police fired warning shots in an attempt to disperse the protesters ('Freeport Indonesia mine clashes leave protester dead', 2011). One of these 'warning' shots claimed the life of a protester who was shot in the chest. The violence surrounding the strikes led to the death of a further three people and injured a dozen others. Freeport eventually agreed to increase wages by 37 per cent. This offer also included improved housing allowances, education assistance and a retirement savings plan for workers (Freeport Indonesia mine clashes leave protester dead', 2011).

Consistent with the argument of this chapter, Ballard (see Ballard & Werden, 2011) argues that the 2011 strikes point to the failed efforts of Freeport in the past to establish a mutually beneficial venture for all stakeholders. Ballard argues that the crucial obstacle to this is the interference of the Indonesian Government, which often regards negotiation on issues in West Papua as threat to sovereignty. The power of Indonesian narratives of national unity will be discussed extensively in the following chapter, but is raised here because the violence and intimidation that marked the strikes reflect Freeport's allowance for stakeholder dialogue to be co-opted by the Indonesian security forces. As Ballard (see Ballard & Werden, 2011) argues, 'the problem is whenever they've [Freeport] been pushed to make a choice, they tend to fit onto the side of Jakarta and the security forces'.

BP

> BP has been well received because the management of the company had already given the first three years of community development – the people know we are part of the company.
>
> (WP3, BP employee)

In contrast to BCL and Freeport, BP's commitment to dialogue with locals affected by the Tangguh LNG project is characterised by participants in this research as somewhat more inclusive and longer-term. Yet the company has also been criticised for failing to include all segments of the community and limitations are identifiable in its approach.

Before BP began constructing the Tangguh LNG project, the company spent three years (2001–3) establishing and implementing numerous environmental and socio-economic development commitments. This forms a stark contrast to the BCL and Freeport cases in which no significant community engagement initiatives were put in place prior to the establishment of the two mines. According to a BP employee, this strategy has worked well because it gave Papuans a sense that BP would recognise the rights of local people (WP3). From the company's perspective, villagers living in proximity to the project are believed to have felt included in the BP project from the moment of production. Through this inclusion, it is anticipated that landowners developed a clearer understanding of the project and the social and environmental effects it was going to create prior to the commencement of operations (WP8, BP employee).

BP adopted this more proactive approach to community engagement, cognisant of the Freeport experience, knowing it would be attempting to establish business operations in an area where resource development had been associated with conflict and human rights violations. BP felt it was taking a serious risk with its international reputation by investing in West Papua. Two crucial steps taken by BP to avoid becoming embroiled in the kind of conflict associated with the Freeport project included the undertaking of the first human rights impact assessment ever to be conducted by a resource company in Indonesia,[7] and the establishment of the TIAP.

The TIAP was established in 2002 'to provide external advice to senior decision-makers regarding non-commercial aspects of the Tangguh LNG Project' (BP, 2015). The panel comprises former US Senator George Mitchell, Lord Hannay of Chiswick from the UK, Ambassador Sabam Siagian from Jakarta, and Reverend Herman Saud from Jayapura. The inclusiveness of the TIAP is therefore questionable, as while it includes a Papuan, it does not include a representative from the local area and all members are male. The panel has been involved in providing regular recommendations to the management of BP, who are then required to respond publicly (through the BP website) to each recommendation. In BP's response to the first TIAP report, the company agreed to the recommendation that it 'continue and intensify the dialogue BP has begun with the central government, regional government leaders in West Papua, NGOs and religious leaders' (BP, 2002, p. 15). The dialogue initiatives that BP commenced in 2002 included local NGO meetings, seminars on BP's community-based security strategy and workshops on revenue management (BP, 2002, p. 6). The establishment of TIAP and public responses to its recommendations have resulted in greater external transparency of the company's activities through the availability of the TIAP reports on BP's website.

Although many Papuans interviewed for this study commended BP for its more comprehensive effort to establish a relationship of trust with affected villages, the TIAP has been criticised by some observers. Hickman and Barber (2011, p. 15) have questioned the 'independence' of the Panel due to the sponsorship it receives from BP. Moreover, the authors argue that while BP has a system of public consultation, 'these events tend to be carefully stage-managed to put BP in a positive light' (Hickman & Barber, 2011, p. 15). The environmental NGO Down to Earth (2003) has also criticised BP for delays between the completion of reports and their publication, and the lack of attention paid to the particular impacts of the project on women.

In line with some external criticism of the TIAP mechanism, annual reports responding to the Panel's recommendations tend not to address the more controversial aspects of the project, particularly land and resource rights. As Down to Earth (2003) claim, 'in fact the Panel avoids this crucial issue by stating that BP's compliance with Indonesian law is outside the scope of the Panel's inquiry'. Down to Earth (2003) also criticise the relative value of BP's efforts to establish dialogue with locals when they have no right to reject the project: 'the whole TIAP mission is based on the understanding that the project will go ahead and the question is how to do it best, not whether to do it at all'.

Despite the external criticism, my fieldwork suggests that BP's efforts to achieve stakeholder dialogue through regular forums with NGOs are at least valued by those involved. As one Papuan NGO worker involved in forums on the Tangguh project stated:

> BP did this well because management of BP knows that they were coming to an area where there has been a problem before. By understanding this case, they are more open with NGOs in order to make relationship with local community. BP also do their social analysis about the effects that can come up after development in the area and involve the local people there. Until now things like instruments to development involve regular communication with NGOs, government, church, and other groups, Muslim and Catholic … Regular meetings every 6 months trying to share dialogue, relating to human rights and environment.
>
> (WP4, NGO worker)

Conclusion

This chapter has identified a number of apparent limitations in BCL, Freeport and BP's attempts to establish dialogue on their business activities in Bougainville and West Papua. The three case studies illustrate the importance of direct dialogue between extractive companies, local communities and their representatives, but have also identified a number of potential difficulties associated with this, such as intergenerational disputes and the presence of the state's security forces. The state, military, the motive of the corporation and the heterogeneity of communities were identified as constraints to effective representation in the two case studies. Conversely, the importance of treating locals with dignity and respect through early, proactive engagement was noted by participants in this study as vital to the development of relationships of mutual trust.

Advancing the argument of this book, the focus of CSR may need to be widened to respond to claims for recognition and representation and not just redistribution. This is different, however, to the kinds of 'cultural recognition' initiatives of Freeport discussed in this chapter. Rather than art exhibitions and food events, this is a call for recognition of the interdependence of the extractive project with a full range of justice claims of the host society. While these claims may include greater respect of cultural traditions, it extends to other concerns such as fears associated with the state's security forces and contests over resource wealth. Without demonstrating a sustained commitment to engage with these deeper issues, it appears that corporations may be limited in their capacity to achieve a 'harmonious relationship'.

An important observation of the discussion of the 2011 workers' strikes at Freeport was the way in which large extractive companies can have their dialogue initiatives co-opted by the state and its security forces. The following chapter expands this discussion through an analysis of the indignity of violence in prising open new conflicts and falsely labelling them as threats to 'national unity'.

Notes

1 Pidgin had become universal on Bougainville by 1972 (Oliver, 1973, p. 187).
2 See Abrash (2002, pp. 2–4) for a discussion of a blocked attempt to initiate a fact-finding mission on human rights in Freeport's Contract of Work area in 1999, sponsored by the Robert F. Kennedy Memorial Center for Human Rights.
3 In May 2015, President Joko Widodo announced that foreign journalists would no longer require special permission to travel to West Papua following international pressure on the Indonesian Government to open up the provinces after two French journalists were detained in 2014 for reporting while on tourist visas (Roberts, 2015). According to Hernawan (2015), however, less than 24 hours after Widodo's announcement, the 'Minister for Security and Political Affairs Tedjo Edhy Purdijatno told Indonesian media that the access will be subject to the scrutiny of an agency. Indonesian military commander General Moeldoko confirmed this statement separately, saying that the government has yet to formulate new rules of the game for foreign journalists.'
4 Sustainable development will be discussed extensively in Chapter 9.
5 For an analysis of the presence of Kamoro artefacts in Freeport buildings, see Jacobs (2012, pp. 121–2).

6 By no means were all of these workers indigenous Papuans, nor Amungme and Kamoro people specifically, as 'in May 1997, for example, there were just 134 Kamoro PTFI employees, less than five percent of the workforce' (Paull *et al.*, 2006, p. 40).
7 This will be discussed in Chapter 7.

Bibliography

Abrash, A. 2002. 'Development aggression: Observations on human rights conditions in the PT Freeport Indonesia contract of work areas with recommendations'. <www.antiochne.edu/wp-content/uploads/2012/08/Development_Aggression.pdf> [accessed 11 May 2015].

Abrash, A. & Kennedy, D. 2002. 'Repressive mining in West Papua', in G. Evans, J. Goodman & N. Lansbury (eds.), *Moving Mountains: Communities Confront Mining & Globalisation*. London: Zed Books, pp. 59–74.

Ballard, C. (Speaker) & Werden, C. (Presenter). 2011. 'Indonesia contributing to problems at Freeport gold mine in Papua'. Radio Australia. <www.radioaustralia.net.au/international/radio/onairhighlights/448360> [accessed 11 May 2015].

Bougainville Copper Limited, BCL Environment and Community Relations Division. n.d. *A Changing Bougainville* [leaflet]. Papua New Guinea.

BP. 2002. 'Tangguh Independent Advisory Panel BP response to the first report on the Tangguh LNG project'. <www.bp.com/content/dam/bp-country/en_id/Documents/TIAPReport/2002%20BP%20Response%20to%20TIAP%20Report.pdf> [accessed 11 May 2015].

BP. 2015. 'Tangguh Independent Advisory Panel'. <www.bp.com/sectiongenericarticle.do?categoryId=9004751&contentId=7008791> [accessed 11 May 2015].

Burchell, J. & Cook, J. 2008. 'Stakeholder dialogue and organisational learning: Changing relationships between companies and NGOs', *Business Ethics: A European Review*, vol. 17, no. 1, pp. 35–46.

Chatterjee, N. & Rondonuwu, O. 2011. 'Indonesia could face more strikes as workers push for higher pay'. Reuters. <www.reuters.com/article/2011/08/29/indonesia-ecoomy-labour-idUSL4E7JQ1JY20110829> [accessed 11 May 2015].

Down to Earth. 2003. 'More doubts emerge over BP's Tangguh project'. <www.downtoearth-indonesia.org/story/more-doubts-emerge-over-bps-tangguh-project> [accessed 11 May 2015].

Filer, C. 1990. 'The Bougainville rebellion, the mining industry and the process of social disintegration in Papua New Guinea', in R. J. May & M. Spriggs (eds.), *The Bougainville Crisis*. Bathurst: Crawford House Press, pp. 73–112.

'Freeport Indonesia mine clashes leave protester dead'. 2011. BBC. <www.bbc.co.uk/news/world-asia-pacific-15237235> [accessed 11 May 2015].

Freeport-McMoRan Copper & Gold. 2006. *Underlying Values: 2006 Working Toward Sustainable Development Report*. <https://www.commdev.org/userfiles/files/1869_file_WTSD.pdf> [accessed 23 July 2015].

Hernawan, B. 2015. 'Papua is not a problem but the way we talk about Papua is', *The Conversation*, 21 May. <http://theconversation.com/papua-is-not-a-problem-but-the-way-we-talk-about-papua-is-41896> [accessed 22 May 2015].

Hickman, A. & Barber, P. 2011. 'Tangguh, BP & international standards: An analysis of the commitments made by BP in relation to BP Tangguh in West Papua and their social and environmental responsibilities'. <www.downtoearth-indonesia.org/sites/downtoearth-indonesia.org/files/Tangguh,%20BP%20and%20International%20Standards%20English%2012%20April%202011.pdf> [accessed 11 May 2015].

Jacobs, K. 2012. *Collecting Kamoro: Objects, Encounters and Representation in Papua (Western New Guinea)*. Leiden: Sidestone Press.

Kapelus, P. 2002. 'Mining, corporate social responsibility and the "community": The case of Rio Tinto, Richards Bay Minerals and the Mbonambi', *Journal of Business Ethics*, vol. 39, no. 3, pp. 275–96.

Kaptein, M. & Tulder, R. V. 2002. 'Toward effective stakeholder dialogue', *Business and Society Review*, vol. 108, no. 2, pp. 203–24.

Latour, B. 2005. *Reassembling the Social: An Introduction to Actor-Network Theory*. Oxford: Oxford University Press.

Lea, D. 1993. 'Melanesian axiology, communal land tenure, and the prospect of sustainable development within Papua New Guinea', *Journal of Agricultural and Environmental Ethics*, vol. 6, no. 1, pp. 89–101.

Leith, D. 2003. *The Politics of Power: Freeport in Suharto's Indonesia*. Honolulu: University of Hawaii Press.

Levine, H. B. 1999. 'Reconstructing ethnicity', *Journal of Anthropology Institute*, vol. 5, no. 2, pp. 165–80.

Matsuno, A., Harsono, A., Noonan, A., Hernawan, B., Kirksey, E., Waluyo, E., Braithwaite, J., Saltford, J., Leadbeater, M., King, P., Drooglever, P. & Chauvel, R. 2011. 'Regarding: International access to and human rights in West Papua'. <http://sydney.edu.au/arts/peace_conflict/docs/Letter_SBY.pdf> [accessed 11 May 2015].

Mena, S., Leede, M. D., Bauman, D., Black, N., Lindeman, S. & McShane, L. 2010. 'Advancing the business and human rights agenda: Dialogue, empowerment, and constructive engagement', *Journal of Business Ethics*, vol. 93, no. 1, pp. 161–88.

Oliver, D. 1973. *Bougainville: A Personal History*. Carlton: Melbourne University Press.

Paull, D., Banks, G., Ballard, C. & Gillieson, D. 2006. 'Monitoring the environmental impact of mining in remote locations through remotely sensed data', *Geocarto International*, vol. 21, no. 1, pp. 33–42.

Pedersen, E. R. 2006. 'Making corporate social responsibility (CSR) operable: How companies translate stakeholder dialogue into practice', *Business and Society Review*, vol. 111, no. 2, pp. 137–63.

PT Freeport Indonesia. 2006. *Grasberg: 2006 Tour Companion*. Grasberg: PT Freeport Indonesia.

Quodling, P. 1991. *Bougainville: The Mine and the People*. St Leonards: Centre for Independent Studies.

Regan, A. J. 2003. 'The Bougainville conflict: Political and economic agendas', in K. Ballentine & J. Sherman (eds.), *The Political Economy of Armed Conflict: Beyond Greed and Grievance*. Boulder, CO: Lynne Rienner, pp. 133–66.

Rifai-Hasan, P. A. 2009. 'Development, power, and the mining industry in Papua: A study of Freeport Indonesia', *Journal of Business Ethics*, vol. 89, no. 2, pp. 129–43.

Roberts, G. 2015. 'Indonesian president Joko Widodo lifts foreign media restrictions in Papua provinces'. ABC News. <www.abc.net.au/news/2015-05-11/indonesia-opens-restive-papuan-provices-to-media/6459068> [accessed 11 May 2015].

Rusmana, Y. 2011. 'Freeport strikers to rally after government-led talks stall'. Bloomberg. <www.bloomberg.com/news/2011-09-25/grasberg-copper-mine-strike-set-to-persist-as-workers-withdraw-from-talks.html> [accessed 11 May 2015].

Tanis, J. 2005. 'Nagovisi villages as a window on Bougainville in 1988', in A. J. Regan & H. M. Griffin (eds.), *Bougainville before the Conflict*. Canberra: Pandanus Books, Canberra, pp. 447–74.

Tonks, G. R. & Dowling, P. J. 1999. 'Bougainville copper: A case analysis in international management'. University of Tasmania, School of Management Working Paper Series, no. 99-08, pp. 1–32.

Unerman, J. & Bennett, M. 2004. 'Increased stakeholder dialogue and the internet: Towards greater corporate accountability or reinforcing capitalist hegemony?', *Accounting, Organizations and Society*, vol. 29, no. 7, pp. 685–707.

Vernon, D. 2005. 'The Panguna mine', in A. J. Regan & H. M. Griffin (eds.), *Bougainville before the Conflict*. Canberra: Pandanus Books, pp. 258–73.

Wanda, S. 2011. 'Thousands of Freeport Indonesia mine workers start 7-day strike'. Reuters. <www.reuters.com/article/2011/07/04/us-freeport-indonesia-strike-idUSTRE 76309R20110704> [accessed 11 May 2015].

Wesley-Smith, T. 1991. 'Papua New Guinea in 1990: A year of crisis', *Asian Survey*, vol. 31, no. 2, pp. 188–95.

'Workers at Freeport mine in Papua to strike again'. 2011. *Jakarta Globe*. <www.thejakartaglobe. com/business/workers-at-freeport-mine-in-papua-to-strike-again/465388> [accessed 11 May 2015].

World Business Council for Sustainable Development (WBCSD). n.d. 'Stakeholder dialogue: The WBCSD's approach to engagement'. <www.wbcsd.org/pages/ edocument/edocumentdetails.aspx?id=195&nosearchcontextkey=true> [accessed 11 May 2015].

7 Corporate security politics

Introduction

The site of interdependence between the three companies and the Bougainville and West Papua conflicts analysed in this chapter is security. The deployment of private and public security forces to protect natural resource projects has been a contributing factor to conflict associated with extractive projects in recent years. Concern about the issue has resulted in international initiatives such as the Voluntary Principles on Security & Human Rights, which aim to assist corporations to adhere to international human rights standards in their security arrangements. These global initiatives have been developed in response to significant scandals in the industry, where the use of private and public security has led to accusations of human rights violations by actors funded by large corporations. The experiences of Freeport in West Papua, Shell in Nigeria and Total/Chevron in Myanmar are particular cases in point.

By comparing the cases of Bougainville and West Papua an important difference between the BCL and Freeport experiences becomes visible. While both companies have been associated with state security forces, this association has been born of quite different approaches. BCL did not explicitly seek the protection of the PNGDF before the conflict, nor was it obliged to engage them under the Bougainville Copper Agreement. Nonetheless BCL became involved in accusations of human rights violations when the PNGDF responded to violent attacks on the mine.

As such, it was BCL's *lack* of preventive security that implicated the company in these accusations. In contrast, Freeport has financially supported the Indonesian security forces as a requirement of its Contract of Work with the Indonesian Government. Consequently, Freeport is perceived to have justified the presence of the Indonesian security forces in areas surrounding the mine. The BP example represents yet another security approach. Through the implementation of a community-based security strategy, BP has explicitly sought to distance itself from the actions of the Indonesian military based on the previous experience of Freeport.

Analysing the security practices of the three companies, this chapter argues that BCL and Freeport are believed to have failed in different ways to recognise the fears about, and hostilities towards, the state's security apparatus. Quite differently, BP is believed to have made some progress, broadly recognising and responding to the apprehension that many Papuans hold towards the Indonesian military. This is believed to have been made possible through the company's willingness to consider alternative models of corporate security, as well as a level of ambivalence about stories of Indonesian state sovereignty over West Papua.

Bougainville

With the exception of the Rorovana landowner protests in 1969 (discussed below), the use of security to protect the Panguna mine has not been a dominant issue in the relatively large body of literature on the Bougainville conflict. This is because the security forces that were employed to protect the mine before the conflict have generally not been accused of violating human rights or violence towards local landowners.

Security before the crisis

When the land that would be used for the development of the mine was first mapped out by CRA, security for company staff was provided by the Australian Administration. As a current executive of BCL explains:

> everything was controlled by the police – the Administration. For example, when the women laid themselves on the ground to resist the mine, it was the police in control of security.
>
> (B1)

An important event for the Administration to handle during the construction of the mine was the Rorovana landowner protests. These protests were staged in response to the Administration's attempt to acquire land for the development of a port and other facilities needed as a part of the mine's infrastructure. The protests were partly motivated by the compensation offer of $105 per acre of land to be used by BCL, plus $2 per coconut tree (Cooper, 1991, p. 62). Instead of responding to the protests through communication and negotiation, the Administration sent riot police to Bougainville to protect company surveyors who were marking the boundaries of the Rorovana land required. This response resulted in a major confrontation on 5 August 1969, between 'bulldozers with lines of riot police carrying batons, shields, rifles and respirators facing a motley crowd of about 65 villagers, men and women and some children, unarmed and quite defenceless' (Cooper, 1991, p. 63).

The Bougainvillean tactics of non-violent resistance hit front-pages back in Australia, where Sydney newspapers published headlines such as, 'Australia's Shame' and, 'Australia's Bullies in New Guinea' (Denoon, 2000, p. 2). According to Braithwaite et al. (2010b, p. 16), the news reports did indeed outrage many Australians, adding 'to the impetus in the Australian Labor movement to push for early independence' for PNG. The Australian Administration's priority at the time, however, was to facilitate PNG's independence and unification into a single state, so there was no attempt made to re-examine 'the social justice of the mine through the lens of the local landowners' (Braithwaite *et al.*, 2010b, p. 16).

One strategy BCL adopted to educate itself about the social impacts the mine might have on Bougainville, was to seek the advice of anthropologist Douglas Oliver. According to Denoon (2000, p. 201), in spite of the Rorovana land-owner protests, Oliver advised BCL that local 'opposition would be limited, and that people would be reconciled to the mine eventually' (Denoon, 2000, p. 201). Oliver's assessment of the situation was so unquestioned within the company's management that it did not treat potential security threats by Bougainvilleans with any seriousness. To be fair to Oliver, his assessment did hold true until the late 1980s.

When the mine began production, BCL deployed large numbers of unarmed private security in place around the mine site. However, the focus of this security was to prevent accidents, rather than deliberate violence (B38, former ABG Department CEO). According to Bougainvillean former BCL employees who participated in this study, the provision of training for BCL employees was generally of a very high standard. However, training to respond to civil disturbance was not provided, as such a scenario was not considered likely. This reflects BCL's belief that the major threats to mining operations did not relate to civil unrest, but were largely environmental, such as earthquakes and landslides (B34, B35, B38). A current BCL executive supports this view stating that:

> when the mine was running we had a well organised unarmed security. Its main reason for being there was to keep people safe and off the mine site.
>
> (B1)

Conflict begins

> The worst mistake [of the PNG Government] was bringing in the police mobile squad. They were the worst criminals. They started subjecting people to torture and frightening people. That really upset the Bougainvilleans. They were forced to take up arms. It turned into an outright war. Became an island-wide thing.
>
> (B35, Bougainvillean former BCL employee)

The legacy of the early approach of the PNG Government in relation to unrest on Bougainville was a disastrous conflict ignited by armed attacks on the mine by members of what became the BRA. As indicated, participants in this research suggest that BCL did not have any strategies in place to deal with such incidents. BCL's position changed dramatically following an ill-informed decision by the PNG Government to send in riot police to bring an end to the violence. Rather than bringing the violence to a halt, the abuses perpetrated by the riot police had quite the opposite effect. Indeed, the introduction of PNG riot police proved to be a decision that would fuel a civil war.

Between 1987 and 1988, the NPLA organised public demonstrations against the mine, culminating in violent attacks on BCL property, including minor looting, arson and the use of explosives (Braithwaite *et al.*, 2010b, p. 23). The most damaging attacks occurred in late November 1988 when electricity pylons of the mine were blown up. In addition to attacks on the pylons, in May 1989 an incident occurred in which a bus was shot at in the area of the mine site:

> two employees were injured. That was it. It was too dangerous to go. Only essential [BCL] staff will remain till further notice. Then they [BCL management] started assessing the seriousness. If one shot was fired, more would be up [more violence could follow].
>
> (B34, Bougainvillean former BCL employee)

A Bougainvillean women's leader living in the vicinity of the mine at the time further recounted,

> at 3.30 we were told the first pylon was blown up. Buses were taking employees and dropping them off. My husband came and said it's bad – four people were shot.
>
> (B32)

A build-up of similar attacks over successive months led to the mine's eventual closure in 1989, at which time all foreign BCL employees were evacuated. A key debate in the Bougainville literature is whether Francis Ona intended to permanently close the mine or whether he 'aspired to reopen the mine under a new income-sharing formula that might one day support an independent Bougainville' (Braithwaite *et al.*, 2010b, p. 23). Regardless of the motivation, the crucial point for Bougainville's security politics at the time was that the Government's response was insensitive to the potential for the behaviour of the PNGDF to exacerbate pre-existing ethnic tensions (Regan, 2001, p. 2).

With the PNG Government unable to absorb the loss of revenue that resulted from the disruption to mining operations, Police Mobile Squads and thereafter the PNGDF were deployed to restore the situation (Rolfe, 2001, p. 41). However, this decision did little to restore peace, but a lot to fuel conflict. One reason that these decisions fuelled rather than neutralised the conflict was that Bougainvilleans were already resentful about the impact that the large numbers of internal migrants, from other areas of PNG, were having on their communities.

Bougainvilleans were angry with the Papua New Guineans, particularly those from the Highlands, who arrived in search of economic opportunities from the mine and as plantation labourers (who had arrived first) but who also created new social problems.[1] In particular, the migrants were held responsible for an increase in violence and harassment towards local women. Tensions ignited when

Highlanders killed a Bougainvillean nurse early in 1989. As a Bougainvillean women's leader recounted:

> the Highlanders were scattered all over the island. It was risky for women because the Highlanders killed a nurse ... Before this, the issue was only about BCL, and then it became chasing squatters. [The murder] happened in 1989 ... [It was] one of the main contributors to why young people joined [the] BRA side.
>
> (B26)

The insertion of the PNGDF into Bougainville can be seen to have further inflamed pre-existing ill will by Bougainvilleans towards Papua New Guineans. Instead of seeing the PNGDF as coming to the aid of local civilians, Bougainvilleans saw 'the colour of their skin' (Regan & Tanis, 2010).

The decision to deploy the PNGDF into Bougainville and the ensuing civil war was indicative of both the company's and the Government's apparent lack of understanding of the social consequences of the mine.

In this way, the apparent failure of BCL and the Government to deal with the social issues that emerged on Bougainville alongside the development of the mine can be seen to have precipitated the violence that followed the deployment of the PNGDF to Bougainville. As Ogan (1999, p. 8) claims, 'the entry of the PNG security forces and their variably brutal and grotesquely ineffectual activities created a qualitative change in a conflict that might otherwise have taken a less catastrophic course'. This 'catastrophic course' was marked by allegations of human rights violations on all sides. The newly formed BRA can be seen to have committed human rights violations that corresponded to the types of violence inflicted by the PNG security forces (Regan, 2001, p. 4).

By the time the conflict had escalated in mid-1989, BCL believed it had lost any opportunity to resolve the problems associated with the mine and felt it had no choice but to evacuate its entire staff. One option that BCL might have considered at this point could have been to announce a pause in operations, and organise a meeting with all factions of landowners. As discussed earlier, in fact the NPLA had called a meeting with BCL, but BCL executives are accused of choosing not to attend (B24, chief/landowner).

The Bougainville conflict, which began with mining-related grievances, gave rise to broader claims for independence when Ona's attacks against the mine and the Government 'struck a responsive chord across all of Bougainville and spontaneous attacks on government and foreign property erupted in many places in sympathy' (Braithwaite et al., 2010b, p. 24). As a Bougainvillean women's leader recounted:

> PNG soldiers were also killing people, the civilians. Everybody was frightened. At the same time, PNG withdrew [government services]. There was no law and order ... they killed many in the mountains. Killing even young children. They wanted to control the situation when BRA started damaging

properties of BCL. PNG withdrew all government workers and sent soldiers to rule this place.

(B26)

The removal of services on Bougainville led to a significant increase in the level of support for the BRA, with some estimates indicating up to 300 armed and active members by 1990 (Wesley-Smith, 1991, p. 189). Not all Bougainvilleans, however, endorsed the actions of the BRA. Localised armed opposition to the BRA coalesced with the BRF in the early 1990s. The BRF fighters blamed the lack of services available to Bougainvilleans on the BRA's violence, and were angered by the criminal behaviour of some BRA combatants (B15, ex-BRA combatant).

Preventive security and the future of the mine

The question that this discussion of BCL's corporate security practices raises is: if BCL had treated the initial protests of Bougainvilleans as a threat to its operations, could the civil war have been avoided, or put differently, 'preventive security' achieved? Alternatively, would the outcome have been more comparable to the repressive actions of the Indonesian security forces around Freeport (discussed in the next section)? The steps taken by the PNG Government in response to attacks against the mine suggest that the Government may have been more inclined to the latter scenario, but the position of BCL remains unclear. A current executive of BCL responded in this way to a question about whether or not current human rights initiatives for the extractive sector would have been effective in the context of the Bougainville conflict:

> there were no voluntary initiatives or human rights standards at the time the mine operated … Contemporary voluntary standards wouldn't change things much.

(B1)

Indeed it is possible to speculate that human rights initiatives such as the Voluntary Principles on Security & Human Rights might have done little to prevent the Bougainville conflict. This is because the perceived lapse in BCL's security approach appears to be related to a lack of foresight as to how the insertion of more Papua New Guineans who impinged on the rights of Bougainvilleans would enflame an already volatile situation.

West Papua

As we have seen throughout this book, conflict in West Papua centres on the contested way in which the territory was incorporated into Indonesia. This incorporation also established one of the key structural features of the conflict: the provocative actions of the Indonesian security forces. These security forces have been accused of human rights violations throughout West Papua in the name of protecting both the 'national unity' of Indonesia and its 'vital national assets', which are understood to include large extractive projects.

The lack of concern for Papuan rights in the context of national development and unity has led Indonesia to be counted as 'one of three countries (along with Colombia and Nigeria) in which human rights in the corporate sphere are most obviously endangered' (Ballard, 2001, p. 9). This has raised concerns within the extractive industry as to whether it is possible to invest in West Papua while maintaining a commitment to international human rights standards (TIAP, 2009, p. 47). Moreover, while the utilisation of state security forces may in the past have paved the way for international companies to enter conflict-sensitive areas (by repressing local protests), it has now become a major reputational concern.

The remainder of this chapter will show how Indonesia's security approach to West Papua is illustrative of a 'contradictory narrative' between protecting the national unity of Indonesia (the perspective of Jakarta) and the violation of Papuan human rights (the perspective of West Papua's independence movement). This contradictory narrative is also reflected in the respective security practices of Freeport and BP.

On the one hand, Freeport (reflective of the Indonesian state view), entered West Papua with the assistance of the TNI, yet has explicitly denied the company's involvement in human rights violations. This denial has relied on a narrative of state sovereignty, which distances the company from accusations of complicity in the behaviour of the Indonesian security forces. In contrast, BP has acknowledged the issue of Indonesian sovereignty as a constraining factor to the protection of human rights in West Papua, but its security practices have not been driven by it. Rather the key driver of BP's security approach is based on:

> the hypothesis that if people feel they benefit from the BP project, they will guard it.
>
> (WP41, BP Indonesia employee)

The chapter will explain how BP's community-based security model may have opened a new space of security in West Papua.

Narratives of unity and threat

In West Papua, the role played by the Indonesian Military (*Tentara Nasional Indonesia*, hereon referred to as TNI) is crucial for understanding corporate security practices in the region. This is not to say, however, that TNI is the only security actor involved in security governance in West Papua. Brimob (Mobil Brigade), Kopassus (Special Forces Command), Kostrad (Strategic Reserve) and provincial police are also engaged in resource sites in West Papua and have competed with TNI over access to wealth from extractive companies. The TNI is afforded more attention in this chapter as it illustrates most clearly the entanglements of extractive companies in broader narratives of nation building vis-à-vis their security practices.

The TNI has been a strong facet of Indonesia's self-constructed identity since it gained independence from the Dutch in 1948. The TNI was a revolutionary army with a mission to build a nation. The success of the TNI in an armed struggle against the Dutch 'gave rise to the perception of the army as the institution that preserved the Indonesian nation and provided the rationale for the military's role in politics' (Rabasa & Haseman, 2002, p. 8). This historical account has not only entrenched a perception amongst Indonesians of the TNI as the 'guardians of national unity', but has been used to justify the TNI's actions against separatist sentiments within Indonesia (Blair & Phillips, 2003, p. 63). More specifically for the purposes of this discussion, it has provided a legitimating rationale for the presence of the TNI in areas surrounding large natural resource projects in the name of protecting the state's assets.

This rationale became most evident when President Suharto gained political leadership of Indonesia and shifted the TNI's attention away from external enemies and towards internal threats to the regime (Ballard, 2001, p. 9). The TNI represented the state's interest and ultimately came to align directly with the interests of Suharto, his party Golkar and his cronies. This mandate for the TNI as the guardian of the regime and its financial resources established the conditions for human rights violations surrounding large extractive projects (Ballard, 2001).

Indonesia has also drawn on a narrative of national unity in response to separatism in West Papua, which, along with Aceh, has felt the full force of the TNI (Rabasa & Haseman, 2002, p. 107). Indeed despite wide reports that the OPM has, 'weakened, lacks ammunition and relies on bows and arrows' the Indonesian Government has maintained, and perhaps even advanced,[2] a militarised approach in Papua for over 40 years (TIAP, 2009, p. 12).

The financial interests of TNI

High numbers of TNI troops continue to be deployed in West Papua and pose a continued threat to cultural expression and Papuan autonomy. As Widjojo argues, political violence in West Papua is psychological and structural. 'The Papuans' experience of political violence nurtured a collective memory of suffering, or what is known as *memoria passionis* [memory of suffering]' (Widjojo, 2010, p. 12).

National stories have been used to justify the large military presence in West Papua. However, the TNI also has a financial interest in maintaining its West Papua presence. According to Blair and Phillips, the TNI must raise a significant proportion of its own revenue due to the fact that it receives only 25–30 per cent of its budget from the national Government (2003, p. 8). The rest is raised through a mixture of activities, including payments by extractive companies for security. On an individual level, soldiers are poorly paid, with mid-ranking soldiers earning $60 to $95 per month and high-ranking officers earning $110 to $350 per month in 2001 (The Economist cited in Blair & Phillips, 2003, p. 62). This situation creates strong individual incentives to compete for resources, and can undermine TNI accountability to civilian authorities (Human Rights Watch, 2009, p. 2).

More specific to the relationship between the military and Freeport is that the TNI's revenue-raising agenda has embroiled Freeport in a number of shooting incidents in areas surrounding the Grasberg mining complex. The economic interests of TNI in Freeport's mining activities have also undermined attempts to control and reform the Indonesian security forces, and have fuelled human rights violations both in the vicinity of major natural resource projects, and throughout West Papua (Human Rights Watch, 2009).

Freeport's security practices and the narrative of state sovereignty

The most visible link between TNI and the Indonesian economy has been the presence of troops around the Grasberg mining area. This presence can be described as one of the most long-standing Papuan concerns regarding Freeport's operations in West Papua. As a Papuan NGO worker stated: 'the problem is because Freeport is making trouble for a very long time. Since the contract [in 1967], Freeport pays security' (WP23).

A particularly significant security issue in the vicinity of Freeport's mining operations was the 1996 riots. Many Papuans believe the riots were orchestrated by the military but were 'accused on Papuan independence organisations' (WP14, Papuan human rights activist). The motivation for these actions is considered to stem from the military's need to source external funding. By orchestrating attacks but attributing them to local separatists, the military can justify their ongoing value to Freeport, and secure well-paid contracts into the future. Similar accusations have been levelled at the military for numerous shooting incidents around the Grasberg mineral district from 2002 to 2011. Responsibility for these violent incidents has been caught in a blame game between Papuan activists and TNI. The Indonesian Government and Freeport have sided with the military by attributing the attacks to separatists seeking to destroy assets of national importance. However, Papuan advocates for independence vehemently deny these accusations.

One of the shooting incidents around the Grasberg mine occurred during August 2002 when teachers working on contract for Freeport, two from the US and one from Java, were killed. Despite a lack of evidence, the military, government officials and Freeport management publicly attributed the attack to Papuan separatists, with a Jakarta court later sentencing a Papuan villager, Antonius Wamang, to life in prison (Kirksey & Harsono, 2008, p. 165). The sentence occurred despite the fact that both police and US intelligence reports linked the murders to the military rather than to Wamang (Kirksey & Harsono, 2008, p. 165). Advocates of Wamang's innocence believe the main suspects involved in the shooting are members of the *Tenaga Bantuan Operasi* (TBO). The TBO is a group of civilians who give logistical assistance to Kopassus personnel. Some of the civilians are believed to be Papuans who are trained in Java to work for the army to instigate violent incidents (WP14, Papuan human rights activist).[3]

According to Ballard and Banks (2009, p. 168), if the military was responsible for the murders, they were likely motivated by Freeport's attempts to wean the security forces off its financial assistance. Freeport's attempts to cease financial ties with the military followed national level reforms, which sought to tighten the control of TNI (Blair & Phillips, 2003, p. 8). However, instead of improving the human rights situation around the mine, these reforms are believed by many Papuans to have created jealousies between the military and the police, both of whom orchestrate attacks in the vicinity of Grasberg in order to secure security payments. The military is then accused of blaming the attacks on the OPM to justify the continuation of their contracts. As a PT Freeport Indonesia employee explained:

> [The] shootings took place because Freeport tried to stop military and only use police. Blame [Kelly] Kwalik[4] and local people on this. They have already enjoyed the cake too much … In 2007 it [Freeport security] changed to policemen. This [promotes] jealousy between the two. When security is taken by policemen, army get jealous of this. They make incident to show they need army.
>
> (WP12)

These suspicions heightened when subsequent shootings took place following further attempts to decrease the company's financial assistance to the military. As Braithwaite *et al.* (2010b, p. 69) note, in July 2009 'there were a further series of perhaps six shooting incidents near the mine in which one Australian mine engineer and two Indonesians were killed and many others were wounded'. In response to the shootings, Papuans and international NGOs demanded that Freeport cease its ties with the Indonesian security forces. Freeport has responded to these demands by pointing to its legal agreement with the national Government that binds it to work with TNI. In a letter addressed to Global Witness, Freeport's Vice President for Communications stated:

> pursuant to the Government's declaration that our company's mining operations are a Vital National Object … there is no alternative to our reliance on the military and police in this regard … The Indonesian Government – not our company – is responsible for employing its security personnel and directing their operations.
>
> (cited in Global Witness, 2005, p. 19)

More broadly, Sethi *et al.* (2011, p. 6) argue that Freeport has considered harassment of indigenous Papuans by the provincial police and TNI as beyond the company's control. As a consequence of Freeport's deference to Indonesian law and sovereignty regarding the actions of the security forces, the company has forgone important opportunities to transform the popular local perception that the company not only operates in its own financial interest, but also in the interests of the Indonesian security forces (WP9, Papuan religious leader).

Others are more understanding of the constraints facing Freeport in changing its security approach, but still critique the lack of will on the part of Freeport to limit the activities of the military around the Grasberg mine. As a former Freeport employee stated:

> Freeport is trying to change – they are more open for human rights – they are taking it seriously. But it will take time because of the surrounding environment. Freeport cannot say it wants less troops … it has had small opportunities … but I don't think they were successful to capitalise because Freeport is too strategic.
>
> (WP11)

A human rights opportunity lost?

In deferring to the sovereignty of the Indonesian Government and its requirement that the Indonesian security forces protect all 'vital national assets', Freeport has distanced itself from responsibility for the actions of TNI in its area of operation. The possibility of conceptualising Freeport's responses to the shooting incidents as a positive human rights opportunity missed was raised in an interview with a former Freeport employee. While he acknowledged that the company recognises that 'Papuans using bows and arrows' did not undertake the shootings, he maintained that 'Freeport is a foreign company – it can't talk about politics – by law it can't interfere' (WP45).

To its credit, Freeport has undertaken a number of human rights initiatives in an attempt to respond to accusations of rights violations in the vicinity of its operations. This includes a 2003 companywide code of conduct as well as the organisation of human rights training for company employees and contracting staff (Sethi et al., 2011). The code of conduct included a commitment to independent auditing and follow-up field visits by the International Centre for Corporate Accountability (Sethi et al., 2011). The audit found that Freeport had taken adequate actions to address numerous concerns identified in the initial audit, including the use of company vehicles to transport military personnel in the mining area, and inadequate employee knowledge of the company's human rights policy (Sethi et al., p. 14). Further, in 2004 President Megawati Sukarnoputri issued President Decree No. 63 on the Security of Vital National Objects. The Decree transferred responsibility for the protection of any sites declared a national asset, including Grasberg, from the military to the police. However, as alluded to earlier, although this did not solve the rivalry between the police and the military, it is believed to have shifted the responsibility and authority over security matters at Grasberg.

As reflected in the above quote by a former Freeport employee, the company faces immense challenges in contributing to security sector reform through its operations in West Papua. Changes in the company's security practices have had perverse results. In particular, Freeport's security practices are embroiled in a complex and dangerous conflict, including competition between security factions over financial gains. In spite of Freeport's attempts to engage with human rights, socio-political unrest in the area of the mine has not subsided and concerns regarding the relationship between Freeport and Indonesian security forces have extended into industrial relations disputes. Between 2011 and 2013, for example, Freeport mining workers staged 17 demonstrations concerning labour rights. In one of these demonstrations, police reportedly fired warning shots at protesting workers (Fadhillah, 2011), causing the deaths of two protesters and leaving six others seriously injured (International Coalition for Papua & Franciscans International 2013, p. 22). While Freeport reportedly acknowledged that 15 people have been killed and 56 people have been injured in shootings along the road leading to the Grasberg mine since July 2009, 'the Indonesian government has responded with additional security forces' (Permatasari, 2012). This raises serious concerns about the possibility of future deaths in areas surrounding the Grasberg mine. It also reflects the lack of momentum generated through previous crises to improve the human rights reputation of the Indonesian Government, its security forces and Freeport.

In saying this, however, Freeport cannot be expected to reform the situation acting alone. Just as the security problem involves numerous actors and motives, any effort to resolve the situation will likely require collaboration between all parties, including local authorities such as regents and governors. It must also be noted that civilian authorities and NGOs also compete for access to financial gain from Freeport. For example, the Governor of Papua, Lukas Enembe, demanded a 10 per cent stake in the company as compensation for years of mining in the province (Somba, 2013). The TNI is only one of many actors in Papua seeking a slice of the Freeport pie. While full analysis of the role of local authorities and their interactions with extractive companies is beyond the scope of this chapter, they are mentioned here to point to an area of future research and to provide a sense of the number of actors who influence the governance of resource sites across different levels and scales. A topic for future research is the strength of local authorities in contributing to resource governance in the context of broader processes associated with the democratisation of Indonesia (Aspinall & Mietzner, 2010).

Tangguh LNG and the development of community-based security

The case of BP's approach to security for its Tangguh LNG project is an instructive contrast to the Freeport project. When BP entered West Papua, the company acknowledged to both stakeholders and shareholders that security would be the most difficult and sensitive issue faced by the Tangguh project. Following the advice of TIAP, BP recognised that Papuans feel significant distrust and fear of the Indonesian security forces based on their prior experience of Freeport. This recognition was a significant element in BP's initiative to undertake a human rights impact assessment for the project. As a BP employee stated:

> Tangguh is the only company with a human rights impact assessment in Indonesia. [It was] the basis of developing community-based security to facilitate and prepare the system for security in the Tangguh area … Because in the human rights impact assessment it already identified the community-based security system in the Indonesian police – but it has never been implemented.
>
> (WP8)

As with Freeport, BP is required to subsidise security expenses mandated by state regulation (Blair & Phillips, 2003, p. 64). However, as an alternative to financially supporting TNI, BP has implemented a community-based security approach. The development of this approach came in response to the recommendation by human rights consultants that 'BP should urge the highest levels of the Government of Indonesia to limit TNI and Brimob deployments and, if necessary, seek support for this position from the U.S. and U.K. governments' (Smith & Freeman, 2002, p. 2).

In response to this recommendation, BP stated:

> as in all countries, the provision of security is ultimately the exclusive prerogative of the state, and we have to work within that framework. Our hope is that the adoption of a community-based regime for Tangguh, in which our stakeholders, particularly those in Bintuni Bay, play an active and integral part of the Project's security, will reduce the risk of human rights incidents from taking place.
>
> (BP, 2003, p. 15)

This statement suggests that although BP has acknowledged that it must operate according to the security regulations set by the Indonesian Government, it can nevertheless adopt proactive strategies that may challenge this requirement. For BP's efforts to reduce the presence of TNI in the Bintuni Bay area, BP's security strategy has been recognised as an innovative model by the UN Global Compact as it 'presents the opportunity to develop mutual trust, respect, and employment in the local community [which] can lead to closer relations and considerably lessen the chances of misunderstanding leading to violence or security issues' (United Nations Global Compact, 2010, p. 17).

BP's security model developed on the basis of a comprehensive consultative process between parties at the local, regional and national levels. During these consultations it was discovered that community-based security could be designed to fall within the parameters of official Indonesian defence doctrine. BP executives uncovered a concept in Indonesian defence doctrine referring to a model of community policing that had never been implemented as a form of corporate security. When this was discovered:

> BP organised a national conference of community security with the national security guardian board, with the generals who train the police on the

philosophy of the country. They advised us to bring this to the national security board for them to agree ... We said it is the same as community-based policing.

(WP8, BP employee, 2010)

An executive of BP Indonesia further described the process:

The concept before it was used; we brought it to the National Defense Institute to discuss entirely. We agree on the type of strategy. They say, 'OK, let the people manage it'. We referred to human rights abuse and how to minimise human rights abuse. A member of the British Embassy was there – the aim was to change the perspective of the Indonesian Government.

(WP41)

This quote illustrates a willingness on the part of BP to resist relying on a story of state sovereignty to justify financially supporting the Indonesian security forces. While the company recognised the constraints it faced in developing the new approach, it did not let those constraints overwhelm the company's ideals and was assisted in this process by its home country government. Significantly in TIAP's 2005 report, the panel quoted the Regional Military Commander as stating, 'while pointing out that Tangguh is a vital national project, he described the principles of ICBS as the new mechanism for security at projects like Tangguh' (TIAP, 2005, p. 25).

The components of integrated community-based security

The main component of BP's ICBS strategy is a social contract, 'between the Project and the community to preserve order and mutual respect, resolving issues through negotiation and discussion rather than confrontation' (BP, 2003, p. 20). One way in which BP has attempted to achieve this goal is to use unarmed locals from the BP area for everyday security of the project, and a commitment to call the police only if a security problem escalates. As a starting point, BP recognised that disruptions to the project were likely to occur, and additional problems could result from the presence of security personnel from different social, cultural and ethnic backgrounds. According to a BP Indonesia executive:

Ninety-three per cent of security guards are Papuan and mostly from the local area. We recruit from local area because during their day off they go back to the village and become a tutor about how to obey the law – especially on alcohol and household abuse ... [They] become a tutor and lead the community to obey the law rather than have a conflict.

(WP39)

In 2007, BP claimed that there were '273 guards in the ICBS programme of whom around 258 are Papuan' (BP, 2007, p. 11). These security guards have all completed, or are scheduled to receive, human rights training by Papuan human rights NGOs. According to a Papuan involved in the human rights training of the guards, the course consists of:

> basic understanding of what human right is and how to handle mass conflict. How to react in case of conflict. Most materials are taken from the general declaration on human rights – the covenant on civil and political rights about social and economic rights – basic principles of human rights ... Then conflict resolution – how security guards make resolution after conflict.
>
> (WP14)

When asked if the respondent believed the training provided was sufficient to avoid human rights violations in the vicinity of the Tangguh project, he stated, 'it depends on the scope of the conflict. Small scale – yes. But if it involves the unity of several tribes it is impossible for them to do it' (WP14). It is BP's policy that the military should be called in to assist with a security disturbance, 'only as a "last resort" upon the coordinated request of BP security and the Papua Police' (TIAP, 2005, p. 24). An executive for BP Indonesia further stated:

> If the problem becomes bigger and can't rely on our security we call the police. And then if they can't handle it they ask the military ... We only call the police – we can't call the military. If the police need more then they call the military.
>
> (WP41)

This statement is in line with BP's initial 2003 response to the human rights impact assessment on the issue of military deployment. BP argued that, 'any attempt to dictate "principles ... to limit military deployments..." with or without BPMIGS support would likely be seen as a transgression of that sovereign right, and have historically been rejected outright' (BP, 2003, p. 18). However, BP also recognised that it could potentially capitalise on the dialogue established with government officials through the development of the ICBS programme, as an opportunity that 'may give BP some ability to influence such issues as the location, strength, and missions of other Police and military deployments' (BP, 2003, p. 18).

Similar to Freeport, however, BP has faced the same problem of the military's history of economic interests in natural resource projects. One of the biggest risks the company has faced in its implementation of ICBS is that Indonesian security forces might orchestrate attacks similar to the shooting incidents around Freeport. Indeed, Indonesian military agents were accused of provoking violence even prior to the construction of Tangguh in 'an unconventional bid for a lucrative "protection" contract' (Kirksey, 2011, pp. 150–1). Kirksey and Grimston also claim that while BP has sought to cut the military out of a security deal, 'the company is using officers from the country's feared Mobile Police Brigade

(Brimob) – which has been accused of numerous human rights abuses' (Kirksey & Grimston, 2003).

Further, even though BP's community-based security approach has largely been well received in West Papua by NGO workers and religious leaders and appears to have gained some acceptance at the local, regional and national levels, not all Papuans are convinced about community security. As a Papuan human rights advocate stated:

> about the [BP's] security system. It is good. Community-based security. The local community guard the company. But I believe Brimob is also inside the company. You cannot say no policemen.

> (WP14)

In addition, it must be acknowledged that much of the data used in this examination of the BP case is drawn from interviews with senior BP employees. Much of this discussion therefore largely reflects the perception of company executives on ICBS. More research is needed into the local realities of ICBS, including any potential unintended consequences of community-based security. At the Porgera mine in PNG, Banks argues that police became 'virtually powerless to act against any segment of the community' because they were so enmeshed in the community through marriages and other local alliances (Banks, 2000, p. 260). This situation meant that on more than one occasion, 'outsiders' were required to bring order to the area (Banks, 2000, p. 260).

Many Papuans acknowledge that while it is too early to herald BP's ICBS security approach as an unmitigated success, they do respect the effort the company has made in comparison to Freeport. Consequently, BP is viewed by the participants in this research (keeping in mind the limits of the data collected) as having made some progress in recognising the fears about, and hostilities towards, the Indonesian security forces. While the company has acknowledged the constraints to eliminating the presence of the TNI and Brimob personnel around the Tangguh project, it is believed by some to have attempted to open a new space of security through interaction with government authorities and trying to learn from the past experience of Freeport.

Conclusion

The participants in this study have evaluated BCL and Freeport as having failed in different ways to recognise the fears and hostilities that Bougainvilleans and Papuans feel towards national security authorities. In Bougainville, BCL's security approach was viewed as symptomatic of the company's colonial view that Bougainvilleans would accept the mine and that security would not be required. One question this raises is, which is preferable: a security approach that rests on the assumption that no civil disturbance will occur, or the imposition of a repressive security force to clamp down on any potential unrest? It was argued that a total lack of security might be equally as problematic as the imposition of a repressive regime. Both these approaches risk a lack of engagement with broader local fears and, in doing so, can increase the likelihood of reactive measures, even panic, when disruptions occur. As we saw with Bougainville, it was the inability of BCL management and the PNG Government to foresee the consequences of sending in riot police and PNGDF into Bougainville that likely transformed a landowner dispute into a civil war.

In contrast to BCL, Freeport is, and was, required by Indonesian law to draw on the state's security forces to protect the mining area. This has implicated the company in numerous shooting incidents that are widely believed to have been orchestrated by the military to justify its presence, and secure ongoing revenue to 'protect' Freeport. This security situation is pathological because it puts both the military and OPM in the position of being able to instigate a security incident, to blame the other as responsible for it, and to be believed by many. It was argued that this scenario has been made possible because of three core issues: national stories relating the development of TNI; national stories relating to unity and disintegration which have characterised Indonesia's security approach towards separatism in West Papua; as well as increased financial benefits to security forces in response to earlier riots. In this way, it appears from the data collected for this study that the security problems surrounding Freeport are not solely about the financial interests of the TNI. While the TNI clearly has financial motives, these motives seem to interact with a 'metanarrative' of Indonesia towards West Papua. Using Fraser's (1996, p. 9) terms, Papuans express feelings of 'lesser esteem, honor, and prestige they enjoy relative to other groups in [Indonesian] society'.

Importantly, BP informants suggest that state narratives and requirements can be challenged or worked around when there is a commitment to recognise the fears of the local community and think creatively about possible alternatives that will meet the needs of all parties. This quality of recognition and engagement with the consequences of the resource project on host communities seems to be a key difference that sets BP's approach apart from the other two case study companies. Thus while Freeport may have a larger CSR budget than BP, it is this type of engagement which may prove more effective and meaningful in the long term. However, given the inherent complexity of any social landscape, it is not necessarily easy to predict the consequences of any business practices, including security arrangements. The following chapter explores the various efforts made by all three companies to predict the social consequences of their business practices, and the limitations of social impact assessments to assist companies in this process.

Notes

1 This will be discussed more extensively in Chapter 10.
2 For example, there are fears that the division of West Papua into three new provinces was a 'covert method of further increasing the massive militarization of Papua' (Ringgi,

2014). It is believed that this would give 'the military the excuse to put more combat troops into each [province]' (Ringgi, 2014).
3 Others are simply civilians who provide basic support to the armed forces, such as food.
4 Kelly Kwalik was a leader of the OPM, killed by Indonesian police in 2009. The police accused Kwalik of a series of attacks in the Freeport mining area in 2002.

Bibliography

Aspinall, E. & Mietzner, M. (eds.) 2010. *Problems of Democratisation in Indonesia: Elections, Institutions and Society*. Singapore: ISEAS Publishing.

Ballard, C. 2001. 'Human rights and the mining sector in Indonesia: A baseline study'. London: International Institute for Environment and Development. <http://pubs.iied.org/pdfs/G00929.pdf> [accessed 7 May 2015].

Ballard, C. & Banks, G. 2009. 'Between a rock and a hard place: Corporate strategy at the Freeport mine in Papua, 2001–2006', in B. P. Resosudarmo & F. Jotzo (eds.), *Working with Nature against Poverty: Development, Resources and the Environment in Eastern Indonesia*. Singapore: ISEAS Publishing, pp. 147–77.

Banks, G. 2000. 'Razor wire and riots: Violence and the mining industry in Papua New Guinea', in S. Dinnen & A. Ley (eds.), *Reflections on Violence in Melanesia*. Annandale and Canberra: Hawkins Press & Asia Pacific Press, pp. 254–62.

Blair, D. C. & Phillips, D. L. 2003. 'Indonesia Commission: Peace and progress in Papua: Report of an Independent Commission Sponsored by the Council on Foreign Relations Centre for Preventive Action'. <www.cfr.org/publication/8281/indonesia_commission.html> [accessed 11 May 2015].

BP. 2003. 'Human rights impact assessment of the proposed Tangguh LNG project'. <www.bp.com/liveassets/bp_internet/globalbp/STAGING/global_assets/downloads/I/hria_response_Tangguh_HRIA_1737.pdf> [accessed 12 January 2011].

BP. 2007. 'BP response to the Tangguh Independent Advisory Panel's fifth report on the Tangguh LNG project'. <www.bp.com/content/dam/bp-country/en_id/Documents/TIAPReport/2007%20BP%20Response%20to%20TIAP%20Report.pdf> [accessed 11 May 2015].

Braithwaite, J., Braithwaite, V., Cookson, M. & Dunn, L. 2010a. *Anomie and Violence: Non-Truth and Reconciliation in Indonesian Peacebuilding*. Canberra: ANU Press.

Braithwaite, J., Charlesworth, H., Reddy, P. & Dunn, L. 2010b. *Reconciliation and Architectures of Commitment: Sequencing Peace in Bougainville*. Canberra: ANU Press.

Cooper, N. 1991. 'Bougainville reconsidered: The role of moral re-armament in the Rorovana land crisis of 1969', *Journal of Pacific History*, vol. 26, no. 1, pp. 57–73.

Denoon, D. 2000. *Getting under the Skin: The Bougainville Copper Agreement and the Creation of the Panguna Mine*. Carlton: Melbourne University Press.

Fadhillah, N. D. S. R. D. 2011. 'Freeport Strike Turns Deadly', *The Jakarta Post*. <www.thejakartapost.com/news/2011/10/11/freeport-strike-turns-deadly.html> [accessed 11 May 2015].

Fraser, N. 1996. 'Social justice in the age of identity politics: Redistribution, recognition, and participation'. The Tanner Lectures on Human Values, Stanford University 30 April–2 May. <http://tannerlectures.utah.edu/_documents/a-to-z/f/Fraser98.pdf> [accessed 11 May 2015].

Global Witness. 2005. 'Paying for protection: The Freeport mine and the Indonesian security forces'. <www.globalwitness.org/sites/default/files/import/Paying%20for%20 Protection.pdf> [accessed 11 May 2015].

Human Rights Watch. 2009. '"What did I do wrong?": Papuans in Merauke face abuses by Indonesian special forces'. <www.hrw.org/sites/default/files/reports/ indonesia0609webwcover_1.pdf> [accessed 11 May 2015].

International Coalition for Papua & Franciscans International. 2013. 'Human rights in West Papua 2013'. <http://humanrightspapua.org/images/docs/HumanRightsPapua 2013-ICP.pdf> [accessed 8 May 2015].

Kirksey, E. S. 2011. 'Don't use your data as a pillow', in A. Waterston & M. D. Vesperi (eds.), Anthropology off the Shelf: Anthropologists on Writing. Chichester: Wiley-Blackwell, pp. 146–59.

Kirksey, E. S. & Grimston, J. 2003. 'Indonesian troops for BP gas project', The Sunday Times, 20 July. <www.thesundaytimes.co.uk/sto/news/world_news/article223564.ece> [accessed 11 May 2015].

Kirksey, E. S. & Harsono, A. 2008. 'Criminal collaborations? Antonius Wamang and the Indonesian military in Timika', South East Asia Research, vol. 16, no. 2, pp. 165–97.

Ogan, E. 1999. 'The Bougainville conflict: Perspectives from Nasioi'. State Society and Governance in Melanesia Discussion Paper, no. 3. <https://digitalcollections.anu.edu. au/bitstream/1885/41820/3/ssgmogan99-3.pdf> [accessed 8 May 2015].

Permatasari, S. 2012. 'Shooting incidents hit Grasberg mine', Sydney Morning Herald, 1 March. <www.smh.com.au/business/shooting-incidents-hit-grasberg-mine-20120229-1u3a6.html> [accessed 11 May 2015].

Rabasa, A. & Haseman, J. 2002. The Military and Democracy in Indonesia: Challenges, Politics, and Power. Santa Monica: RAND.

Regan, A. J. 2001. 'Why a neutral peace monitoring force?', in M. Wehner & D. Denoon (eds.), Without a Gun: Australians' Experiences Monitoring Peace in Bougainville 1997–2001. Canberra: Pandanus Books, pp. 2–18.

Regan, A. J. & Tanis, J. 2010. 'New economic interests and the future of peace-building in Bougainville'. Paper presented at the State, Society and Governance in Melanesia and Resource Management in Asia-Pacific conference, Australian National University, Canberra.

Ringgi, H. Y. 2014. 'Papua's response to the gift of special autonomy plus'. Open Democracy. <https://www.opendemocracy.net/hipolitus-yolisandry-ringgi/papua%E2%80%99s-response-to-gift-of-special-autonomy-plus> [accessed 11 May 2015].

Rolfe, J. 2001. 'Peacekeeping the pacific way in Bougainville', International Peacekeeping, vol. 8, no. 4, pp. 38–55.

Sethi, S. P., Lowry, D. B., Veral, E. A., Shapiro, H. J. & Emelianova, O. 2011. 'Freeport-McMoRan Copper & Gold, Inc.: An innovative voluntary code of conduct to protect human rights, create employment opportunities, and economic development of the indigenous people', Journal of Business Ethics, vol. 103, no. 1, pp. 1–30.

Smith, G. A. & Freeman, B. 2002. 'Human rights assessment of the proposed Tangguh LNG project: Summary of recommendations and conclusion'. <www.bp.com/liveassets/ bp_internet/globalbp/STAGING/global_assets/downloads/I/hria_summary_Tangguh_ HRIA_1736.pdf> [accessed 12 January 2011].

Somba, N. D. 2013. 'Papua administration wants 10% of Freeport', *The Jakarta Post*, 19 April. <www.thejakartapost.com/news/2013/04/19/papua-administration-wants-10-freeport.html> [accessed 11 May 2015].

Tangguh Independent Advisory Panel (TIAP). 2005. 'Third report on Tangguh LNG project'. <www.bp.com/content/dam/bp-country/en_id/Documents/TIAPReport/2005%20TIAP%20Third%20Report.pdf> [accessed 11 May 2015].

Tangguh Independent Advisory Panel (TIAP). 2009. 'Seventh report on the Tangguh LNG project and overview of panel's experiences (2002–2009)'. <www.bp.com/content/dam/bp-country/en_id/Documents/TIAPReport/2009%20TIAP%20Seventh%20Report.pdf> [accessed 11 May 2015].

Tangguh Independent Advisory Panel (TIAP). 2014. 'First report on operations and proposed expansion of the Tangguh LNG project'. <www.bp.com/content/dam/bp-country/en_id/Documents/TIAPReport/2014%20TIAP%20First%20Report_rev2.pdf> [accessed 11 May 2015].

United Nations Global Compact. 2010. 'Doing business while advancing peace and development'. <www.unglobalcompact.org/docs/issues_doc/Peace_and_Business/DBWAPD_2010.pdf> [accessed 11 May 2015].

Vernon, D. 2005. 'The Panguna mine', in A. J. Regan & H. M. Griffin (eds.), *Bougainville before the Conflict*. Canberra: Pandanus Books, pp. 258–73.

Wesley-Smith, T. 1991. 'Papua New Guinea in 1990: A year of crisis', *Asian Survey*, vol. 31, no. 2, pp. 188–95.

Widjojo, M. S. (ed.) 2010. *Papua Road Map: Negotiating the Past, Improving the Present, and Securing the Future*. Jakarta: LIPI.

8 Social impact assessments

Introduction

The problem this chapter explores is the limited capacities of large corporations to predict the likely social impacts of their business activities on local communities, other than to broadly recognise that resource development may initiate rapid and fundamental change. As O'Faircheallaigh (1999, p. 64) argues:

> a project or development will often have consequences that cannot be predicted at the time of the SIA [social impact assessment]. In addition, a series of relevant factors, for example, people's values (including their attachment to traditional ways of life), government policies, and the nature of the development in question – will change over time, undermining the validity of the assumptions that underlay the original study.

The focus of this chapter is different to the discussion in Chapter 5 about the creation of new divisions over access to resource wealth. This chapter focuses on the social impacts of resource development beyond competition for revenues. These impacts include ethnic tension, new class relations and the weakening of traditional social structures.

Through a discussion of the social impact and monitoring assessments of BCL, Freeport and BP, this chapter will show how the three resource projects have been associated with a number of new social problems that were not identifiable during the initial stages of operations. Moreover the focus of this chapter is the sixth site of interdependence, social impacts.

Consistent with the broader argument of this book, we will again see how distributing material resources to local communities is not always sufficient to resolve local grievances. Rather, the three cases illustrate the value of a continuous commitment to engage with the consequences of resource development on local communities, and to use local grievances as the basis for a more meaningful engagement.

Social impact assessments

'Social impact assessments' (SIAs) are the most commonly used tool by the extractives industry to identify the positive and negative *potential* 'social' impacts of an extractive project. Social impacts refer to changes in local social and cultural systems through, for example, the distribution of new forms of wealth to certain members of the population, changes in the natural environment and the migration of different ethnic groups into resource-producing regions.

Defined broadly, SIAs include:

> processes of analysing, monitoring and managing the intended and unintended social consequences, both positive and negative, of planned interventions (policies, programs, plans, projects) and any social change processes invoked by those interventions. Its primary purpose is to bring about a more sustainable and equitable biophysical and human environment.
>
> (Vanclay, 2003, p. 5)

SIAs are not a new phenomenon, having originally emerged in the 1970s in response to new environmental legislation in the US (Freudenburg, 1986, p. 451). As a result, they have been closely associated with environmental impact assessments (EIAs). Despite the close association with EIAs, analysts such as Lockie (2001, p. 277) argue that SIAs are less substantive as the 'social' represents a far less predictable domain than the environment. This complexity is evident in Latour's (2005, p. 5) understanding of the social as not a 'thing among other things, like a black sheep among other white sheep, but a *type of connection* between things that are not themselves social'.

SIAs are undertaken by a range of actors, including employees of resource companies, consultants and/or regulatory agencies of host governments. They are often carried out because companies are required to do so by government regulations (Banks, 1999, p. 4) as part of the project approval process (O'Faircheallaigh, 1999, p. 63). SIAs can also be structured according to the regulatory requirements of the financial lenders of a resource project, such as the World Bank and the Asian Development Bank. Moreover, a new field of applied social research has emerged alongside the development of SIAs with numerous academics, business associations and NGOs involved in the creation of new methodologies and models.

Despite the diversity of methods and models, the dominant criticism regarding SIAs is that the extractives sector privileges 'technocratic rationality' based on the view that, 'it is possible to control the actual or potential opposition of local landowners' (Filer, 1990, p. 98). Consequently, those affected by an extractive project are not necessarily empowered to track and define the more 'subjective' social impacts associated with the exploitation of natural resources, such as new fears (for example, the use of the military as a source of project security) and aspirations (for example, preferences among a younger generation to gain employment within large corporations). Indigenous groups are therefore often excluded from the process as they lack 'access to the "technical" information and expertise required to ensure effective participation' (O'Faircheallaigh, 1999, p. 64). As Lockie (2001, p. 279) argues:

> in privileging the quantifiable, technocratic rationality empowers governments and developers by highlighting apparently positive impacts, such as

regional economic and employment growth, while ignoring those that are not measurable; the variable impact of changes within affected communities; and the subjective and cultural meanings that these changes hold within communities.

This claim links with Latourian theory (2005, p. 6), which posits that the meaning of the social has shrunk over time, 'starting with a definition which is *coextensive* with all associations, we now have, in common parlance, a usage that is limited to what is left *after* politics, biology, economics, law, psychology, management, technology, etc.'.

Indeed a narrow understanding of the social as something that is measurable can drive out other important effects such as 'the cumulative and longer term impacts that a succession of projects can have on indigenous communities' (O'Faircheallaigh, 1999, p. 64). Further, critics of SIAs argue that the process generally falls short of its greater potential. As Joyce and MacFarlane (2001, p. 3) write:

> at one end, the SIA is a dynamic, ongoing process of integrating knowledge on potential and real social impacts into decision-making and management practices; at the other end, it is a static, one-shot technocratic assessment undertaken to gain project approval of financing, with little or no follow through. Most SIAs fall somewhere on a continuum between the two.

This quote indicates that while large corporations do recognise that their operations are likely to have significant social impacts, it is 'no easy task to devise a program which can actually limit or control the community breakdown process' (Filer, 1990, p. 106). Extending this critique of SIAs, the remainder of this chapter highlights the difficulty that BCL, Freeport and BP have had in diagnosing, predicting and resolving the social impacts of their business practices. This is evident in the disparity between the social impacts identified and the CSR projects implemented.

Bougainville

To BCL's credit, the company attempted to understand the potential social impacts that the mine might cause. These attempts were undertaken despite the absence of any formal requirement imposed on BCL and it is only with hindsight that they can be viewed as inadequate. As discussed previously, BCL sought the advice of Douglas Oliver, who coordinated a research team at the Australian National University funded largely by BCL and which produced much of the available information on social change in Bougainville (Wesley Smith, 1992, p. 413). In 1973, BCL also sponsored a socio-economic survey (Scott & Company, 1973), with the aim of understanding the potential consequences of the mine on PNG's economy and society, as well how PNG's economic and social environment might influence BCL's business activities (Scott & Company, 1973, p. 4).

Population growth and in-migration

The earliest concerns and/or predictions regarding the social impacts of the Panguna mine related to population growth. Bougainville's population had grown steadily since the 1930s and accelerated in the 1970s and 1980s. By 1989, language groups such as the Nasioi and Nagovisi had one of the highest rates of population growth in the world (3.5 per cent) (AGA, 1989, p. 4.1). According to Connell (1990, pp. 47–8), the main concern regarding this population growth was that it would result in future land shortages, put pressure on local resources and lead to greater demand for modern sector employment. These issues did not eventuate as the war greatly reduced the population in areas surrounding the mine, both through conflict-related deaths and by causing New Guineans, Chinese and Australians to flee.

In 1968, Oliver (1968, p. 218) advised BCL that population concerns were a dominant theme in local resentment of the mine. Bougainvilleans believed BCL was 'looting' their island, leaving them with nowhere to live or plant crops. Moreover, some Bougainvilleans believed there would be nothing left to mine once PNG gained independence from Australia (Connell, 1990, p. 48).

In terms of how population growth would influence BCL's business activities, Oliver (1968, p. 219) advised management that local concerns about land acquisition would continue to increase. Oliver thus sent a warning signal to BCL that any further pressures placed on land through population growth would be problematic and would exacerbate these concerns. What the company understood less well, however, was the way in which the in-migration of New Guineans, especially Highlanders, in search of economic opportunities would lead to ethnic tensions (Vernon, 2005, p. 267).

While Oliver (1968, pp. 228–9) did warn the company that 'direct or *uncontrolled* contacts between CRA personnel (Europeans, Asians, "Redskins" and non-local Bougainvilleans) and local Bougainvilleans are going to result in incidents detrimental to CRA's interest', he did not foresee migrants remaining on Bougainville if they did not gain employment at the mine. Inability to predict this outcome is reflected in the only recommendation Oliver put forward to BCL in regard to avoiding racial conflict: that BCL develop its proposed mining town of Arawa in a sparsely populated area away from local villages (Oliver, 1968, p. 229). The number of migrants was significant, with estimates that the squatter population amounted to approximately 4,400 people, with only 54 per cent engaged in some type of employment and about two-thirds of children in these settlements not attending school (AGA, 1989, p. 4.7).

Despite the chronological link between the establishment of the mine and the proliferation of squatter settlements on Bougainville, BCL claimed the problem of 'vagrant migration' was an issue between the provincial and national Governments (Bougainville Administration, n.d., p. 15). However, neither the provincial nor central government has been seen to have adequately dealt with the situation. An Applied Geology Associates (AGA) review of the impacts of the mine claimed, 'after much discussion of possible policies, there was little direct action either to reduce squatter numbers or to upgrade welfare services in squatter settlements' (AGA, 1989, p. 4.6). BCL's argument was that although the provincial government was keen to restrict migration from other provinces, 'political implications at the National level have continued to militate against positive action' (Bougainville Copper Limited, n.d., p. 14).

Employment

BCL's responsiveness to the interests of the national Government also dominated its employment practices. As an executive of BCL stated, 'there was a preference towards PNG but the trouble was [that] it was not to Bougainville separately' (B2). As former Chairman of BCL, Don Carruthers (1990, p. 62), explains:

> the Company and the Papua New Guinea Government saw Bougainville Copper as an operation for the country as a whole. For this reason it was felt that employment opportunities should be available for people throughout the country, with the main criterion being suitability for the job.

Accordingly, BCL executives proudly reported their indigenous employment figures, with estimates that during the construction period, approximately 10,000 people were employed, of whom 6,000 were indigenous (Moulik, 1977, p. 12). In spite of these figures a number of criticisms were levelled at BCL for its employment policies. For example, Denoon (2000, pp. 168–9) highlights the low wages of Bougainvillean employees in contrast to expatriates. However, this is also true of foreign professionals working on Bougainville today, and is not on the face of it a criticism unique to BCL.

Participants in this research also indicate conflicting views as to whether Bougainvilleans were treated fairly in regard to employment levels and conditions. While some Bougainvilleans said, 'BCL was a very good company to work for because they looked after the employees' (B5, Bougainvillean former BCL employee), others criticised the lack of opportunities for Bougainvilleans to elevate to senior positions. For example, one disgruntled Bougainvillean former employee of BCL claimed:

> [BCL] should have provided the opportunity to elevate Bougainvilleans to senior levels. It was an injustice. I was convinced I should be up there [on the board of directors] after 16 years.
>
> (B6, ABG Department CEO/former BCL employee)

Either way, the main social impacts associated with employment did not take the form of tensions between staff over wages, but rather what employees did with this money when they returned to their villages.

One of the most important problems associated with the transition of an increasing proportion of the Bougainvillean population participating in the labour market was the breakdown of traditional village culture, or what Filer refers to as a 'process of local social disintegration' (Filer, 1990, p. 1). A crucial impact of more opportunities for employment on Bougainville was that it resulted in gradual changes within traditional village authority. Bougainvilleans identified the potential for this to occur early in the life of the mine and Oliver relayed this concern to the company's management through the following account:

> CRA will have a bad effect on our young people. They go there, earn lots of money and many evil ways and when they come home they will not do as we tell them anymore.
>
> (Oliver, 1968, p. 214)

This concern became a reality in the 1970s when it appeared that men in some villages were beginning to usurp women's rights over land, as well as their authority over younger men (Togolo, 2005, p. 283). In spite of this transformation, Togolo (2005, p. 283) argues that Filer's (1990) use of the concept social 'disintegration' is an inappropriate characterisation for all of Bougainville's villages. In Togolo's view, senior women in villages such as the Torau continued to play an important role in the community. Moreover, Togolo (2005, p. 283) argues that 'despite social tensions, the quintessential elements of the society held together'. Nonetheless changes in village authority can be seen to have had crucial implications on the control of the younger generation who were enjoying the benefits of a cash income for the first time. As a consequence of the breakdown of traditional forms of authority and the fact that many young men became more interested in employment at the mine than traditional farming occupations (Moulik, 1977, p. 186), village elders found it hard to maintain social control.

Income derived from new forms of employment also led to the creation of a 'class struggle' (Filer, 1990, p. 90), with increasing economic inequality between those who were engaged in some form of employment and those who were not. One consequence of this inequality was that it left many young men who were not working for the mine without a source of income at a time when significant changes were occurring within their village culture. Although BCL executives claim the company was not in a position to 'offer anything to young men outside employment' (B2, BCL executive), the lack of opportunities the mine created for a significant proportion of young men motivated them to join the BRA. As Regan (1998, p. 275) claims, 'BRA's strongest support came from frustrated young men with few economic opportunities for whom membership of the BRA gave power and status.'

Despite the scale of the aforementioned community disruption, BCL did in fact adopt numerous social and employment policies, 'unusual for mining companies in less-developed countries at that time' (Harvard Business School, 1974, p. 8). Unfortunately, many of BCL's community development initiatives (such as scholarships, medical aid and community grants) 'may have produced *negative* results' (Oliver, 1968, p. 224). Oliver's main criticism of BCL's early social initiatives was that they were implemented without an adequate understanding of possible consequences. Oliver's advice to improve these initiatives was for BCL to gain a more adequate understanding of the events and general social trends on the island (Denoon, 2000, p. 167). Oliver believed this knowledge would enable the company to implement community projects that would target actual rather than imagined needs of those affected by BCL's operations.

West Papua

The social impacts of Freeport and BP in West Papua are similar to those discussed for Bougainville. They include: the in-migration of people from other parts of Indonesia who have come to dominate local space, as well as limited opportunities for Papuans to elevate to senior employment positions.

As has been highlighted throughout this book, Freeport had little concern for environmental and social issues in the early stages of its business activities in West Papua (Rifai-Hasan, 2009, p. 29). The 1967 Contract of Work with the Indonesian Government did not include regulatory requirements concerning social or environmental impact assessments. Further, the company did not seek the advice of anthropologists or other consultants in the way that BCL did in the initial stages of the Panguna mine.

In spite of the lack of attention to addressing potential social impacts, Banks (1999, p. 4) argues that various forms of social monitoring of Freeport's mining activities in West Papua have occurred from time to time, but not until the 1990s (Ballard & Banks 2009, p. 7). For example, Chris Ballard and Glenn Banks spent 12 months working with Kamoro and Amungme communities on the UNCEN-ANU Baseline Study in the Freeport Contract of Works area over the period 1997–9 (Paull et al.,2006, p. 37). The study, which was in part sponsored by Freeport, established a 'baseline account of the living conditions and aspirations of the indigenous landowning Amungme and Kamoro communities against which subsequent progress in their status could be gauged' (Ballard & Banks, 2009, p. 151).

It was not until 1995, however, that the Indonesian Government approved the first environmental impact assessment (called the *Analisis Mengenai Dampak Lingkungan* [Integrated Environmental and Social Impact Assessment] or 'AMDAL' in the Indonesian context) (Paull et al., 2006, p. 36). Under the AMDAL process, social impacts are included in the analysis of environmental impacts; however, 'the social impacts of mining are even less well catered for than the environmental impacts' (Ballard, 2001, p. 14). This supports broader critiques that the social consequences of resource development are primarily considered as add-ons to the more comprehensive environmental monitoring requirements (Banks, 1999, p. 1). Moreover, even though the Indonesian Government reluctantly established the AMDAL assessment process (Leith, 2003, p. 155) and 'despite several written reports and letters from various government agencies pointing out breaches of government regulations, Freeport has consistently stated that it complies in all material respects with Indonesian law in terms of its operation' (Ballard & Banks, 2009, p. 164).

In contrast to Freeport, and as a result of the more substantive social and environmental regulations with which major extractive companies must now comply, BP was obliged to engage in a more rigorous social impact process prior to the construction of the Tangguh project.

According to BP's Summary Environmental Impact Assessment (SEIA), environmental studies in the area of the Tangguh LNG project commenced in 1998 (BP, 2005, p. 1). However, it was not until 2000 that detailed environmental and social impact assessments were carried out (BP, 2005, p. 1). The exchange of land for the Tangguh project occurred in 1999. This means that the exchange took place before any considerable social and/or environmental impact processes had taken place. Therefore it is reasonable to question how much knowledge landowning clans had of the social and environmental changes that would occur before 'agreeing' to 'sell'.

On 25 October 2002, the Indonesian Government ruled that the Tangguh project had complied with its environmental impact analysis (BP, 2005, pp. 1–2). In order to be granted approval under the AMDAL process, BP was required to produce three reports: an environmental impact assessment analysing the project's environmental and social impacts; an environmental management plan which outlined mitigation plans; and an environmental monitoring plan which detailed the monitoring and compliance plans (Hickman & Barber, 2011, p. 5). In addition to AMDAL, BP has been required to produce social impact reports, plans and monitoring processes in order to secure the backing of international financial donors, the Asian Development Bank and the Japanese Bank for International Development. These documents include: an Indigenous Peoples' Development Plan (BP, 2006), a Resettlement planning document (BP, 2006), as well as the publication of annual reports by the TIAP.

Population growth and in-migration

In spite of BP's and Freeport's (later) attempts to minimise the social impacts of their business operations, both projects have led to considerable population growth and tensions along ethnic lines. However, the situation for Papuans is arguably worse than for Bougainvilleans for two reasons. First, the Grasberg mine has resulted in an influx not just of economic migrants, but also of large numbers of Indonesian military. Second, the domination of local space by non-indigenous Papuans has been perceived by Papuans as a deliberate strategy on the part of the Indonesian Government to 'Indonesianise' West Papua.

Before the fall of Suharto in 1998, the Indonesian Government sponsored an official policy of transmigration to West Papua in order to relieve population pressure from over-populated areas of Indonesia, as well as to provide a supply of cheap labour to foreign-owned plantations (Leith, 2003, p. 96). Because the large number of migrants resulted in indigenous Papuans becoming a minority on their own land, many Papuans viewed the policy as a deliberate attempt by the

Government to subsume Papuan identity within a singular 'Indonesian' identity (Elmslie, 2011). The experience of ethnic marginalisation has been perceived as historically entwined with Freeport's mining activities, as the Indonesian Government has targeted Freeport's Contract of Work area and surrounds for the placement of transmigration settlements (Braithwaite et al., 2010, p. 75). The Amungme and Kamoro peoples thus claim that Freeport is not only responsible for the presence of these settlements, 'but also their economic viability and continuation' (Leith, 2003, p. 207).

Like the squatter settlements surrounding the Panguna mine, large numbers of Indonesian migrants and non-local indigenous Papuans arrived in areas surrounding the Grasberg complex in search of economic opportunities. The Amungme and Kamoro communities of Freeport's Contract of Work area had gone from making up greater than 95 per cent of the population in 1967 to less 15 per cent in 1998 (Paull et al., 2006, p. 40). Moreover, the town of Timika that services the mine is one of the most highly populated in the province (Ondawame, 1997), and in 2006 had the 'highest rate of growth of any urban community in Indonesia' (Paull et al., 2006, p. 36).

Again, similar to the Bougainville case, rapid population growth associated with mining in West Papua resulted in greater competition for economic opportunities (International Centre for Corporate Accountability, 2005, p. 21). Compounding this, Cook (2001) claims one of the greatest sources of antagonism has been an influx of neighbouring tribal groups into the vicinity of the Amungme and Kamoro communities. According to Cook, tensions between the Amungme and the Kamoro and neighbouring groups have exceeded those between Papuans and Indonesians[1] as they share a long history of tribal warfare. This claim is supported by Leith (2003, p. 96) who argues that:

> this volatile mix of rival *sukus* [tribal groups] forced into close proximity (rather than conflict between Indonesians and Papuan residents) has, to date been the cause of the greatest tension and violence in the area.

As discussed in Chapter 5, Freeport is accused of exacerbating tensions in the mid-1990s, by including tribal groups that the Amungme and Kamoro resented for encroaching on their land as beneficiaries of the One Per Cent Trust Fund. In this way, the contested distribution of the Fund is believed to have heightened pre-existing conflict between tribes (Soares 2004, p. 136). More importantly, TNI is accused of provoking inter-tribal conflict to justify their security services. This new kind of conflict has been referred to as 'military wars' (Braithwaite et al., 2010, p. 118). Wanting to prove that the security situation in the Freeport area under the leadership of the police is worse, TNI is considered to have manipulated traditional fighting. This has occurred by supplying guns to one side thereby altering the rules and means of traditional warfare (see Braithwaite et al., 2010, pp. 117–18).

BP has made an explicit attempt to avoid significant migration into the communities surrounding the Tangguh project. The strategies employed by BP include: a policy of no on-site recruitment at the LNG plant; programmes to limit construction worker off-duty activities in and around the Bintuni Bay area; affirmative action policies relating to local employment; returning employees home for rest periods and when their employment ends; paying wages in places where people are originally hired; and accommodating workers in closed camps.

According to BP, the aim of these measures is to 'avoid the "honey-pot" syndrome and the impact of excessive spontaneous in-migration into the Bintuni Bay area' (BP, 2007, p. 11). As an executive of BP Indonesia stated:

> the strategy is to recruit from open ports around Papua and send back to post rather than have them marginalise local people. We are giving the chance for local workers first and then we look for another one. Start with locals. We are not aiming to make discrimination but it is designed to manage expectations and reduce jealousy.
>
> (WP39, BP Indonesia executive)

Additionally, BP has initiated programmes to counter the negative impacts associated with in-migration such as increased pressure on existing infrastructure and services; greater competition for jobs and training; crime; violence; alcohol abuse; prostitution; ethnic tension; and the erosion of traditional cultures (BP, 2015). In spite of these initiatives, BP claims that it is ultimately the central government that is responsible for restricting access to the area surrounding the Tangguh project. It claims:

> ultimately, in-migration policy is a matter for the Indonesian government. We can offer advice and advocate specific actions – but cannot successfully address the issue acting alone.
>
> (BP, 2012)

The TIAP supports this view, asserting that it is up to local leaders to decide the restrictions that should be placed on migrants. Consequently, the TIAP advised BP that its core responsibility is to maintain programmes to limit worker off-duty activities and 'benefit to the maximum extent possible the original members of the community and support them economically' (TIAP, 2002, p. 25).

This mirrors requirements at PNG resource sites which require the developer to 'give preference in training, employment and business development opportunities to local landowners, followed by people of the affected area, followed by people of the host province, followed by other PNG citizens' (Filer, 2008, pp. 124–5). However, the unintended result of this practice is the increasingly contested notion of local identity at these sites (Banks, 2008), which also appears evident in West Papua.

In 2009, the TIAP reported that a process was underway to regulate immigrant activities through a deposit of fees for transportation back to the migrants' place of origin, limitations on the length of stay and permissible activities (TIAP, 2009,

p. 55). These regulations were developed in response to the TIAP's findings in 2009 that:

> there are large numbers of migrants in each of the RAVs [resettlement affected villages]. Their population has grown from 1,074 to 2,153, with Onar having the most dramatic growth of almost 300%.
>
> (TIAP, 2009, p. 50)

This result, however, also revealed an unintended consequence of BP's compliance with the Asian Development Bank's requirements on the forced relocation of villages surrounding the Tangguh project. These requirements include the development of new housing and community facilities (see BP, 2006). According to the TIAP, the new housing and community facilities that BP was obliged to provide were the main attraction for the arrival of large numbers of migrants to these villages. An Indonesian NGO worker involved in monitoring the Tangguh project told the author that many of the houses BP built for the relocated villagers have since been sold by local Papuans to migrants from Java (WP30, Indonesian NGO worker). This suggests the houses provided were either inappropriate for their lifestyle, that the gains of selling outweighed the loss of the house, or possibly a combination of both.

While the TIAP does not go so far as to suggest locals have been selling the houses provided to them by BP, it does suggest that:

> many of the migrants are sharing or renting homes of the original residents. This has raised tensions over agricultural and fisheries resources, village governance, population management, and social issues including prostitution, alcohol and gambling.
>
> (TIAP, 2009, p. 50)

According to Down to Earth (2005, p. 9), migrants are particularly interested in staying with the locals so that they can gain employment with BP in positions that are set aside for indigenous Papuans (discussed in the following section). The migrants do this by seeking the recommendation of the village head and Village Development Committee that BP classify them as 'local people'. In return, the migrants pay the village head between Rp 50,000 and Rp 1 million (US$5–100) and give cigarettes to the committee leader (Down to Earth, 2005, p. 9).

Employment

As discussed in relation to Bougainville, employment practices and the income they generate can have a number of important flow-on effects detrimental to the welfare of local communities, such as the breakdown of traditional village structures and increased economic inequality. Although the employment practices of Freeport and BP are believed to have led to similar effects in West Papua, there a number of important differences.

The first difference is that unlike BCL, Freeport was not quick to localise the mine's workforce. It is possible that as a consequence of the close relationship between the company and the Suharto regime, Freeport did not share BCL's concern that the government might one day fully nationalise the mine. Suharto was more interested in signalling to the international community that Indonesia was 'open for business'. As a result, Freeport is accused of largely neglecting the professional development of indigenous Papuans for over 25 years, and it is only since the mid-1990s that the company has adopted an affirmative action employment policy.

One of the most significant policies Freeport implemented in the 1990s was a commitment to double the employment of Papuans at the mine by the year 2000, and to double it again by the year 2006 (International Centre for Corporate Accountability, 2005, p. 9). While both these targets were exceeded and represent a considerable improvement (Braithwaite et al., 2010, p. 74), by 2008 the number of Papuans directly employed by Freeport amounted to only 3,352 (29 per cent) out of a total workforce of 11,659 direct employees (PT Freeport Indonesia, 2008, p. 23). Moreover, Freeport took 25 years longer than BCL to reach the same proportion of indigenous employment. However, as was the case on Bougainville, the achievement of employment targets in West Papua has not necessarily resulted in satisfaction among the indigenous workforce. As a Papuan member of the Tongoi Papua claimed:

> The relationship inside is good but sometimes in promotion it is different. I don't know what they say – it's always special for their people [Indonesians].
>
> (WP24)

One consequence of competition between Indonesians and Papuans for Freeport employment is that, similar to Bougainville, it has created a new kind of class struggle, 'between those who have jobs and those who do not, and those that have supervisory positions (overwhelmingly migrants) and those who do not' (Braithwaite et al., 2010, p. 16). Competition for Freeport employment, therefore, has added a class dimension to ethnic tension between Papuans and migrants from other parts of Indonesia.

In response to Papuan concerns relating to the perceived lack of opportunity to elevate to senior positions, Freeport was advised in 2005 to move away from a sole focus on employment targets. As the report of the International Centre for Corporate Accountability (2005, p. 11) states:

> the issue about Papuan employment cannot end with reaching an employment goal alone; it must also deal with on-going issues of Papuan employee satisfaction, fair treatment for Papuans in the workforce and enhanced opportunities in the future.

This recommendation was based on Freeport's slow progress in providing training and apprenticeships to Papuans. For example, it was not until 2003 that Freeport formed the Nemangkawi Mining Institute, which provides apprenticeships and career development opportunities for hundreds of Papuans and other Indonesians each year (PT Freeport Indonesia, 2008, p. 23). Freeport's delayed commitment to local training and education has been blamed for the small numbers of Papuans possessing the skills required to achieve employment with the company.

BP: employment at Tangguh

One major difference in the employment practices at Tangguh is that BP has been obliged under the AMDAL process to favour local people since the initial stages of construction. Specifically, BP is required to give preference to applicants from the nine directly affected villages surrounding the Tangguh project.

BP's employment obligations include a commitment to a gradual increase in the number of Papuan employees. Targets have been set at 31 per cent initial operations stage, 62 per cent after ten years, and 85 per cent after 25 years (BP, 2005, p. 35). In regard to the initial stage, BP committed to employ at least one person from each of the 700–800 households in the nine directly affected villages to help construct the LNG facility (BP, 2005, p. 15). In 2009 the TIAP (2009, p. 20) reported that BP had successfully achieved this commitment, confirming that job offers were made to at least one member in every family.

A concern regarding Tangguh's construction workforce was that it was only short-term. While a cohort of 5,800 workers was required to construct the facility, this number dropped to just 450 when operations began (Hickman & Barber, 2011, p. 13). Hence, the biggest concern for BP and its advisers in regard to employment was how to limit the potential negative effects of a sudden, yet temporary, increase in employment opportunities.

One strategy BP deployed to mitigate the potential negative impacts of short-term employment was by financing a vocational training centre for workers in carpentry, plumbing, electricity and welding (BP, 2007, p. 12). The aim, according to BP, was 'to support the transition of [the] construction workforce to non-Project employment as construction related employment starts to decline' (BP, 2007, p. 17). In contrast to the view of the BCL executive who claimed that the company could not offer opportunities outside of the mine, BP believed it could provide skills beyond those needed by BP in order to reduce the potential for long-term dependency (BP, 2007, p. 3).

Recognising that contractors would recruit most of the construction workforce, the TIAP panel also advised BP to encourage its contractors to train and recruit indigenous Papuans (TIAP, 2002, p. 23). While TIAP were aware that BP did not have direct control of its contractors (TIAP, 2003, p. 13), the panel stressed the issue of employment was one of the key expectations and primary benefits to be derived from the project (TIAP, 2003, p. 20). Consequently, BP wrote into the terms and conditions of its contracting agreements a requirement that contractors employ a certain percentage of Papuans (TIAP, 2006, p. 16).

By 2006, the TIAP panel reported, 'thus far, BP and its contractors have met most of their obligations for employment of local villagers and Papuans' (TIAP,

2006, p. 16). However, the panel did add, 'because so few Papuans are skilled in the areas needed, many of these jobs are short term and have little potential for advancement' (TIAP, 2006, pp. 16–17). Like Freeport, BP has argued that its need for skilled workers has constrained its capacity to employ indigenous Papuans.

By 2007 the construction workforce at the Tangguh project peaked at more than 10,000 people, of whom 3,000 (30 per cent) were Papuan, including 608 (about 6 per cent) from the directly affected villages (TIAP, 2008). In this way BCL, Freeport and BP can be seen to have all shared the 30 per cent 'local' employment figure, with the main differences being the length of time required to reach this figure, and the temporal nature of employment at the Tangguh site.

Despite the achievements of BP's local employment targets, the TIAP has maintained pressure on the company to educate the construction workforce on the demobilisation process in order to mitigate the impact of any shock or disappointment when employment ceases (TIAP, 2008, p. 3). In 2009 the TIAP reported that the demobilisation process was well under way, with most Papuan employees having returned to their homes and most, but not all, non-Papuans having left West Papua (TIAP, 2009, p. 4). BP provided temporary assistance to employees from the nine affected villages in their return to traditional fishing, and some were provided training for employment in the operations phase of the project (TIAP, 2009, p. 4).

In spite of the post-employment provisions put in place by BP, the TIAP maintains that the limited employment and other economic opportunities for Papuans will remain a serious issue for the long term (TIAP, 2009, p. 69). However, the panel's 2011 report (TIAP, 2011, p. 5) claims, 'regional and local leaders, although anxious for more employment and advancement of Papuans, are pleased at BP's efforts and accomplishments thus far'.

Conclusion

This chapter argued that BCL, Freeport and BP business activities in Bougainville and West Papua have been associated with considerable community disruption within local communities, such as population growth, class struggle and transformations of traditional forms of authority. It was argued that the problems brought about by these changes were not necessarily anticipated during the initial stages of the resource projects due to inherent difficulties in the prediction of future social and political trends.

In relation to the Bougainville case, the data suggest that BCL did not foresee that many migrants would be attracted to remain on Bougainville despite not securing employment at the mine. Consequently the company and government had few measures in place to regulate migration to Bougainville once the mine opened, and were unable to address the proliferation of squatter settlements.

In relation to the West Papua case, Freeport has been accused locally of not having adequate strategies in place to engage with the potential social impacts of its mining operations. This was demonstrated by the slow localisation of the mine's workforce and provision of training to indigenous Papuans. In contrast, BP has been obliged to engage in a more rigorous SIA process as a result of new Indonesian and international regulations. In spite of this, the Tangguh project has produced similar social problems to those that affected communities surrounding the BCL and Freeport mines. However, BP is considered by some to have made a significant effort to engage with and mitigate these negative social impacts as they arose (TIAP, 2011, p. 5). BP's strategies have not been completely successful in alleviating all negative impacts. The data collected for this study suggest that a positive perception appears to have been maintained overall due to the company's successful strategy of ongoing engagement with the TIAP and designing community development projects to target the social problems associated with the project. Whether this holds true for the next 20 years, however, is not yet known.

A common theme in both the Bougainville and West Papua cases has been the importance of empowering locals to define for themselves the impacts associated with natural resource development, something which has only recently become accepted. The next chapter explores this in more depth, through a discussion of local inclusion in environmental protection measures.

Notes

1 It is important not to dismiss the tensions that do exist between the Indonesian migrants and Papuan residents as a result of 'widespread Indonesian racism … which blames them for being "primitive", "stupid", "lazy" and worse' (Braithwaite *et al.*, 2010, p. 76).

Bibliography

Applied Geology Associates (AGA). 1989. *Environmental, Socio-Economic and Public Health Review of Bougainville Copper Mine, Panguna*. Christchurch: Applied Geology Associates.

Ballard, C. 2001. 'Human rights and the mining sector in Indonesia: A baseline study'. London: International Institute for Environment and Development. <http://pubs.iied.org/pdfs/G00929.pdf> [accessed 7 May 2015].

Ballard, C. & Banks, G. 2009. 'Between a rock and a hard place: Corporate strategy at the Freeport mine in Papua, 2001–2006', in B. P. Resosudarmo & F. Jotzo (eds.), *Working with Nature against Poverty: Development, Resources and the Environment in Eastern Indonesia*. Singapore: ISEAS Publishing, pp. 147–77.

Banks, G. 1999. 'Keeping an eye on the beasts: Social monitoring of large-scale mines in New Guinea'. Resource Management in Asia-Pacific, Working Paper 21. Research School of Pacific and Asian Studies, Australian National University.

Banks, G. 2008. 'Understanding "resource" conflicts in Papua New Guinea', *Asia Pacific Viewpoint*, vol. 49, no. 1, pp. 23–34.

Bougainville Administration. n.d. 'Awareness materials: Establishing representative structures for landowners of BCL mining-related leases'.

BP. 2005. 'Summary environmental impact assessment: Tangguh LNG project in Indonesia'. <www.adb.org/sites/default/files/project-document/69276/ino-tangguh-lng-project.pdf> [accessed 12 May 2015].

BP. 2006. 'Indigenous peoples development planning document'. <www.adb.org/sites/default/files/project-document/68965/38919-01-ps-ipdp.pdf> [accessed 12 May 2015].

BP. 2007. 'Indonesia: Tangguh liquefied natural gas project'. <www.adb.org/documents/indonesia-tangguh-liquefied-natural-gas-project> [accessed 12 May 2015].

BP. 2012. 'In-migration'. <www.bp.com/sectiongenericarticle.do?categoryId=9004769&contentId=7008850> [accessed 15 August 2011].

BP. 2015. 'Tangguh LNG'. <www.bp.com/sectiongenericarticle.do?categoryId=9004779&contentId=7008759> [accessed 8 May 2015].

Braithwaite, J., Braithwaite, V., Cookson, M. & Dunn, L. 2010. *Anomie and Violence: Non-Truth and Reconciliation in Indonesian Peacebuilding*. Canberra: ANU Press.

Carruthers, D. 1990. 'Panguna impact (2): Dialogue with the chairman of BCL. Transcript of interview conducted by Jim Griffin and Don Carruthers', in P. Polomka (ed.), *Bougainville: Perspectives on a Crisis*. Canberra: Strategic and Defence Studies Centre, Australian National University.

Connell, J. 1990. 'The Panguna mine impact (1)', in P. Polomka (ed.), *Bougainville: Perspectives on a Crisis*. Canberra: Strategic and Defence Studies Centre, Australian National University.

Cook, C. D. 2001. 'Papuan gold: A blessing or a curse? The case of the Amungme', *Cultural Survival*, vol. 25, no.1. <www.culturalsurvival.org/ourpublications/csq/article/papuan-gold-a-blessing-or-a-curse-the-case-amungme> [accessed 12 May 2015].

Denoon, D. 2000. *Getting under the Skin: The Bougainville Copper Agreement and the Creation of the Panguna Mine*. Carlton: Melbourne University Press.

Down to Earth. 2005. 'Tangguh – ignoring the reality'. <www.downtoearth-indonesia.org/story/tangguh-ignoring-reality> [accessed 8 May 2015].

Elmslie, J. 2011. 'West Papuan demographic transition and the 2010 Indonesian census: "Slow motion genocide" or not?' Paper presented at the Comprehending West Papua Conference, 23–24 February, University of Sydney, Sydney.

Filer, C. 1990. 'The Bougainville rebellion, the mining industry and the process of social disintegration in Papua New Guinea', in R. J. May & M. Spriggs (eds.), *The Bougainville Crisis*. Bathurst: Crawford House Press, pp. 73–112.

Filer, C. 2008. 'Development forum in Papua New Guinea: Upsides and downsides', *Journal of Energy & Natural Resources Law*, vol. 26, pp. 120–50.

Freudenburg, W. R. 1986. 'Social impact assessment', *Annual Review of Sociology*, vol. 12, pp. 451–78.

Harvard Business School. 1974. *Bougainville Copper Limited*. Boston: Harvard Business School.

Hickman, A. & Barber, P. 2011. 'Tangguh, BP & international standards: An analysis of the commitments made by BP in relation to BP Tangguh in West Papua and their social and environmental responsibilities'. <www.downtoearth-indonesia.org/sites/downtoearth-indonesia.org/files/Tangguh,%20BP%20and%20International%20Standards%20English%2012%20April%202011.pdf> [accessed 12 May 2015].

International Centre for Corporate Accountability. 2005. *Audit Report: Human Rights, Employment and Social Development of Papuan People in Indonesia*. New York.

Joyce, S. A. & MacFarlane, M. 2001. *Social Impact Assessment in the Mining Industry: Current Situation and Future Directions*. London: International Institute for Environment and Development (IIED) – Mining, Minerals and Sustainable Development.

Latour, B. 2005. *Reassembling the Social: An Introduction to Actor-Network Theory.* Oxford: Oxford University Press.

Leith, D. 2003. *The Politics of Power: Freeport in Suharto's Indonesia.* Honolulu: University of Hawaii Press.

Lockie, S. F. 2001. 'SIA in review: Setting the agenda for impact assessment in the 21st century', *Impact Assessment & Project Appraisal,* vol. 19, no. 4, pp. 277–87.

Moulik, T. K. 1977. *Bougainville in Transition.* Canberra: Development Studies Centre, Australian National University.

O'Faircheallaigh, C. 1999. 'Making social impact assessment count: A negotiation-based approach for indigenous peoples', *Society & Natural Resources,* vol. 12, no. 1, pp. 63–80.

Oliver, D. 1968. 'Some social relational aspects of CRA copper-mining on Bougainville (condensed version)', in D. Denoon (ed.), *Getting under the Skin: The Bougainville Copper Agreement and the Creation of the Panguna Mine.* Carlton: Melbourne University Press.

Ondawame, J. O. 1997. 'The impacts of Freeport's mining activities on the Amungme and Kamoro peoples in West Papua'. Paper presented at the Visions and Actions for Peace Conference at the Australian National University, Canberra.

Paull, D., Banks, G., Ballard, C. & Gillieson, D. 2006. 'Monitoring the environmental impact of mining in remote locations through remotely sensed data', *Geocarto International,* vol. 21, no. 1, pp. 33–42.

PT Freeport Indonesia. 2008. 'Core values: 2008 working toward sustainable development report'. <www.fcx.com/sd/pdfs/WTSD_2008.pdf> [accessed 11 May 2015].

Regan, A. J. 1998. 'Causes and course of the Bougainville conflict', *Journal of Pacific History,* vol. 33, no. 3, pp. 269–85.

Rifai-Hasan, P. A. 2009. 'Development, power, and the mining industry in Papua: A study of Freeport Indonesia', *Journal of Business Ethics,* no. 89, no. 2, pp. 129–43.

Scott, W. D. & Company. 1973. *A Study of the Impact of the Bougainville Copper Project on the Economy and Society of Papua New Guinea.* Port Moresby: W. D. Scott and Company.

Soares, A. D. J. 2004. 'The impact of corporate strategy on community dynamics: A case study of the Freeport mining company in West Papua, Indonesia', *International Journal on Minority and Group Rights,* vol. 11, no. 1, 115–42.

Tangguh Independent Advisory Panel (TIAP). 2002. 'First report on Tangguh LNG project'. <www.bp.com/content/dam/bp-country/en_id/Documents/TIAPReport/2002%20 TIAP%20First%20Report.pdf> [accessed 12 May 2015].

Tangguh Independent Advisory Panel (TIAP). 2003. 'Second report on Tangguh LNG project'. <www.bp.com/content/dam/bp-country/en_id/Documents/TIAPReport/2003%20 TIAP%20Second%20Report.pdf> [accessed 12 May 2015].

Tangguh Independent Advisory Panel (TIAP). 2006. 'Fourth report on Tangguh LNG project'. <www.bp.com/content/dam/bp-country/en_id/Documents/TIAPReport/2006%20 TIAP%20Fourth%20Report.pdf> [accessed 12 May 2015].

Tangguh Independent Advisory Panel (TIAP). 2008. 'Sixth report on the Tangguh LNG project'. <www.bp.com/content/dam/bp-country/en_id/Documents/TIAPReport/2008%20 TIAP%20Sixth%20Report.pdf> [accessed 12 May 2015].

Tangguh Independent Advisory Panel (TIAP). 2009. 'Seventh report on the Tangguh LNG project and overview of panel's experiences (2002–2009)'. <www.bp.com/content/dam/ bp-country/en_id/Documents/TIAPReport/2009%20TIAP%20Seventh%20Report. pdf> [accessed 12 May 2015].

Tangguh Independent Advisory Panel (TIAP). 2011. 'First report on operations phase of the Tangguh LNG project'. <www.bp.com/content/dam/bp-country/en_id/Documents/TIAPReport/2011%20TIAP%20First%20Report%20on%20Operations%20Phase.pdf> [accessed 12 May 2015].

Togolo, M. 2005. 'Torau responses to change', in A. J. Regan & H. M. Griffin (eds.), *Bougainville before the Conflict*. Canberra: Pandanus Books, pp. 274–90.

Vanclay, F. 2003. 'SIA principles: International principles for social impact assessment', *Impact Assessment and Project Appraisal*, vol. 21, no. 1, pp. 5–11.

Vernon, D 2005, 'The Panguna mine', in A. J. Regan & H. M. Griffin (eds.), *Bougainville before the Conflict*. Canberra: Pandanus Books, pp. 258–73.

Wesley-Smith, T. & Ogan, E. 1992. 'Copper, class, and crisis: Changing relations of production in Bougainville', *The Contemporary Pacific*, vol. 4, no. 2, pp. 245–67.

9 Environmental damage

Introduction

This chapter focuses on the seventh site of interdependence between the companies and the root causes of conflict in Bougainville and West Papua: environmental damage. As discussed in Chapter 8, concern for the social impacts associated with resource development has often formed a component of larger assessments of environmental impacts. In practice, however, and based on Western technocratic conceptions of the environment and reliance on scientific analysis, large corporations are inclined to treat the 'social' and the 'environmental' as separate domains.

Beginning with a discussion of 'sustainable development' discourse, Western conceptions of the environment will be contrasted with those of Melanesian cultures. The work of Escobar (1995) and Banerjee (2003) will be drawn on to question the model of development that tends to be ascribed to and perpetuated by multinational resource extraction companies. This theoretical paradigm will then be applied to the Bougainville and West Papua cases. Through this analysis the chapter seeks to demonstrate that corporate and state actors do not always share the same cultural attachments to land as local communities. Yet these actors usually make decisions relating to environmental management. This has a tendency to provoke conflict as it can trigger strong feelings of injustice relating to the control of land and the denial of local wisdom. The chapter explains that by learning to be more interdependent with indigenous peoples, resource companies might be able to develop more meaningful, less Western and more socially and spiritually engaged forms of ecological interdependence.

Sustainable development

The concept of 'sustainable development' emerged in the 1980s alongside heightened concerns about the deterioration of the environment, natural resources and the consequences for economic development (Banerjee, 2003). These concerns emerged alongside greater awareness of the ways in which human activity might threaten the future survival of the planet (through problems relating to global warming, ozone depletion, declining biodiversity, environmental pollution and the scarcity of natural resources) (Shrivastava & Hart, 1995). Therefore, sustainable development has been 'part of a broader process of the problematisation of global survival' (Escobar, 1995, p. 194).

The term sustainable development came to prominence following a report compiled by the World Commission on Environment and Economic Development in 1987, chaired by the former Prime Minister of Norway, Gro Harlem Brundtland. The 'Brundtland report' defines the goal of sustainable development as 'meeting the needs of the present without compromising the ability of future generations to meet their own needs' (WCED, 1987).

Following the publication of the Brundtland report, there has been greater recognition by the private sector that 'the economy and society depend on the biosphere and environmental processes occurring within them' (Dunphy et al., 2000, p. 22). This reflects a reworking or new understanding of the relationship between nature and society in which there is greater recognition that the future of the global economic system is dependent on the future of the planet itself.

Heightened attention to the environmental costs of economic development has led to the emergence of numerous regulatory initiatives concerning environmental protection by the extractives industry. This includes the conduct of environmental impact assessments prior to the development of large resource projects, as well as the implementation of independent monitoring and evaluation processes throughout the life of the project. It is also customary for large natural resource extraction companies to publish 'sustainable development reports' alongside other CSR commitments on company websites.

While the adoption of the sustainable development discourse by the extractives industry has been far-reaching, there are many concerns relating to its intent and implications. The dominant concern relates to its impact at the 'broader level of the political economy' (Banerjee, 2003, p. 145). The main concern is that notions of sustainable development advance Western assumptions that economic growth is an assured good. Situating his critique within a broader analysis of 'development' as a 'historically singular experience' Escobar (1995, p. 195) argues sustainable development:

> focuses less on the negative consequences of economic growth on the environment than on the effects of environmental degradation on growth and potential growth. It is growth (read: capitalist market expansion), and not the environment, that has to be sustained.

In this way Escobar derides the sustainable development discourse as a 'feat of Western rationality' (1995, p. 192) that is intended to create the impression that only minor adjustments to the market system are needed to launch an era of environmentally sound development (1995, p. 197).

There are two aspects of Escobar's critique that are particularly important in the context of this chapter. The first relates to the capacity of sustainable development to lead to greater environmental protection. The second is the criticism of the assumption 'that the benevolent (white) hand of the West will save the

Earth' (Escobar, 1995, p. 193). Moreover aside from scepticism that sustainable development will trigger the institutional reform required to reconcile economic development with environmental protection, Escobar argues that the discourse fails to facilitate a move 'away from conventional Western modes of knowing in general in order to make room for other types of knowledge and experience' (1995, p. 216). The sustainable development discourse, in Escobar's view, thus fails to encourage corporations to engage with less Western and perhaps more meaningful, forms of environmental protection.

Sharing Escobar's (1995) two-pronged critique of sustainable development, Banerjee (2003) asks, 'Who sustains whose development'? Banerjee (2003, p. 144) claims:

> as with development, the meanings, practices, and policies of sustainable development continue to be informed by colonial thought, resulting in dis-empowerment of a majority of the world's populations, especially rural populations in the Third World.

As a result of the colonial logic that underpins the global economy (see Chapter 3), Banerjee (2003, p. 144) characterises sustainable development as a 'unitary system of knowledge', which instead of promoting an alternative path to development, focuses on sustaining the global economy more or less as it currently exists. Thus in Banerjee's view, sustainable development is more likely to further marginalise or co-opt 'traditional' forms of knowledge than empower alternative environmental management practices, or alternative means to economic development more broadly.

Building on the work of Escobar and Banerjee, it will be argued that Melanesians hold a more 'holistic' (Banks, 2002, p. 41) conception of the environment than that which tends to dominate Western business practice. In Melanesian societies, environmental damage or ecological problems are rarely solely about the 'environment', but are also about cultural identity, land control and access to resources. It appears from the data collected for this study that these issues cannot necessarily be solved through corporate environmental strategies alone, and require a more integrated, wider-reaching response.

Melanesian conceptions of the environment

In contrast to Western conceptions of the environment as separate from society, environmental consciousness in Melanesian societies has been described as fusing 'the social, cultural, political, economic, and environmental landscapes' (Banks, 2002, p. 41). Land forms the basis of group membership and nationality (Ballard, 1997, p. 48) and is a source of political power and cultural sustenance. Indeed in contrast to the West there are no clear distinctions 'between the environment and the rest of one's daily life' (Banks, 2002, p. 41).

Melanesian conceptions of the environment have led some Western environmentalists to characterise Melanesians as 'noble primitive ecologists' or 'natural conservationists' (Macintyre & Foale, 2002). The idea of the 'noble primitive ecologist' is perhaps as problematic as contests over the Noble Savage debate that have dogged anthropologists over successive generations (Ellingson, 2001). Indeed Macintyre and Foale (2002) contest the 'noble primitive ecologist' characterisation claiming there is no such thing as a 'natural conservationist ethic in Melanesia'. Those who do make this claim, according to Macintyre and Foale, fail to acknowledge the 'degrading ecological transformations brought about by indigenous inhabitants' themselves. The authors argue that even in cases where companies are required to negotiate the terms of access to land with the customary owners, they generally do not demand stricter environmental controls (Macintyre & Foale, 2002). Rather, they demand more money. Based on this, Macintyre and Foale (2002) argue that their main concern is not the preservation of the environment per se, but the lack of utilisable resources and amenity.

Macintyre and Foale's critique does not contradict the characterisation of Melanesians as holding a more holistic conception of the environment. Rather what the authors object to is the portrayal of Melanesians as 'natural stewards of their environment', which has the effect of obscuring the issues that most concern them. Thus, supporting the Escobar and Banerjee critique of sustainable development, environmental management practices based on Western conceptions of the environment can curtail the priorities of non-Western resource producing communities.

Banks (2002, pp. 39–40) argues that while many observers continue to frame the impacts of mining operations in Melanesia as solely 'environmental' or 'ecological', the impacts most fundamentally concern the control of resources. Banks suggests that a better means of understanding the environmental impacts of resource extraction in Melanesia is to 'look at the way in which control over a range of resources is affected by the mining operations' (Banks, 2002, pp. 40–1). This includes subsistence, political and social resources and systems of rights and responsibilities. This understanding of Melanesian conceptions of the environment is supported by Ballard (1997, p. 50), who claims that the local landscape pervades every aspect of social life:

> this sense of identity-through-place finds expression in the common statements that water from the streams of one's own land is the sweetest – all other streams taste different and this taste is one of the markers of difference that establishes identity.

Echoing Escobar's (1995, p. 197) concern that the sustainable development discourse creates an impression that only minor adjustments to the global economy are needed, Banks (2002, pp. 60–1) concludes his analysis by stating that:

> for mining companies to consider only the environmental aspects of their operation, ignoring the cultural, economic, political, and social realities of resources use and control in the areas in which they operate, also provides those companies with another 'easy out'.

Instead of corporations engaging with the complexity of the environmental impacts of resource development in Melanesian societies, Banks (2002, p. 60) argues that the tendency is to adopt 'technological fixes' that are asocial, do not include locals and, consequently, do not respond to their highest priorities.

Bougainville

> The mine caused a lot of pollution in the Jaba River. The water became blue and it still is. There is no life in the river. You cannot eat the fish. It used to be a big source of food.
>
> (B16, Rorovana resident)

Mining at Panguna brought considerable environmental change, the most visible of which is the giant hole of the mine pit that covers 400 hectares – land that is lost forever (Denoon, 2000, p. 159). While BCL began producing environmental reviews in 1984, no pre-mine environment assessment was required and no environmental impact assessment was produced by the company or the Administration (AGA, 1989, p. 1.1).

To construct the mine, approximately 220 hectares of tropical rainforest had to be cleared, as well as volcanic ash and weathered rock removed (Brown, 1974, p. 20). On a daily basis, this resulted in the disposal of approximately 150,000 tons of rock and tailings waste (Brown, 1974, p. 19). BCL was permitted under the Bougainville Copper Agreement to discharge this waste into the Kawerong River at Panguna, which then flowed into the Jaba River[1] (Denoon, 2000, p. 159; Tanis, 2005, p. 452). Reflective of the difficulties associated with predicting the 'social' impacts of mining at the beginning of construction, however, the tailings and waste rock disposal sites ended up covering much larger areas and were in different locations to those originally planned by BCL or agreed to by the Australian Administration (AGA, 1989, p. 8.3). In addition, the 'behavior of the river and spread of the tailings has been contrary to what was originally predicted' (Brown, 1974, p. 24).

The mine was constructed at a time when pollution was not a strong political issue (Brown, 1974, p. 19) and technology was more limited than it is today. For example, in the late 1960s, technology had not yet been developed to carry slurry over long distances[2] (Vernon, 2005, p. 269) and was subsequently discharged directly into the Kawerong River. The impact this would have on the river system was underestimated by BCL as it was told by hydraulic experts that river deposition would carry 80 per cent of tailings of tailings out to sea, when in fact only some 60 per cent was carried out to sea (Vernon, 2005, p. 269).

The disposal of this waste significantly altered the Kawerong–Jaber river valleys, resulting in the loss of freshwater and fish resources for possibly up to several generations[3] (AGA, 1989, p. 8.5; Brown, 1974, p. 22). As most fish species in Bougainville need to spend part of their life in the sea, all fish in the Jaba River were depleted due to the physical and chemical barriers tailings posed to their migration (AGA, 1989, p. 7.28). Tailings spread out over 1,700 ha on either side of the Jaba River (Brown, 1974, p. 19), destroying areas of rainforest important for hunting (AGA, 1989, p. 8.6). The gradual build-up of the riverbed also increased the risk of flooding and the spread of sediment killed trees in the rainforest (Brown, 1974, p. 25).

The spread of tailings threatened several villages, with approximately 800 people holding rights to land in the tailings lease area and 1,400 holding fishing rights on the two rivers (Brown, 1974, p. 25). Mining significantly decreased the land-holdings of some of these people, resulting in significant and permanent loss of food and materials (AGA, 1989, pp. 8.2–8.3). As a study by AGA (1989, p. 725) found, 'even in villages where land losses have been relatively slight, some clans and households may now have very poor or non-existent access to land, and be almost wholly dependent on purchased food'. Re-vegetation in some areas affected by tailings and waste rock is near impossible, with experiments indicating that species of nutritional and commercial value for locals cannot be restored to their original state (Connell, 1991, p. 67).

Thus, although landowner opposition which marked the construction of the mine diminished over time in part because of the modernisation benefits it seemed to offer (AGA, 1989, p. 8.1), it became increasingly obvious that a significant amount of land had been destroyed and would never be of any economic or social use again (Boege, 1999, p. 213). As the AGA (1989, p. 7.26) report noted: 'this resentment has followed the situation where villagers have assumed that at least a proportion of their land would eventually revert to something approaching its historic use' only to find that 'village land [that] has been used in the mining operations will not revert to land of any real economic or social value'.

This disappointment developed in spite of attempts by BCL to show some Bougainvilleans the effects that mining would have on the environment. Prior to the construction of the mine BCL took several Bougainvillean employees to see mines in Australia. The logic was that the Bougainvilleans could witness first-hand the environmental impacts of a large open cut mine and explain to their villages what they had seen when they returned. When I asked a former Bougainvillean employee of BCL if this occurred, he stated:

> Yes, BCL took us to go to Australia and I did see environmental devastation of the mines there.
>
> (B14, former BCL employee)

Despite this commitment, BCL management believe the strategy failed because of the lack of vocabulary to explain what they had seen. As a current executive of BCL states:

> there is a problem with this strategy. People cannot return and convey what they saw. It is really hard especially in Pidgin because of the lack of vocabulary. An example is helicopters. The word used to refer to helicopters means 'Jesus' mixer' as they imagined Jesus to be 'up there' and thought of

the propeller as a giant mixing machine. Now we show a three-dimensional video instead.[4]

(B1, current executive of BCL)

Language is not necessarily the constraint in these situations. In a discussion of 'study tours' to the Porgera mine in Enga Province, West (2006, pp. 296–307) argues that it is often the signs of modernity and its contradictions that people focus on, rather than the environmental damage that mining creates (West, 2006, pp. 306–7). Similarly, Filer and Macintryre (2006, p. 223) explain the limitations of a visit to Bougainville by landowners from Lihir in New Ireland Province, writing that:

> while mining company managers hoped that such visits would ensure that local people had a clear understanding of the nature and extent of the physical changes to be inflicted on their environment – particularly the size of the hole in the ground – visitors tended to notice the material advantages that people enjoyed.

In spite of the early benefits mining creates, for an overcrowded population that was dependent on agriculture, and would again be dependent on agriculture once the mine closed, loss or damage to the land was over time seen as threatening the basis of future survival (Connell, 1991, p. 67). These impacts were not solely 'environmental' or 'ecological' (Banks, 2002, p. 39); other effects included the loss of connection with ancestors through the destruction of cemeteries and loss of cultural values associated with traditional lifestyles (AGA, 1989, p. 8.2). Land for the affected villages, therefore, was not just a commodity that could be leased by BCL. As three Bougainvillean students wrote in 1974:

> Land is our physical life [and] our social life; it is marriage; it is status; it is security; it is politics; in fact, it is our only world... We have little or no experience of social survival detached from the land. For us to be completely landless is a nightmare which no dollar in the pocket or dollar in the bank will allay; we are a threatened people.

(Dove et al., 1974, p. 182)

It was this fear – fear about the survival of the traditional culture and aspirations to control the future – which BCL appears to have been unable to respond to. This was reflected in landowner responses to compensation payments for damages recognised as legitimate by the company that were soon judged to be inadequate. For example, compensation was paid to individuals at a rate of A$20 per person per year for the loss of fish in the Jaba River, with approximately A$412,000 paid to about 1,400 people as of 1974 (Brown, 1974, p. 26).

Although compensation was an important source of cash income, disagreements occurred between BCL environment staff and villagers over issues such as whether fish stocks had returned to normal in certain areas and whether mining chemicals were responsible for fish disease (AGA, 1989, p. 7.28–9). The more significant contest, however, was that landowners felt neither the company nor the government was doing enough to respond to their concerns (AGA, 1989, p. 8.1). Consequently, compensation payments became the focal point for any real and perceived grievances against BCL and the PNG Government (AGA, 1989, p. 8.1). As Vernon (2005, p. 270) reflects:

> If the weather seemed wetter or drier than before, then BCL was to blame. If the crops were not as prolific, or the game not as abundant, as they had been – then the mining operation was probably the cause. Various illnesses were obviously caused by chemical pollution – or so it seemed to many people in central Bougainville.

Escalating complaints and the felt experience of a lack of responsiveness by the company and Government directly linked environmental management to the onset of conflict. Paradoxically, however, it was an attempt to understand the environmental impacts of the mine that seems to have resulted in this outcome. In mid-1988, escalating landowner complaints coincided with a visit to Panguna by the PNG Ministers for Minerals and Energy. This visit

> resulted in the commissioning by the PNG Department of Minerals and Energy of a New Zealand consultancy firm, Applied Geology Associates (AGA), to determine the social and environmental impact, both past and future, of mining operations at Panguna.
>
> (Quodling, 1991, pp. 30–1)

Six consultants and two assistants along with the cooperation of landowners conducted the review (AGA, 1989, p. 1.1). Study activities included briefings from BCL, the NSPG, landowner associations and individual villagers; inspection tours of the mine; village meetings; sampling of water, sediment and soils; and a workshop by the review team to discuss the study's interim findings (AGA, 1989, p. 1.1).

Instead of resolving concerns about the environmental damage caused by the mine, however, the study further angered the landowners. According to BCL, the report ignited tensions as it failed 'to attribute a wide range of environmental concerns to mining activities'[5] (BCL, 2010–11). Yet the consultants believe the review had in fact been 'prejudged' by the landowners as 'yet another excuse for delaying delivery of recognition and payment for their loss and for what they believe to be a rightful share of benefits from the mine profits' (AGA, 1989, p. 8.2). As a Bougainvillean civil servant recounted:

> Environmental damage is getting worse by the day but always hear from BCL that everything was 'hunky dory'. PNG sponsored a survey because of pressure from the landowners … It said there was no environmental damage and Ona stormed out of the meeting. It was the beginning of the end.
>
> (B13)

Further, a member of the AGA team, John Connell, recounted:

> AGA limited consultants expressed the view that although environmental damage from mining operations was substantial there was no direct evidence of significant levels of chemical pollution and thus it was unlikely that Bougainville Copper Limited's operations were responsible for the loss of wildlife, declining agricultural production or a range of human illnesses.
>
> (Connell, 1991, p. 71)

Rather than attribute these concerns to mining at Panguna, the AGA report suggested they were the inevitable result of development. The study also found that the poor performance of subsistence and cash crops was linked to diseases common in other gardens remote from the mine (AGA, 1989, p. 7.30).

In response to this conclusion, Francis Ona condemned the AGA study a 'whitewash' (Vernon, 2005, p. 270) and other landowners rejected the findings. As one landowner stated, 'we have seen the destruction, we cannot trust them' (B20, ABG Department CEO/landowner). Therefore,

> an inquiry that was intended to aid the resolution of land-owners' grievances had merely emphasised ... that they would be most unlikely to receive high levels of compensation ... and thus may have proved to be something of a catalyst for conflict.
>
> (Connell, 1991, pp. 71–2)

For the villages that were experiencing the daily effects of environmental pollution and disruption to their livelihoods, the findings of the study contradicted their views on the cause of a number of environmental issues and became 'symptomatic of wider problems' (Banks, 2002, p. 42). While the study found that many of the concerns could in fact be resolved in the long term through remedial action and better understanding by all parties, the problem was that they had already been raised with the Government and BCL without a satisfactory response. Failure to respond in a way deemed adequate by the landowners 'increased the certainty in people's minds that they are caused by the presence of the mine and its discharges, and that no one is willing to admit this to them' (AGA, 1989, p. 7.31).

The dilemma the Panguna mine represents is that it is unlikely that one can have such a large mine without significant damage to the natural environment. One avenue where corporations are advised to respond to this dilemma is to ensure 'community involvement in the decision-making that affected them, their resources, and their environments' (Banks, 2002, p. 59). Such an approach requires engagement with environmental impacts beyond those that can be scientifically measured and causally linked. As the events associated with the AGA study illustrate, attempts to evaluate the social and environmental impacts of mining are conditioned by a variety of pre-existing factors, such as feelings of frustration and distrust. Moreover, there are practical limits to community participation in the kinds of environmental management adopted by the extractives industry, such as the specialised knowledge required to scientifically evaluate environmental changes and limited authority to exercise regulatory powers (O'Faircheallaigh, 2007, pp. 320–37).

West Papua

There are more similarities than differences between West Papua and Bougainville when it comes to environmental damage. Tailings waste from the Grasberg mine has created similar, but possibly even worse environmental impacts to the Panguna mine. The land affected also holds particular spiritual and cultural importance for indigenous Papuans. While the environmental footprint of BP's Tangguh LNG project has not been as large as the two mines (as it does not require a mountain to be dug out), the project has not been able to avoid some notable environmental degradation.

As discussed in relation to Bougainville, the environmental impacts of resource development appear to feed into a broader distrust of Freeport, BP and the Indonesian Government to protect local community interests. The major difference between the two cases is that Freeport's operations in West Papua have extended into a new era of environmental consciousness. In contrast, the Panguna mine ceased operations when environmental awareness was more emergent than ubiquitous in resource development activity. Despite, or perhaps because of the greater scrutiny, accusations against Freeport of severe environmental damage continue to tarnish the company's international reputation (Greenpeace, 2012). Core concerns relate to Freeport's riverine disposal of tailings waste, overburden and insensitivity towards the original owners of the land.

Environmental criticisms related to BP's Tangguh LNG project relate to the lack of local involvement in environmental management processes, as well as the social and cultural impacts associated with BP's marine exclusion zone. These concerns reinforce the claim made in relation to Bougainville that interests relating to environmental damage feed into broader fears relating to cultural survival and the future of individual and group identity.

Freeport

> Every time they come they give hope. You can improve development. They give good dreaming for us. But after that they give not hope but killing and that is land. Land is the mother. They can get everything from the land – food, build their house, water from the river. In the forest they can implement their knowledge. That's why they say when the Government and the Company destroy my own land it seems like they kill us. We could lose everything.
>
> (WP1, Papuan NGO Worker)

Freeport's 1967 Contract of Work contained no environmental restrictions and no environmental impact assessment was conducted prior to the construction of the Ertsberg mine. At the time, almost complete control of the land rested with the Suharto regime (Abrash, 2001). The financial and political influence of Freeport combined with the regime's primary interest in pursuing national development rather than the protection of Papuans resulted in a situation in which environmental regulation was neglected. The Indonesian Government did not take an active interest in the environment until the mid-1990s (Paull et al., 2006, p. 36) and compliance with environmental regulations under Suharto was not necessarily difficult (Leith, 2003, p. 155).

With approximately 3 billion tons of tailings waste and waste rock amounting to 6–7 billion tons, Grasberg will produce one of the largest volumes of waste by any single industrial activity in the world (WALHI, 2006, p. 26). Waste management has been the primary concern relating to the environmental impact of Freeport's mining activities in West Papua. Mining at Grasberg generates two main forms of waste: waste rock that is stored in a waste dump in the Wanogong River; and tailings waste that is discharged into the Ajkwa River system (Paull et al., 2006, p. 36).

The quantity of tailings waste discharged into the Ajkwa River system has increased over time, from 7,000 tons per day (tpd) at the start of operations to the approval of 300,000 tpd in 1997. This is more than double the amount of tailings waste that BCL disposed into the Kawerong (140,000 tpd) (Leith, 2003, p. 166). Akin to BCL, however, Freeport utilises a riverine tailings disposal method, claiming that the construction of a tailings dam is unfeasible because of high rainfall and seismic activity in the area (WALHI, 2006, p. 25). A pipeline is also considered impractical due to the steep terrain and risk of landslides (WALHI, 2006, p. 25). Consequently, the bulk of the waste is emptied into what has become an enormous tailings dam in the lowlands (Leith, 2003, p. 167).

The impact of tailings waste on the lowlands environment is controversial (see Leith, 2003, pp. 166–71). Specific effects identified by Indonesian NGO WALHI (2006, p. 111) include: smothered vegetation, risks to threatened wildlife species, pollution of freshwater aquatic life, the destruction of between 21 and 63 km² of mangrove forests and higher than minimum levels of copper in fish. Tailings waste has also altered the river system, with estimates that the Ajkwa River is carrying over ten times more sediment than its natural carrying capacity (Leith, 2003, p. 167). While not all Kamoro have been impacted by tailings waste, they are the ones who have been most affected by tailings waste through the loss of sago gardens, trees traditionally used to build canoes for fishing, as well as fish species.

While Freeport has compensated the villages that formerly owned the land where the tailings are deposited in the form of community development projects (including: homes, schools, markets, places of worship, reclamation and economic development (MMSD, 2002, pp. J-11–J-13)), their relevance has been questioned as tailings waste is not the only threat to the Kamoro. As Muller writes:

over-logging and over-fishing by Indonesian entrepreneurs, and the permanent loss of land and natural resources to Indonesian settlers, to highland
migrants, and to urbanization without reasonable compensation, constitute
a bigger challenge for the Kamoro than the effects of Freeport tailings.

(Muller cited in Pouwer, 2010, p. 255)

The highlands land of the Amungme has also been impacted by Freeport's mining operations. WALHI (2006, pp. 56–61) highlights the dangers associated
with waste rock dumps, quality of ground water, odours caused by chemicals,
and the destruction and alienation of areas of practical and spiritual importance
(WALHI, 2006, p. 62). Similar to the Bougainville experience, therefore, these
impacts are not just 'environmental', but are also seen as a threat to cultural survival. As Beanal (1997) writes:

when we say that the environment for us is our 'mother' we mean that human
beings are an integral part of the environment and therefore each one of
us has to be mindful of and accountable to the limitations of the environment. Modern people do not recognize the special relationship of indigenous
people to the environment. But for the indigenous people, their view of their
natural surroundings teaches them ecologically sound principles to care for
the environment in a sustainable way. For the indigenous people, destroying
the environment means damaging the lives of human beings.

National and international critics

As stated earlier, the establishment of the Grasberg mining complex coincided
with a greater focus internationally on the environmental impacts of development. Notably, Freeport has been accused of breeching numerous Indonesian
environmental regulations, which are believed to have not been enforced due
to the company's financial and political influence (WALHI, 2006, p. 8). Some
of these charges include: failing to comply with government orders to amend
dangerous waste management practices; negligence in waste rock management;
refusal to build a tailings containment dam; illegal disposal of tailings into the
highlands river system; pollution of the river system; breeches of regulatory
water quality standards; and the discharge of acid rock drainage without a haz-
ardous waste license (WALHI, 2006). Freeport however, claims that the tailings are non-toxic and consistently states that it complies with Indonesian law
(Leith, 2003, p. 170). The Indonesian Government has never challenged this
claim (Paull et al., 2006, p. 36) and numerous environmental audits sponsored
by Freeport support the company's compliance with Indonesian law. As a 2014
audit states:

The analysis on legal performance of PTFI environmental management
concluded that PTFI has fulfilled the requirements and its obligation
outlined in the various government regulations, Ministry Environment

decrees, as well as letters from the Governor of Papua and Regent of Mimika.

(PT.LAPIITB, 2014, p. 4)

In spite of numerous commitments to environmental management (such as voluntary external environmental audits every three years), Freeport's performance in practice has been challenged through a variety of means both national and international. One of the most high-profile protests is a lawsuit filed in the US courts by an Amungme landowner, Tom Beanal (*Beanal v. Freeport-McMoRan*). The lawsuit highlights the effects of mining activity on both the immediate mine area, as well as the downstream environment. The suit focuses on Freeport's disposal of tailings into the Ajkwa River, which led to approximately 120 km^2 of dead trees and thick tailings sludge (Banks, 2002, p. 44). Beanal also alleges 'Freeport's mining operations resulted in "cultural genocide" by destroying the Amungme's habitat and religious symbols' (Business & Human Rights Resource Centre, n.d.). In spite of considerable support among indigenous community members (Abrash, 2001) the case was dismissed in 1998 'on the basis that the environmental and human rights abuses alleged by Beanal were not violations of the "law of nations"' (Business & Human Rights Resource Centre, n.d.). While Beanal appealed this ruling, the dismissal was affirmed in 1999 and Beanal has since accepted positions at the company as a PT Freeport Commissioner and as Vice President of the People's Development Foundation[6] (Abrash, 2001).

The perspective that Freeport's environmental damage has been 'unnecessary' also led the Overseas Private Insurance Corporation (OPIC)[7] to revoke Freeport's $100 million political risk insurance in 1995, OPIC's first ever cancellation. OPIC stated in a letter addressed to Freeport that it would exercise its statutory charge under the US Foreign Assistance Act of 1961 to 'ensure that overseas investment projects do not pose unreasonable or major hazards or cause the degradation of tropical rainforests in developing countries' (OPIC, 1995). Based on a monitoring visit of Freeport's operations in West Papua in 1994, OPIC highlighted numerous environmental problems relating to: tailings, acid rock drainage including overburden management, solid and hazardous waste management, environmental monitoring activities and reclamation efforts (EnviroSearch International, 1994, p. 1). Nevertheless, OPIC reinstated the policy (but only until 31 December 1996) on the condition that OPIC would be allowed to monitor the implementation of recommended changes and that Freeport would initiate a $100 million mine closure fund (Leith, 2003, p. 176). Yet in another twist of events, Freeport then cancelled its insurance with OPIC, claiming that political risk insurance was no longer the best use of the company's shareholder dollars (Park, 2010).

In 2006 Norway's government pension fund also declared divestment from Freeport primarily on environmental grounds. The organisation claimed that:

the Grasberg mine's riverine tailings disposal threatens 'irreversible' effects, posing 'unacceptable risks' and creating severe environmental damage … of importance to future generations.

(cited in Nostromo Research, 2006)

The pension fund also highlighted the company's intention to continue its existing waste management system, in spite of the World Bank's declaration that it was an unacceptable means of disposal (Ministry of Finance, Norway, 2006). In 2011 the New Zealand superannuation fund also came under pressure to follow Norway and divest from Freeport, but dismissed the call on the basis that:

> For us, walking away might be simpler and quicker than staying engaged, it might avoid critical coverage, but it changes nothing ... a properly considered responsible investment approach should also include a significant element of seeking to change company behaviour as it is that, not walking away, which makes the biggest impact on the people and environments most affected by problematic company behaviour.
>
> (New Zealand Superannuation Fund, 2011, pp. 1–2)

Freeport's turn to science

Although Freeport expressed a commitment to environmentally sustainable development in 1989 (Leith, 2003, p. 163), it was not until 1996 that the company voluntarily committed to external environmental assessments every three years. This commitment, however, did not necessarily move Freeport towards a closer engagement with the full range of concerns related to the environment and cultural survival of the Amungme and Kamoro. Rather, Freeport turned to scientific forms of authorisation (through, for example, ISO 14001 certification across all of the company's operating facilities).[8] This is reflected in Freeport's description of its approach to sustainable development as 'based on our objective to be compliant with laws and regulations and to minimize environmental impacts using risk management strategies based on valid data and sound science' (Freeport-McMoRan Copper & Gold, n.d.). Freeport's environmental strategy, therefore, is managed through analyses in which the criteria for evaluating environmental impacts are scientifically constituted (Macintyre & Foale, 2002).

Macintyre and Foale (2002) argue that the reliance on scientific analyses by corporations and consultants is a response to environmentalists from developed industrial nations, rather than local communities. The limitation of this approach is that corporations end up drawing on concepts that are generally unknown and inaccessible for locals (Macintyre & Foale, 2002). Freeport's reliance on scientific legitimacy instead of engaging with the complex local understandings also supports Escobar's critique of sustainable development discussed earlier in this chapter, as a commitment to sustaining current models of growth and development (Escobar, 1995, p. 193). Escobar argues, 'the question in this discourse is what kind of new manipulations we can invent to make the most of the Earth's "resources"' (Escobar, 1995, p. 193). This critique is evident in the following statement by Freeport on sustainable development:

> As the earth's population continues to grow along with the global standard of living, the demand for our metals rises. We will respond to increased demand by expanding our operations; however, our ability to

reduce or mitigate certain impacts, such as total greenhouse gas emissions and total water consumption, will be challenged as we evaluate how we can be more efficient.

(Freeport-McMoRan Copper & Gold, n.d.)

This quotes reveals that Freeport's understanding of sustainable development is not necessarily based on a commitment to meaningful engagement with local communities. Rather the focus is on how best to maintain company efficiency in the context of a growing demand for metals.

In one external audit of Freeport's operations in West Papua, MWH reported that the company was diligently following the sustainability guidelines of the International Council on Mining & Metals, which incorporate ten principles for the implementation and integration of sustainable development within the corporate decision-making process (MWH, 2008). However, Freeport has only published the executive summary of the MWH report, with no reference to the environmental concerns of the Amungme and Kamoro peoples. Instead, the report highlights Freeport's compliance with all regulatory and sampling requirements and claims that the company demonstrates a strong commitment to continuous improvement. For example, the report states, 'current PTFI [PT Freeport Indonesia] management practice of controlled riverine tailings transport and deposition to an engineered area remains the best option available for the operation' (MWH, 2008).

The MWH report depicts Freeport in a positive light, but makes no mention of consultation with landowners in the research for the report, nor the concerns expressed by environmental NGOs about Freeport's disposal of tailings waste. As with BCL in Bougainville, therefore, the company is perceived locally as having relied on external scientific evaluation to distance itself from the perspectives of those who depend on the land for cultural and physical survival.

BP's Tangguh LNG project

Environmental footprint of BP is very small. Only footprint is where the LNG plant is. You don't need to dig a mountain.

(WP8, BP employee)

In 2000 BP rebranded itself from British Petroleum to 'bp: beyond petroleum' in an attempt to portray the company as 'one that incorporated solar energy in its portfolio and was willing to move away from oil' (Beder, 2002, p. 26). As a part of this rebranding, BP adopted a new green, yellow and white sun logo named 'Helios', 'after the Greek god of the sun' (BP, 1996–2015). BP has failed dramatically, however, in its pitch to the world that it is an unusually 'green' extractive company. In 2005 a refinery explosion in Texas killed 15 BP workers and injured 170 others. That same year, a BP oil leak in Alaska resulted in some

4,800 barrels of oil being spread into the Alaskan snow (Lustgarten, 2010). In April 2010 BP received worldwide media coverage following the explosion at the Deepwater Horizon oil rig in the Gulf of Mexico that killed 11 people and released nearly 5 million barrels of oil into marine waters (Robertson & Krauss, 2010). The changes to BP's corporate image occurred just before the construction of the Tangguh project. However, the company's record of environmental failure over the past decade has raised genuine concerns in West Papua of the potential for disaster at the Tangguh LNG project.

The environmental impact assessment for the Tangguh project undertaken by the Central AMDAL Evaluation Commission of the Indonesian Government Ministry of the Environment was approved by BPMigas in 2002. Comprising three documents, the assessment evaluates the Tangguh project against Indonesian regulations concerning issues such as noise, atmospheric emissions, water quality and sanitary wastes. The key anticipated impacts of the Tangguh project relate to pollution of the Bintuni Bay area, restricted access to traditional food sources, waste generation from industrial and community activities, the level of CO_2 emissions, and air quality impacts (BP, 2005).

BP claims that the assessment was undertaken, 'by soliciting the views of many stakeholders, particularly the people living in nearby villages and communities' (Delaney, 2005), with 'at least 1,622 people in the villages and towns [having] registered their names and participated in the consultations' (BP, 2005, p. 53). BP also cites the names of villages where consultations took place, the dates of the consultations and number of attendees (BP, 2005, pp. 83–4). However, in a joint letter addressed to the Asian Development Bank in opposition to the US$350 million loan it provided for the Tangguh project, three Indonesian NGOs have contested BP's environmental impact assessment process:

> the process of environmental impact assessment for the Tangguh project was seriously flawed, without meaningful consultation of affected communities, and was a 'rubber stamp' process since the national government granted the Tangguh license before the EIS [Environmental Impact Study] was even completed.
>
> (WALHI, JATAM & KAU, 2005)

As discussed in Chapter 8, the NGOs contest BP's social and environmental impact assessment process as it was conducted after the exchange of land. Landowners and NGOs have understandably viewed this 'cart before the horse' chronology of the environmental impact assessment process with scepticism. Indeed questions have been raised about the degree of local empowerment in decisions relating to the environment when BP had already acquired control of the land. In this way even though BP had made a commitment to consult locals on the environmental impacts of their operations, the consultation process has been perceived by some Papuans as a disingenuous empty gesture. As Down to Earth (2008) claims:

> perhaps this is an indication that the gap between the realities of this big multi-national corporation and local Papuan villagers is too big to be bridged in this way, and that Tangguh's presence remains an imposition on the local landscape and society.

This quote reinforces Escobar's (1995, p. 197) point that sustainable development discourse indicates that only minor adjustments to, rather than a radical rethinking of current economic models, is required to launch an era of environmentally sound resource development.

Similar to the Bougainville copper mine and Freeport cases, a crucial environmental concern regarding the Tangguh project to date has centred on disruptions to traditional food sources. As a journalist based in West Papua stated:

> Environmental effects in Bintuni are getting more complicated ... they destroy fish and shrimp – the main food for the local people.
>
> (WP10)

This is partly due to pollution caused by a massive increase in shipping in and around the Bintuni Bay area. As a result, shrimp, fish and sago that indigenous groups in the area depend on as a source of income have been affected (JATAM, 2003). However, an additional disruption to food sources has been caused by BP's safety exclusion zone, which comprises a total area of approximately 4,555 ha or 0.5 per cent of the Bearau and Bintuni Bay area (BP, 2005, p. 35).

The prohibition of fishing boats in the Bearau and Bintuni Bay area has affected communities who have traditionally relied on fish close to the shoreline. According to a Papuan human rights advocate, this has led many villagers to travel further out to sea despite a lack of skills or equipment for deep-sea fishing (WP14, Papuan human rights activist). While BP has attempted to respond to this situation by providing villagers with a motorboat, this has created jealousy between landowning groups. As an Indonesian human rights activist based in Papua explains:

> BP collaborated with the local government to provide a motor boat for people of New Tanah Merah to catch fish. But when they reach the area there is anger and jealousy of the landowners there ... because their area is used by BP too but they didn't get anything.
>
> (WP14, human rights activist)

The activist claims that the local government tried to intervene by issuing a statement to villagers suggesting they consider alternative sources of food and livelihood. A concern of Papuans observing the Tangguh project is that villagers who cannot access traditional food sources will end up becoming dependent on BP. One Papuan peace activist related:

Now people can't sail freely as this is a company area … If they want to or not they must depend on BP. In a long time it may be a similar situation to Freeport where the people depend on the company.

(WP30, Papuan peace activist)

An additional concern connected to the environmental impacts of the Tangguh project highlighted during my fieldwork was BP's environmental record in other areas of the world. Respondents expressed concern that if a disaster similar to the 2010 Gulf of Mexico oil spill were to occur in West Papua, the Indonesian Government would not work to guarantee the protection of Papuans, or adequately restore the environment. Reinforcing the arguments made in relation to the BCL and Freeport cases, therefore, the environmental impacts associated with resource development cannot be considered in isolation from issues of trust between local communities, governments and corporations.

Conclusion

By drawing on an analysis of the environmental damage caused by the activities of BCL in Bougainville and Freeport and BP in West Papua, this chapter argued that the environmental impacts of large-scale mining and gas projects can be conditioned by a broader range of factors, specifically feelings of frustration, mistrust, jealousy and concerns about cultural survival.

While there has been a global increase in expectations that the private sector practise sustainable development, the cases reveal that these processes do not guarantee holistic responses to the social and environmental impacts of development. Through a discussion of the work of Banerjee (2003) and Escobar (1995), this was found to be attributable to the general focus of concepts of sustainable development on sustaining the global economic system, rather than Indigenous cultural relationships to land. Policies of sustainable development occur within a global economic system that is dominated by a Western ontology that views the environment and society as separate, and struggles to incorporate other ways of being in which distinctions between society and environment are less clear.

With the power to control the land, the power to control the science and the power to decide who is included and excluded from environmental management practices in the hands of Western corporations, it appears that locals have few opportunities to share alternative models of development and environmental protection. As noted in the discussion of Bougainville, one identified avenue for redressing this imbalance is to open spaces in which corporations are able to learn from non-Western conceptions of the environment, through the inclusion of locals in environmental impact assessments. In doing so corporations might learn more 'holistic' forms of ecological interdependence and local communities can have traditional ecological knowledge respected and used to inform decisions that will shape their future. It is important to note, however, that there are a number of practical limitations to community involvement in environmental management and the involvement of local leaders can result lead to negative perceptions of them by other members.

The next chapter expands this discussion of local participation in decisions relating to resource development through a discussion of the contemporary situations in Bougainville and West Papua. It argues that the three companies have important opportunities to make progress towards the achievement of 'bottom-up' resource development through participation in local reconciliation.

Notes

1 Tailings waste also affected the Pagala, Nonopa and Ore Rivers (Tanis, 2005, p. 452).
2 In 1986, BCL built a 33 km tailings pipeline from the concentrator to the Jaba delta. The pipeline was more than 70 per cent complete when the mine closed (Vernon, 2005, p. 269).
3 Sediment also eliminated fish from the river, resulting in compensation payments of $20,000 annually until 1975 (Denoon, 2000, p. 159).
4 This, however, is not a very convincing argument as surely the Bougainvilleans would have returned with photographs of the mines they visited that would have been given to them by their hosts.
5 Landowners blamed chemicals from the mine for a number of occurrences including: disappointing performance of food and cash crops; dust effects on plants; health problems; and the disappearance of flying foxes (AGA, 1989, p. 7.30).
6 Beanal reportedly reflects on this acceptance with bitterness (Abrash, 2001) as other Amungme leaders no longer trust him (Shari, 2000) even though he believes it was the only option left available to him in defending his people (Abrash & Kennedy, 2002).
7 For more detail on the OPIC case, see Leith (2003) and Park (2010).
8 The ISO 14000 family of standards provides practical tools for companies and organizations of all kinds looking to manage their environmental responsibilities (ISO, n.d.).

Bibliography

Abrash, A. 2001. 'The Amungme, Kamoro & Freeport: How indigenous Papuans have resisted the world's largest gold and copper mine', Cultural Survival, vol. 25, no. 1. <www. culturalsurvival.org/ourpublications/csq/article/the-amungme-kamoro-freeport-how-indigenous-papuans-have-resisted-worlds-> [accessed 11 May 2015].

Abrash, A. & Kennedy, D. 2002. 'Repressive mining in West Papua', in G. Evans, J. Goodman & N. Lansbury (eds.), Moving Mountains: Communities Confront Mining & Globalisation. London: Zed Books, pp. 59–72.

Applied Geology Associates (AGA). 1989. Environmental, Socio-Economic and Public Health Review of Bougainville Copper Mine, Panguna. Christchurch: Applied Geology Associates.

Ballard, C. 1997. 'It's the land stupid! The moral economy of resource ownership in Papua New Guinea', in P. Lamour (ed.), The Governance of Common Property in the Pacific Region. Canberra: National Centre for Development Studies and Resource Management in Asia-Pacific, Australian National University, pp. 47–65.

Banerjee, S. B. 2003. 'Who sustains whose development? Sustainable development and the reinvention of nature', Organization Studies, vol. 24, no. 2, pp. 143–80.

Banks, G. 2002. 'Mining and the environment in Melanesia: Contemporary debates reviewed', The Contemporary Pacific, vol. 14, no. 1, pp. 39–67.

Beanal, T. 1997. 'Speech presented at Loyola University, Chicago', 28 April. <www.
austinchronicle.com/issues/vol16/issue36/pols.environs.xtra.html> [accessed 12
May 2015].

Beder, H. 2002. 'bp: beyond petroleum?', in E. Lubbers (ed.), *Battling Big Business: Countering
Greenwash, Infiltration and other Forms of Corporate Bullying*. Devon: Green Books,
pp. 26–32.

Boege, V. 1999. 'Mining, environmental degradation and war: The Bougainville case',
in M. Suliman (ed.), *Ecology, Politics and Violent Conflict*. London: Zed Books,
pp. 211–27.

Bougainville Copper Limited. 2010–11. 'Chronology of events'. <http://bcl.nlawebdesigns.
com/bougainville/chronology-of-events.html> [accessed 2 May 2015].

BP. 1996–2015. 'The BP brand'. <www.bp.com/en/global/corporate/about-bp/our-brands/
the-bp-brand.html> [accessed 12 May 2015].

BP. 2005. 'Summary environmental impact assessment: Tangguh LNG project in Indonesia'.
<www.adb.org/sites/default/files/project-document/69276/ino-tangguh-lng-project.
pdf> [accessed 12 May 2015].

Brown, M. J. F. 1974. 'A development consequence: Disposal of mining waste in
Bougainville, Papua New Guinea', *Geoforum*, vol. 18, pp. 19–27.

Business & Human Rights Resource Centre. n.d. 'Freeport-McMoRan lawsuits (re
West Papua)'. <http://business-humanrights.org/en/freeport-mcmoran-lawsuits-re-
west-papua-0#c9323> [accessed 12 May 2015].

Connell, J. 1991. 'Compensation and conflict: The Bougainville copper mine, Papua New
Guinea', in J. Connell & R. Howitt (eds.), *Mining and Indigenous Peoples in Australasia*.
Sydney: Sydney University Press, pp. 54–75.

Delaney, E. 2005. 'Reply from Emma Delaney', 19 October. <www.minesandcommunities.
org/article.php?a=4948> [accessed 12 May 2015].

Denoon, D. 2000. *Getting under the Skin: The Bougainville Copper Agreement and the
Creation of the Panguna Mine*. Carlton: Melbourne University Press.

Dove, J., Miriung, T. & Togolo, M. 1974. 'Mining bitterness', in P. G. Sack (ed.), *Problems
of Choice: Land in Papua New Guinea*. Canberra: ANU Press.

Down to Earth. 2003. 'More doubts emerge over BP's Tangguh project'. <www.
downtoearth-indonesia.org/story/more-doubts-emerge-over-bps-tangguh-project>
[accessed 12 May 2015].

Down to Earth. 2008. 'Multinational corporations lining up to profit from West
Papua's resources'. <www.downtoearth-indonesia.org/story/multinational-corporations-
lining-profit-west-papuas-resources> [accessed 12 May 2015].

Dunphy, D., Benveniste, J., Griffiths, A. & Sutton, P. 2000. *Sustainability: The Corporate
Challenge of the 21st Century*. Sydney: Allen & Unwin.

Ellingson, T. J. 2001. *The Myth of the Noble Savage*. Berkeley: University of California Press.

EnviroSearch International. 1994. 'Final report: Environmental review of P.T. Freeport
Indonesia copper and precious metals mine Irian Jaya, Indonesia. <http://web.archive.
org/web/20060113104955/www.austinchronicle.com/issues/dispatch/2005-09-23/
FreeportEnvReview.pdf> [accessed 12 May 2015].

Escobar, A. 1995. *Encountering Development: The Making and Unmaking of the Third World*.
Princeton: Princeton University Press.

Filer, C. & Macintyre, M. 2006. 'Grass roots and deep holes: Community responses to
mining in Melanesia', *The Contemporary Pacific*, vol. 18, no. 2, pp. 215–31.

Freeport-McMoRan Copper & Gold. n.d. 'Environment'. <www.fcx.com/sd/env/index.
htm> [accessed 12 May 2015].

Greenpeace. 2012. 'Ranking – Public eye awards'. <www.publiceye.ch/en/ranking/> [accessed 22 April 2012].

ISO. n.d. 'ISO 14000 – Envrionmental Management'. <www.iso.org/iso/home/standards/management-standards/iso14000.htm> [accessed 23 July 2015].

JATAM. 2003. 'Behind the BP Tangguh project propaganda'. <http://wpik.org/Src/286686.html> [accessed 12 May 2015].

Leith, D. 2003. *The Politics of Power: Freeport in Suharto's Indonesia*. Honolulu: University of Hawaii Press.

Lustgarten, A. 2010. 'Gulf oil spill isn't BP's only recent black eye', *The Daily Green*, 20 April. <http://preview.www.thedailygreen.com/environmental-news/latest/bp-gulf-oil-spill-0430> [accessed 12 May 2015].

Macintyre, M. & Foale, S. 2002. 'Politicised ecology: Local responses to mining in Papua New Guinea'. Resource Management in Asia-Pacific, Working Paper 33. <www.crawford.anu.edu.au/rmap/pdf/Wpapers/rmap_wp33.pdf> [accessed 12 May 2015].

Mining, Minerals and Sustainable Development (MMSD). 2002. 'Mining for the future – Appendix J: Grasberg riverine disposal case study'. International Institute for Environment and Development and World Business Council for Sustainable Development, no. 68c. <http://pubs.iied.org/pdfs/G00563.pdf> [accessed 12 May 2015].

Ministry of Finance, Norway. 2006. 'Norway disinvests from Freeport: Press release'.<www.minesandcommunities.org/article.php?a=220> [accessed 12 May 2015].

MWH. 2008. 'Audit report: 2008 external environmental audit'. <www.fcx.com/sd/pdfs/audits/Executive_Summary_2008.PDF> [accessed 12 May 2015].

New Zealand Superannuation Fund. 2011. 'Guardians respond to Metro magazine story, December 2011 issue'. <https://www.nzsuperfund.co.nz/news-media/guardians-respond-metro-magazine-story-december-2011-issue> [accessed 12 May 2015].

Nostromo Research. 2006. 'Norway throws out Freeport'. <www.minesandcommunities.org/article.php?a=4154&l=1> [accessed 12 May 2015].

O'Faircheallaigh, C. 2007. 'Environmental agreements, EIA follow-up and aboriginal participation in environmental management: The Canadian experience', *Environmental Impact Assessment Review*, vol. 27, no. 4, pp. 319–42.

Overseas Private Investment Corporation (OPIC). 1995. 'Letter from the Overseas Private Investment Corporation to Freeport-McMoRan cancelling $100,000,000 of risk insurance'. <www.utwatch.org/corporations/freeportfiles/opic-letter.html> [accessed 12 May 2015].

Park, S. 2010. *World Bank Group Interactions with Environmentalists: Changing International Organisation Identities*. Manchester: Manchester University Press.

Paull, D., Banks, G., Ballard, C. & Gillieson, D. 2006. 'Monitoring the environmental impact of mining in remote locations through remotely sensed data', *Geocarto International*, vol. 21, no. 1, pp. 33–42.

Pouwer, J. 2010. *Gender, Ritual and Social Formation in West Papua: A Configurational Analysis Comparing Kamoro and Asmat*. Leiden: KITLV Press.

PT.LAPIITB. 2014. '2014 External environment audit'. <www.fcx.com/sd/pdf/audits/Executive_Summary_2014.PDF> [accessed 12 May 2015].

Quodling, P. 1991. *Bougainville: The Mine and the People*. St Leonards: Centre for Independent Studies.

Robertson, C. & Krauss, C. 2010. 'Gulf spill is the largest of its kind, scientists say', *The New York Times*, 2 August. <www.nytimes.com/2010/08/03/us/03spill.html?_r=4&fta=y> [accessed 12 May 2015].

Shari, M. 2000. 'Freeport McMoRan: A pit of trouble', *Business Week*, 31 July. <https://www.globalpolicy.org/the-dark-side-of-natural-resources-st/water-in-conflict/40140.html> [accessed 23 July 2015].

Shrivastava, P. & Hart, S. 1995. 'Creating sustainable corporations', *Business, Strategy, Environment*, no. 4, pp. 154–65.

Stempel, J. 2013. 'Rio Tinto wins end to human rights abuse lawsuit in U.S.', *The Star Online*, 29 June. <www.thestar.com.my/story/?file=%2f2013%2f6%2f29%2fworldupdates%2frio-tinto-wins-end-to-human-rights-abuse-lawsuit-in-us&sec=Worldupdates> [accessed 12 May 2015].

Tanis, J. 2005. 'Nagovisi villages as a window on Bougainville in 1988', in A. J. Regan & H. M. Griffin (eds.), *Bougainville before the Conflict*. Canberra: Pandanus Books, pp. 447–74.

Vernon, D 2005, 'The Panguna mine', in A. J. Regan & H. M. Griffin (eds.), *Bougainville before the Conflict*. Canberra: Pandanus Books, pp. 258–73.

WALHI. 2006. 'The environmental impacts of Freeport-Rio Tinto's copper and gold mining operation in Indonesia: Executive summary'. <www.minesandcommunities.org/article.php?a=978> [accessed 12 May 2015].

WALHI, JATAM & KAU. 2005. 'Tangguh LNG project-Papua-Indonesia'.<www.forum-adb.org/inner.php?sec=13&ref=extras&id=21> [accessed 12 May 2015].

West, P. 2006. 'Environmental conservation and mining: Strange bedfellows in the eastern highlands of Papua New Guinea', *The Contemporary Pacific*, vol. 18, no. 2, pp. 295–313.

World Commission on Environment and Development. 1987. 'Report of the World Commission on Environment and Development'. <www.un.org/documents/ga/res/42/ares42-187.htm> [accessed 12 May 2015].

10 Local reconciliation

Introduction

A key conclusion of Chapter 9 was the importance of empowering locals to define the environmental impacts associated with resource development, and for companies to engage meaningfully with their concerns about the future. The final site of interdependence, addressed in this chapter, is aspirations to define the future. The chapter argues that participation in local reconciliation processes offers the greatest opportunity for resource companies caught up in conflict to make progress on their relationships with local communities. Drawing on the contemporary situations of Bougainville and West Papua, the chapter explores possibilities open to BCL, Freeport and BP to reconcile past damage and to contribute to peace building in Bougainville and West Papua more broadly. By engaging in processes of local reconciliation, the three companies may have an important opportunity to shift from 'top-down' to 'bottom-up' resource development.

The business and peace literature

As discussed in Chapter 1, the potential for the private sector to contribute to peace building has gained significant interest from scholars, international organisations and NGOs. We saw that this has resulted in the development of a budding scholarship on 'business and peace'. While acknowledging that important questions have been raised in this literature regarding the role of business in conflict and post-conflict settings, an important limitation has also been identified. That is, the development of this scholarship has tended to occur in the absence of an adequate understanding of how and why the voluntary social and environmental initiatives already pursued by the extractive industry might have unintended violent consequences. Examples identified include: the breakdown of traditional village authority through changes to employment opportunities; divisions among landowners over access to resources; and the development of new infrastructure attracting large numbers of migrants. One limitation of the business and peace literature, therefore, is that it has not developed on the back of a deep understanding of the paradoxes of CSR.

Rather than generate broad strategies that are applicable to all societies affected by conflict, the logic underlying this book is that when companies idiosyncratically engage with the ways in which their work may aggravate sources of conflict in particular locations, they are in a better position to implement strategies to counter these dynamics (Banfield *et al.*, 2005). Such an engagement is what this book has attempted by exploring the core sites of interdependence between BCL, Freeport and BP with the root causes of conflict in Bougainville and West Papua. Through conceptualising business activity as interdependent with, rather than separate from, the root causes of conflict, it may become easier to identify a range of measures that a corporation might implement in order to contribute to peace in that area. Boege and Franks (2011, p. 4) distinguish between two post-conflict scenarios which mining companies might operate within:

- post-conflict development of new mines or reopening of old mines where mining was a factor in prior violent conflict;
- post-conflict development of new mines where mining was not a cause of the violent conflict, or where there was no pre-conflict mining.

These kinds of distinctions make it easier to develop appropriate corporate strategies according to specific operational scenarios. For example, in cases where mining was *not* a factor in prior violent conflict, it might be possible for corporations to foster stability through performing their core business activities (Bais & Huijser, 2005, p. 124), such as the creation of new employment opportunities. In cases where mining *was* a factor in prior violent conflict, the same 'opportunities' may actually prolong or ignite conflict depending on the way they are distributed (Chapter 5), and the historical context in which they are deployed (Chapter 3).

The aim of this chapter, therefore, is to progress our understanding of the transformative potential of engaging with the interdependencies between business and conflict. In this way the 'Interdependent Engagement' framework is only relevant for large corporations where resource development has been a contributing factor to conflict. In cases where resource development 'was a factor in prior violent conflict' (Boege & Franks, 2011, p. 4), a detailed analysis and acknowledgement of the roles that corporations have played in the conflict can be seen as the first step to identifying a 'conflict sensitive' business strategy.

In saying this, however, it is important to recognise differences in perspectives of conflict cross-culturally (Banks, 2008), such as the Western view of conflict as having a distinct beginning and end point. In contrast, Melanesian conceptions of conflict do not necessarily have such a clear linearity. For example, in a discussion of Huli disputes in PNG, Goldman (2003, p. 4) writes that 'many claims would lay dormant until such time as a strategically significant dispute arose allowing claimants to "activate" past unresolved disputes in a sequenced set of claims'. The kind of analysis and acknowledgement required by corporations therefore needs to be grounded in a locally informed view of the conflict and conflict resolution, rather than one that is developed by 'outsiders'.

Bougainville

As discussed in Chapter 2, a process is currently under way in Bougainville[1] to negotiate the island's political future as well as the possibility of reopening the Panguna mine. From 2007 onwards, support for reopening the Panguna mine began to build among the Bougainville political elite, mainly due to a requirement in the 2001 Bougainville Peace Agreement that a referendum on Bougainville's independence from PNG be held sometime between 2015 and 2020 (McKenna, 2014). Many Bougainvilleans believe that neither meaningful autonomy nor independence will be economically viable without a substantial source of revenue (Jennings & Claxton, 2013, p. 7). This support is based on the view that Bougainville requires a reliable source of economic development for an independent future to be feasible. In this regard Chairman and Managing Director of BCL, Peter Taylor, claims that the Panguna mine is potentially:

> large enough to support the Bougainville economy and also to produce a large number of jobs and businesses that always develop around a major project. There are stats [statistics] about how many direct employees will lead to how many indirect employees and the ratio is about 5 to 1 so if we are employing 3000 people you can expect another 15,000 people to be employed locally.
>
> (Taylor & Garrett, 2011)

In addition, the mine is estimated to have a life of approximately 24 years, 'processing between 60 million and 90 million tonnes of ore per annum' (Taylor, 2015). In this way Panguna is considered to be a viable option to support an independent Bougainville for at least 15 years. If the Bougainville Government and landowners deem these 15 years of mining a success, there is also the potential for new mining projects to be developed on other parts of the island.

To gauge local support for the resumption of mining at Panguna, the ABG and the PNG Government agreed in 2008 that the Bougainville Copper Agreement should be reviewed. As the Agreement has not been reviewed since the 1970s, landowners and the Bougainville Government have been left with uncertainty on a number of important issues such as the availability of revenues from Panguna in the future, and the responsibility for stabilising the mine site if it is never to reopen (Bougainville Administration, n.d., p. 6). For these and other outstanding issues to be clarified, the Agreement must be renegotiated.

Reflecting the significant changes that have occurred on Bougainville,[2] the two governments also agreed that the BCA review would include the ABG and representatives of landowners from areas impacted by the mine. For the first time, the right of Bougainvilleans to be consulted on whether they want mining was being recognised. To ensure the widest representation of landowners in the review process, from March 2010 the ABG embarked on a process of consulting landowner communities about how they would be represented (Regan, 2014, p. 88). During consultations from 2010 to 2011, the communities requested, and the ABG agreed to, the establishment of nine separate associations and one umbrella body for customary landowners from BCL's mining-related leases and nearby areas.

According to the Bougainville Administration, the aim of establishing these associations is to recognise that while each mining-affected area has distinct needs and concerns, they also need to develop the capacity to speak with one voice when they begin negotiations on the future of the mine (Bougainville Administration, n.d., p. 8). The inclusivity of these consultations, however, has been challenged, especially with regard to the involvement of youth, women and children[3] (Jubilee Australia, 2014, p. 6). Moreover, reflecting the sensitivity of the mine issue and the fact that reconciliation between the 'old' and 'new' Panguna landowners has only very recently occurred, it took many months for these landowning groups to agree to work together (Nisira & Garrett, 2011). Despite this, Regan reports that the process to date has been fruitful:

> the people are very clear, they know what their problems are and they are identifying them with tremendous clarity and great emotion. They really feel they have suffered, they are aware that they are the real victims of mining, and they are not opposing mining, for the future for the most part, but they are saying if it is to happen again, then it is to be done very differently and they, amongst others, have to be looked after in very different ways.
>
> (Regan & Garrett, 2011)

Consequently, the emphasis in the literature on business fostering peace through contributing to a sense of community is relevant to the Bougainville case. As we will see, this is due to the fact that BCL itself is expected to participate in some form of reconciliation before it would be in a position to play a lead role in the reopening of the mine.

In 2012 the ABG and the landowner associations jointly established a consultative process to consider the future of negotiations about Panguna. The ABG and the PNG Government also established a Joint Panguna Negotiating Consultative Committee (JPNCC) comprising representatives of PNG, the ABG, landowner associations and BCL (Regan, 2014, p. 88). Having met several times per year, all parties of the JPNCC agreed that if Panguna were ever to reopen, it would require not just a review of the BCA, but an entirely new agreement (Regan, 2014, p. 90). This was based on a view expressed in public consultations that it would be unacceptable 'for the first Bougainville mining law to give any form of recognition to the BCA, or to any mining exploration or development licences granted to BCL under the grossly unfair colonial mining law operating in the 1960[s]' (Regan, 2014, p. 90). Further, landowner representatives increasingly expressed the view that any new Agreement must be under ABG law. When the ABG passed the August 2014 Bougainville Mining (Transitional Arrangements) Bill, BCL was stripped of all lasting tenements, instead vesting it with an exploration license over its former Special Mining Lease. This puts BCL in the position of an exploration licence holder that has discovered commercially exploitable minerals and so wishes to negotiate grant of tenements for development of the resource (Taylor, 2015). In response, Rio Tinto, majority (53.83 per cent) shareholder in BCL, has announced a review of its investment in BCL (Taylor, 2015); so negotiations on the future of Panguna will not be considered further until the review is complete.

Three of the obvious possibilities[4] the parties to the review process must consider are: (1) the mine never opens again; (2) the mine opens again as a BCL operation; (3) the mine opens again under control of some other company (Bougainville Administration, n.d., p. 4). In order to illustrate the potential roles that BCL might play in Bougainville's future, each of these options will be explored in more detail. This discussion will be followed by suggestions on how and why BCL might participate in local reconciliation processes on Bougainville.

Option 1: the mine never opens again

> If the mine reopens there will be another war. That's what I predict.
> (B19, Bougainvillean landowner, 2010)

Despite considerable support among Bougainvilleans that the mine should reopen, this view is not without dissent. Numerous high-profile individuals express concerns that reopening the mine could jeopardise Bougainville's peace process. The main fears are that:

- the Bougainville Government will not have the capacity to contain local interests;
- there is the potential for warlords to emerge; and/or
- unresolved conflicts might erupt, which have the capacity to turn deadly due the many weapons that continue to be available on the island (Regan & Tanis, 2010).

In addition, there are concerns that the resumption of mining will lead to a resurgence of the social and environmental problems that plagued Bougainville during the operating years of the mine. As one Bougainvillean stated:

> we have already seen the damages. There are a lot of fears. Not only about the mine but fear of the PNG military coming back. Even the loss of land.
> (B25, Me'ekamui spokesman)

While there are no official groups opposing the mine as such, there are a number of well-known Bougainvilleans opposing the resumption of operations. Prior to his death in 2013, Damien Dameng, a strong complainant of the impacts of the mine on traditional values during the 1970s and 1980s, continued to oppose mining (Taylor & Garrett, 2011). Those who share Dameng's view believe that instead of reopening the mine, stakeholders of the review should:

work on the exit strategy and fill that bit [the mine pit] and make it conducive for cultivation.

(B20, ABG Department CEO/landowner)

In addition to Dameng, Chris Uma, leader of the Bougainville rebel group the
'Original Me'ekamui', has expressed reservations about the resumption of min-
ing. Uma's opposition is due to numerous outstanding issues between landowners,
BCL and the National and Provincial Governments. Uma states:

Bougainville is not yet normal, there are issues we still have to sort out first.
Things like compensation, I also want the mine pit measurement looked at
and people compensated fairly for the damages done to this hole. We have
to address and settle this before we can start talking about mine reopening.

(cited in Kenneth, 2011)

This quote, and other statements made by Uma on Australian radio programmes
(Uma et al., 2011) indicate that Uma does not entirely rule out the resumption
of mining on Bougainville. However, he does hold a firm view that the parties
to the negotiation process must deal with the unresolved issues of compensation
and environmental restoration, before any commitments are made on the future
of the mine. Should these issues not be adequately dealt with, the potential for
armed conflict is high. Moreover a report by Jubilee Australia (2014) argues that
opposition to opening the mine is near universal. Based on 65 interviews with
people in the Panguna mine lease areas and a discussion group with 17 participants, the report identifies three reasons for this opposition: negative social and
environmental consequences; the role of the mine in sparking the conflict; and
lack of meaningful reconciliation and justice. This finding, however, has been
contested by the President of Bougainville, John Momis (2014), who argues:

The Report is factually inaccurate, biased, methodologically unsound, and
dishonest in claiming that interviews with 65 individuals selected by its
authors allows it to represent the voices of 300,000 Bougainvilleans.

In particular, Momis (2014, pp. 1–2) criticised Jubilee's lack of consultation with
the ABG in compiling the report, and contends that:

the vast majority of those consulted do favour reopening the mine if it can
be done in a way that avoids the past environmental and social impacts and
conflict it engendered, and if Bougainvilleans can share fully and fairly in the
economic benefits mining can generate.

Another possible reason for not reopening is that the very high expectations of
landowners and other Bougainvilleans as to the compensation for past damage
(environmental, etc.) and for damage and injury suffered during the conflict will
make the reopening economically unviable.

Option 2: the mine opens again as a BCL operation

> People would prefer to work with the devil they know. They [BCL] will understand what they did wrong.
>
> (B11 ABG Department CEO)

While no systematic survey research evidence is available, based on observations of the negotiations, Regan and Tanis (2010) suggest that a significant number of Bougainvilleans support reopening the mine. Moreover, all three Bougainvillean leaders who have served as President (Kabui, Tanis and Momis) have supported the resumption of large-scale mining, either at Panguna or elsewhere.

Should Bougainvilleans decide to reopen the mine, fieldwork observations suggest that BCL may be the preferred operating company. Some of the Bougainvilleans the author spoke to explained this preference on the basis that 'it's better the devil you know', believing that BCL will accept some responsibility for what went wrong, something they fear a new company may not. Additionally, there appears to be a perception on Bougainville that because BCL was the company which created many of the social and environmental problems that have plagued Bougainville since the 1970s, it should also be BCL that comes back to fix these problems. As a Bougainvillean ex-BRA combatant stated:

> they [BCL] can just come back. They can do reconciliation with landowners and start a new chapter. BCL has to come back because it did that [the social and environmental damages] no other company can come back.
>
> (B28)

Underlying this seeming openness to BCL is also trust that the company has learned from its mistakes, and as a consequence, will be more committed to protecting the rights of landowners and their environment in the future. As two Bougainvillean landowners stated:

> I only deal with BCL. They have been here. They did the environmental damage. I will only talk to BCL. They know me.
>
> (B18, landowner group chairman)

> BCL already learned its mistakes. There will be better things with BCL again.
>
> (B20, ABG Department CEO/landowner)

Within these statements there is also a sense of confidence among Bougainvilleans that they have the capacity to hold BCL socially and environmentally accountable. As one Bougainvillean landowner stated, 'people are willing to sit with BCL to once again remind them what stimulated them to take up arms' (B20, ABG Department CEO/landowner). Alongside the idea of inviting BCL to reopen Panguna, therefore, is a strong expectation that the suffering of Bougainvilleans during the previous mining experience will be acknowledged. As such, the future of mining is inextricably tied to the Bougainvilleans' understanding of the past and their aspirations to define the future. However, continued support for BCL on Bougainville is likely to depend on how it handles outstanding issues such as compensation and environmental damage. As the following landowners stated:

> You [BCL] must pay out the damages [first] or we can find another company.
> (B24, chief/landowner)

> What we want is compensation for the damage. If they cannot sort out the [existing] problems they cannot come.
> (B27, former BCL employee/landowner)

Option 3: the mine opens again under control of some other company

While numerous companies have been raised as potential alternatives, competition at the corporate level to reopen the Panguna mine is not believed to be fierce. This is due to two main factors. First, before the passing of the new ABG mining law, BCL held the legal rights to the mining-lease areas and remaining infrastructure. This meant that unless Rio Tinto and/or the PNG Government became interested in selling their investment, it was unlikely that another company could obtain a legal right to reopen Panguna (Taylor & Garrett, 2011). Second, an investment of approximately US$5.2 billion is required to reopen the mine (Hoyle, 2014). The ABG believes that there are only four or five companies in the world that have this capacity. Consequently, the companies that have been raised as potential competitors to BCL are believed to only want a slice of equity in the mine, rather than operating status.

Despite these claims, the ABG has reportedly held discussions with several resource companies. For example, an Australian company with links to the China Nonferrous Metals and Mining Company, Ord River Resources, is believed to have held talks in 2007 with the ABG about reopening Panguna. Ord River heightened public speculation over the future of the mine when it issued several press releases (Ord River Resources, 2007a, 2007b) stating that talks with the Bougainville Government were 'progressing nicely'. However, these talks came to an abrupt end in 2007, when the ABG reportedly ended discussions on the basis that the mine was too sensitive an issue to discuss in the absence of a Bougainville mining policy ('ABG pulls out', 2007).

Invincible Resources has also been involved in public debate and speculation on Bougainville since the late President of Bougainville, Joseph Kabui, gave the company 70 per cent control over Bougainville's future mineral resources[5] ('Leader denies Bougainville', 2008). The deal was criticised for its lack of transparency, following the revelation that the ABG received K20,000 (AU$8000) for 'capacity building' (The Devui Committee, 2008, p. 5). The fund was allegedly used by some members of the ABG for their own purposes ('The killer deal', 2008). Many Bougainvilleans were also angry with the deal as it was made during a period in which it had been made 'clear that they were not prepared to return to foreigners mining their land' (Rabasca, 2009). Despite these concerns, there was enough support within the Bougainville Government to oust members of the Bougainville Executive Council who were acting in favour of Ord River.

While Invincible's influence in Bougainville had largely ended by early 2010, the company's promoter, Lindsay Semple, was soon back, 'this time with another Canadian company, Morumbi Resources Inc., a small oil producer in Canada that Semple convinced could make its fortune in Bougainville' (Regan, 2014, p. 86). According to Regan (2014, p. 86):

> working with Bougainvillean partners, Morumbi subsidiaries signed seven MOUs with different Bougainville landowner companies established by Morumbi and its Bougainvillean partners ... [that] ... purport to give Morumbi exclusive mineral exploration and development rights over large areas of Bougainville for up to fifty-five years.

Responding to landowner complaints about a lack of consultation and approval of the sale of their rights, the ABG stepped in with 'transitional' mining legislation which, in part, provided provisions that the 'Morumbi MOUs would have no legal effect' and a restriction that no more than two major mines can operate at any one time on Bougainville 'because of concerns that the push from Morumbi for MOUs over many different parts of Bougainville could result in as many as six or seven major mines' (Regan, 2014, p. 87).

Following Kabui's death in 2008, there has been a succession of two Presidents of Bougainville with different approaches to the mine issue. According to Braithwaite *et al.* (2010b, p. 129), James Tanis 'has been genuinely open to listening to the diverse and conflicting positions of his people in a new bottom-up attempt to forge a consensus on the future of the mine'. Tanis' logic is that for the Bougainville peace process to be sustainable, the conflict must be taken back to where it started. This links to the earlier discussion about why some Bougainvilleans seem to prefer BCL to other companies. As Patrick Nisira (Nisira & Garrett, 2011) claims:

> because of Panguna, Bougainville went down the drain and we believe that if we can fix Panguna, if we can stabilise Panguna, we can help Bougainville [stand] on its [own] two feet again.

While there are hopes on Bougainville that the current President and former PNG Ambassador to China, Momis, will continue the progress made on the mine issue by Tanis, some fear his close links to China will lead him to prefer Chinese investors regardless of the support of landowners. However, from 2011, Momis ceased to look at China and accepted the need to deal with BCL, at least initially. He did so for two reasons: (1) landowner views on preferring the 'devil they know', and (2) concern that simply ousting BCL could lead to legal battles that would result in the resource being effectively 'locked up'. But Momis and other leaders' ambivalence regarding BCL, which mirrors broader ambivalence to BCL, is reflected in the loss of BCL tenements under the new Mining Act.

The huge investment required to reopen Panguna, coupled with the tension surrounding local dealings with Invincible Resources and Morumbi, has meant that it is less likely, though not impossible, that the mine will reopen under a new company. While BCL is clearly attempting to capitalise on the negative experience of the failed Invincible and Ord River deal, Taylor's reflection on the competition facing BCL does, at least for some, seem to ring true, 'having seen the alternatives, the Bougainvilleans are saying, they actually prefer Bougainville Copper to reopen the mine' (Taylor & Garrett, 2011).

Distributive vs. symbolic reparation

Given the apparent support that currently exists for BCL to reopen Panguna, the idea of a role for BCL in peace building processes is a possibility worth pursuing. From BCL's perspective nothing is off limits for talks about reopening the mine, with Peter Taylor encouraging landowners to set the agenda for negotiations themselves (Taylor, 2015). Bougainville, therefore, represents a unique opportunity to explore the local expectations of a company involved in prior violent conflict in return for a new social licence to operate.

My Bougainville interview data suggest there is an expectation for BCL to make both material and symbolic reparations for the injustices that have been experienced, not just before the conflict, but also what happened to people as a result of the conflict. As discussed earlier, there is a strong 'material' expectation for BCL to resolve the outstanding issue of compensation. This includes discussions about how to calculate and distribute 1990 rent and compensation payments for more than 800 groups with customary ownership of blocks in the three main leases, given that large numbers of the 'title-holders' listed in 1989 have since died (Office of the Principal Legal Adviser, 2014).

Despite the firmness with which compensation is being demanded, there is also awareness on Bougainville of the social problems that monetary compensation has caused in the past, such as intergenerational disputes. Some Bougainvilleans are suggesting that an apology and/or reconciliation with BCL should also take place. While the ultimate aim of this would be to rebuild relationships, reconciliation would be the start of this process, not the end. As one Bougainvillean peacemaker stated:

> They [the landowners] will want the company to apologise … The company could participate in peace building by the executives participating in a reconciliation ceremony. Compensation can be paid later.
>
> (B12, peacemaker)

This statement implies that Bougainvilleans appear to be hoping for a compensation deal negotiated from a foundation of reconciliation. If another company were to reopen the mine, the expectations would likely be different. An apology on behalf of the company for past harms would not be required. This is not to say, however, that the company would not need to engage with the association of the mine with conflict. In such a scenario, the company might adopt other strategies which demonstrate an awareness of past grievances and how they might be avoided in the future. The point is that in either scenario, the company may need to consider measures that engage meaningfully with the past. Without such engagement, it is conceivable that a new or reopened resource project may provoke resentment in unpredicted ways. The following section explains how BCL's participation in reconciliation could take place.

Reconciliation with BCL

According to Boege and Franks (2011, pp. 36–7) if BCL were to participate in customary peace building processes on Bougainville, the company would 'essentially have to behave as if it were another "clan"'. This would require BCL to make material reparations for the harms caused (for example, compensation), as well as take practical steps to remedy those harms. The key here is to acknowledge the suffering of those who have been affected and to seek their forgiveness. To do this, current and former BCL executives will be required to put aside their own cultural interpretations of justice and prioritise 'local ways of doing things' (Boege & Franks, 2011, p. 38).

According to one Nasioi man, Bougainville's justice system is particularly difficult for foreigners to understand as it emphasises forgiveness over punishment (Mekea, cited in Howley, 2002, p. 102). Bougainvilleans do not consider legal revenge and punishment a necessary part of justice (Howley, 2002, p. 103). As Mekea claims:

> in its simplest form, it [Bougainvillean reconciliation] is just a question of two people saying 'I did you wrong and you did me wrong. I forgive you and you forgive me'. That is what happens in its most simple form. Of course there will be an exchange of goods, money, pigs and shell-money. People in other cultures do not really understand this. They prefer punishment and putting people in jail.
>
> (Mekea, cited in Howley, 2002, p. 102)

It is likely that BCL executives may want to avoid participation in this type of reconciliation, particularly through fear of admissions that might be used in litigation. However, even allowing for these risks, engagement in local reconciliation could be a win–win scenario for both BCL and landowners. For example, there is evidence in the regulatory literature that suggests where symbolic reparation is made (for example, an apology), victims are less likely to seek redress through judicial mechanisms (Healy, 2011, p. 269). Local reconciliation could thus be an attractive option for BCL whose parent company, Rio Tinto, had been caught in a lengthy lawsuit in the US. Although the case was eventually dismissed in 2013 as a result of a US court's decision on jurisdictional and other technical issues (see Stempel, 2013), in return for a suite of reparative and reconciliatory measures (which could include investment of the resources that would otherwise go to fighting a legal case into community development projects), BCL could ask for all the leaders of Bougainville to commit not to take further legal action. On the other hand, this kind of strategy may be viewed by critics as buying off local opposition, opening the company to a different kind of reputational damage.

The US lawsuit mentioned above involves serious allegations[6] against Rio Tinto that should not be dismissed lightly. However, there are concerns as to how representative the case is and the benefits that can be derived from a court battle in the US. By participating in a process that holds meaning for locals, BCL could be in a better position to be 'truthful with the people on what happened in the past' (B10, Bougainvillean small-scale miner) and apologise for the social and environmental damage that mining brought to the island. If landowners then invited BCL to reopen Panguna, it would send a strong message to both current and future shareholders that Bougainville Copper represents a secure investment. Importantly, therefore, both BCL and landowners have an interest in exploring alternative redress mechanisms that draw upon local reconciliation processes.

My fieldwork observations suggest Bougainvilleans consider an apology a small ask of the company, but a significant test for how culturally sensitive BCL would be if it were to reopen Panguna. As the following Bougainvillean women's leaders stated:

> cultural/symbolic recognition – it's our way of thinking. It is good manners. If they [BCL] were culturally sensitive, it would come naturally.
>
> (B5, former BCL employee/women's leader)

> It can be small but people will appreciate it. They should speak and say sorry about the damages. The people will speak about the loved ones and they will invite the spirits to invite them back.
>
> (B31, women's leader)

Regarding how reconciliation between Bougainvilleans and BCL could take place, it is best to think of reconciliation as an ongoing process that involves 'shallow and weak' forms of restoration. For example, 'shallow reconciliation' between Bougainville and BCL has already started by way of invitations to Peter Taylor as Chairman of BCL and Paul Coleman as PNG Manager for BCL in mid-2012 to visit Bougainville for the first time since the closure of the mine. In addition, a delegation of senior Australian diplomats was allowed to see the mine site for the first time in two decades (Taylor & Garrett, 2011). For 'deep reconciliation' to occur, there appears to be an expectation that current and former

BCL executives should go to Bougainville to participate in 'a meeting, and then a ceremony' (B28, Bougainvillean ex-combatant) to begin this process.

Local reconciliation[7] efforts have been central to conflict resolution in Bougainville and began almost as soon as the conflict (Regan, 2010). Although 'every village-level story of reconciliation was unique' (Braithwaite *et al.*, 2010b, p. 67), traditionally, Bougainvillean reconciliation ceremonies involve a feast during which 'former adversaries may feast, drink, and dance together; chew betel nut together; and symbolically break spears and arrows' (Boege and Franks, 2011, p. 38). While Bougainvilleans recognise that 'injustice is deep and it will not heal overnight' (B31, Bougainvillean women's leader), there remains a strong faith in the customary reconciliation process to restore relationships and to 'heal the pain' (B31, Bougainvillean women's leader). There seems to be a sense of confidence that if BCL were to engage in the 'Bougainville way' of reconcili-ation, there would be a strong foundation for a new working relationship. This is evident in the success of local reconciliation in the Bougainville peace process which analysts describe as consisting of two stories: the story of top-down peace resulting in a political settlement between PNG and Bougainvillean factions, and the story of 'zones of local reconciliation' (Braithwaite *et al.*, 2010b, p. 68). As Braithwaite *et al.* (2010b, p. 68) write:

> Most accounts assume the top-down story is the master narrative and the bottom-up reconciliations are subsidiary. But in important ways the bottom-up micro-narratives subsume and infuse the top-down peace.

Prospects and obstacles

A customary reconciliation process known as *Bel Kol*[8] (translated as a cooling of the heart) between BCL, landowners, ABG, ex-combatants and community leaders is now under active consideration (Bougainville Copper Limited, 2013, p. 5). Consideration of this began when Paul Coleman visited Buka in 2012 and met the ABG and about 40 Panguna landowner representatives. It was the land-owners who said they wanted BCL to re-establish a presence in Bougainville, not yet for purposes of reopening the mine (a matter left to after negotiations) but rather to begin evaluation on the extent of the damage done, local community needs and to do the work (including impact studies) needed before negotiations.

The landowners agreed that before a presence could be established, *Bel Kol* was required. BCL then agreed to explore what would be involved. According to Momis (2014, p. 5):

> The initiative originated in a July 2012 joint request from over 40 Panguna lease area landowner leaders attending a meeting with BCL and the ABG. The landowners requested BCL to establish an office in Arawa (central Bougainville) to enable it to clean-up potentially dangerous chemicals left by the mine, evaluate its environmental damage, and undertake community projects identified by the people. But the landowners insisted on first taking

initial steps towards customary reconciliation with BCL through a preliminary Bel Kol ceremony.

BCL agreed to this suggestion with the current Chairman of BCL stating that:

> as a gesture of goodwill, the company will make a significant contribution, towards vocational training upgrades, village literacy programs and malaria mitigation. After the Bel Kol ceremonies, in which BCL management will participate, three conflict memorials will be erected. In return, BCL has asked for open access to Panguna and the SML, assurances of safety, and a written invitation to establish a presence in Arawa, as a base for field work, baseline studies and social mapping previously mentioned, and for the recruitment of local people to participate in the evaluation and de-risking programs.
>
> (Taylor, 2014)

The *Bel Kol* therefore symbolises the beginning of a long process of reconciliation in Bougainville where it has long been recognised 'that reconciliation takes decades rather than years' (Braithwaite *et al.*, 2010b, p. 67). Moreover, there are no guarantees that this kind of acknowledgement of previous errors will result in a more considered approach in the future. Even if BCL were invited back to Bougainville and were willing to make reparations for the past, future harmful practices, intentional or otherwise, will always be a risk.

Negotiations on the potential for BCL to return to Bougainville are also occurring at a time when it is unclear who the ultimate governing authority will be after the referendum on independence. To add further uncertainty, the outcome of the referendum will be subject to ratification by the PNG Parliament (Jennings & Claxton, 2013, p. 5). Some fear the potential for future bloodshed if the PNG Parliament votes down Bougainvillean independence (Jennings & Claxton, 2013, p. 5). In this context, BCL would once again be required to straddle two governing authorities with divergent interests.

It is not certain, however, that PNG's refusal to ratify a vote for independence would re-ignite conflict (Jennings & Claxton, 2013, pp. 6–7). Nor is it certain that an influx of money into Bougainville would spark envy from the rest of PNG. This is due, in part, to a lack of capacity and appetite for renewed hostilities and the fact that PNG is no longer economically dependent on Bougainville's natural resources (Jennings & Claxton, 2013, p. 8). There are many possibilities that could unfold on Bougainville as it approaches the 2015–20 referendum on independence. This chapter has merely explored some of the potential peace building opportunities which BCL might consider if it were invited to return to Bougainville.

West Papua

In comparison with Bougainville, reconciliation in West Papua is at an early stage. Indeed it is not at a stage where the conflict itself has ended. Serious problems continue to characterise West Papua as a 'Land of Conflict', rather than the 'Land of Peace' to which many indigenous Papuans aspire. This is evident in the contemporary continuation of human rights abuses and inequalities discussed in chapters 3 to 9. These persistent problems pose significant challenges to the nascent initiatives to promote reconciliation that have emerged in West Papua.

While human rights groups and church groups represent the 'key pressures for peace' (Braithwaite *et al.*, 2010a, p. 134), lack of momentum towards achieving reconciliation in Papua has become a defining feature of the conflict itself. As Braithwaite *et al.* (2010a, p. 115) argue, 'the Papua conflict is distinguished by how little determined local or international mediation and reconciliation has occurred'. Analysts such as Rees *et al.* (2002, p. 2) attribute the slow progress in resolving the Papua conflict to a 'lack of political will to promote processes of reconciliation on the part of the many actors, both within Papuan civil society and in State authorities'. One problem associated with this lack of political will is that it sets up 'high expectations of an immediate outcome rather than seeing reconciliation as an ongoing process' (Rees *et al.*, 2002, p. 2).

The difficulty of achieving momentum towards reconciliation in West Papua is most evident in the relationship between indigenous Papuans and the Indonesian Government. One significant example is reflected in the divergent responses to the failure of the Special Autonomy Law (2001). While both Papuans and the Indonesian Government agree that the Special Autonomy Law has failed (Chauvel, 2011), there are disparate views as to why, and what an appropriate way forward might be. As Chauvel (2011) explains:

> Papuan responses to the failure have been demands for a referendum or dialogue with Jakarta. The government, however, has preferred to see Papua's problems as ones of socio-economic backwardness, as well as corruption and poor governance.

These conflicting views highlight the commitment that will be required to agree to working together to find a solution to the West Papua conflict. On the Papuan side, some proponents believe their only real chance to initiate peaceful dialogue with Jakarta will be to move away from the historical emphasis on a referendum for independence. Father Neles Tebay, for instance, argues that 'Papuans need to make clear that the issue of Papuan independence will not be on the agenda' (2009, p. 3) if they are to get Jakarta to agree to participate in dialogue on the West Papua conflict. Tebay does not dismiss the importance of the rectification of history for indigenous Papuans; however, he argues that developing trust between the two parties so that a long-term process of reconciliation can take place is a higher priority. With this goal in mind, Tebay called for an 'internal dialogue' among Indigenous Papuans to address questions such as:

> What are the features of 'Papua, Land of Peace'?
> What are the problems that impede 'Papua, Land of Peace'?
> What are the causes of these problems?

What solutions are required to address these problems?

What solutions are required to address the root causes of these problems?

What policies must be taken to prevent these problems from occurring in the future?

What roles should be played and tasks undertaken by various parties (government and civil society) to bring about 'Papua, Land of Peace'?

(Tebay, 2009, p. 26)

The current situation in West Papua, therefore, is one of developing a collective vision for the future. Due to the 'curses and opportunities' that characterise natural resource development in West Papua, the remainder of the chapter will be devoted to exploring the potential roles for Freeport and BP to support the emerging vision of 'Papua, Land of Peace'.

Expectations of Freeport and BP

The initial stages of reconciliation centre on the relationship between West Papua and Jakarta, Papuans and the Indonesian military, as well as among Papuans caught on different sides of the conflict (Braithwaite *et al.*, 2010a, p. 115). In this context, reconciliation between indigenous Papuans and large natural extractive companies is not high on the agenda.

Papuans would certainly welcome reconciliation with extractive companies, and Freeport in particular; however, there are significant obstacles to achieving this in the absence of the resolution of fundamental issues with the Indonesian Government. This is due to the sensitivity of the Indonesian Government when it comes to foreign 'interference' in Indonesia's domestic affairs. As one Papuan activist stated:

it would be great if they [Freeport] apologised but I'm not sure if it will be done. Indonesia has a government and this government has sovereignty to the people. If Freeport apologises to the people … it will make the Indonesian government very ashamed.

(WP30, Papuan activist)

What this statement demonstrates is that expectations for symbolic reparation from Freeport do exist in West Papua. However, as Indigenous Papuans currently have the higher priority of dialogue with Jakarta, their expectations of Freeport and BP are less defined than those discussed in relation to the Bougainville case. As a result there is less detail in the West Papua data for what might be expected of Freeport and BP in processes of reconciliation. Instead, the West Papua data support the criticism made by Rees *et al.* (2002) that reconciliation in West Papua currently emphasises immediate outcomes rather than long-term solutions. For example, according to my fieldwork observations, the two expectations of Freeport are that the Grasberg mine be closed, and that an Indigenous Papuan be made the President of Freeport, Indonesia. International law would hardly lend support to Papuan efforts to sustain such claims.

The expectation that a Papuan should be made the next President of Freeport is particularly strong in the mining town of Timika. This view is based on the belief that if a Papuan were made President of Freeport, the company would be in a better position to conduct mining in a way that would respect the rights of Papuans. As one Papuan NGO worker stated:

> it must be clear within the corporation that the next President in Freeport is Papuan. We hope that this is the time to take our rights and also lead our corporation... We believe that when a Papuan becomes head [President] – it will change. Right now, I'm under an Indonesian person. When it [the President] is a Papuan, it will be more safe and there will be more support for our [community development] programmes.
>
> (WP33, Papuan NGO worker)

A former Freeport employee responded to how credible an option this is for the company to consider:

> Yes, to an extent. But who should be promoted? I prefer educational pro-grammes that give better results... But people are not patient enough to wait. They see the position as a political position, like a Bupati [regency head]. They say local people can be elected but they don't see the [import-ance of] qualifications.
>
> (WP45)

Given Freeport has been comparatively slow to initiate Indigenous training and affirmative action policies, asking Papuans to be patient and wait for a Papuan qualified to take up the Presidential position is a big ask. On the Papuan side, a demand that a Papuan be President of Freeport is not particularly strategic. A Papuan as CEO of the operating company in West Papua will still have to answer to the CEO of the holding company and the Board at corporate headquar-ters in the US. These real controllers could surround a 'Papuan President' with their own men and women and hold back bonuses if the President did not do their bidding. Moreover, as discussed in Chapter 9, involvement in the company by Papuan leaders (such as Tom Beanal) can be a difficult individual experience and shift relationships of trust between community leaders.

A second Papuan view is that the solution to the problems associated with resource development is that 'all mines be closed' (ICG, 2011, p. 3). While the ICG have criticised this suggestion as 'more focused on problems than solutions' (2011, p. 3), McKenna and Braithwaite (2012) argue that openness to a resource exploitation pause could be an option worth pursuing. While it is not in Papuan interests to blow up pylons to attack the Freeport mine, the authors argue that negotiations with Freeport and BP to adopt a resource exploitation pause could produce long-term solutions. The aim would be to shift the current relation-ship of 'win for the investor, lose for Papuans' to a win–win for Papuans and foreign investors. By leaving the resources in the ground for a period of time, the resources may increase in value[9] and create an opportunity for new environmental technologies to be developed to manage the catastrophic environmental impacts of mining, and simultaneously provide a powerful leverage for Papuans to lobby Jakarta for peaceful dialogue, as well as changes in the conduct of natural resource exploitation generally. The main obstacle in pursuing this idea is whether such a pause would be a credible option in the eyes of Freeport, given the potential loss of revenue from days of production.

While ideas as to how Freeport and BP can become involved in promoting reconciliation in Papua are still evolving, there are nevertheless options worth considering.

The Papua Peace Conference

In 2011 significant progress was made on 'unifying Papuan civil society and activist groups in the interest of resolving the multi-dimensional conflict' (ICG, 2011, p. 2). The Papua Peace Conference held in Jayapura, 5–7 July 2011, marked this progress. Organised by the Papua Peace Network and chaired by Father Neles Tebay, the conference attracted over 500 participants (consisting of religious groups, customary groups, women, academics, students and resistance groups) who came together under the theme 'Let us together make Papua a Land of Peace'.

As discussed earlier, a key objective for Papuans committed to initiating dialogue with Jakarta has been the achievement of internal dialogue among Papuans themselves. In this regard the conference was hailed a success by all participants (ICG, 2011, p. 1). Significantly, participants at the conference included a representative of the Indonesian Government, the coordinating Political, Legal and Security Affairs Minister, Djoko Suyanto. The conference thus exceeded expectations of fostering internal dialogue between Papuans, by also making an initial step towards dialogue with Jakarta.

Two additional achievements marked the conclusion to the conference. First, five Papuans (Rex Rumakiek, John Otto Ondawame, Benny Wenda, Octovianus Mote and Leoni Tanggahma) were appointed to pursue formal negotiations with Jakarta. Second, a list of 44 'Indicators of Papua, Land of Peace' was developed. These indicators, drafted by the Papua Peace Conference participants, emphasise the complex political, economic, environmental and socio-cultural injustices that lie at the heart of the Papuan conflict. However, the most important feature of the indicators is that they incorporate a vision of the resolution of these injustices. For example:

> if one problem was exploitation of natural resources by various non-Papuan parties, one indicator of a peaceful Papua would be a thorough mapping of indigenous Papuan land, with customary rights legally recognised.
>
> (ICG, 2011, p. 2)

The 44 indicators thus provide an important insight into how indigenous Papuans see their current circumstances, as well as a collective vision for how peace could be achieved.

From 'top-down' to 'bottom-up' CSR in Papua

Throughout this book, it has been argued that Freeport is perceived locally to have failed to capitalise on opportunities to respond to local grievances in a way that could contribute to peaceful development in West Papua. Although Freeport has made significant contributions towards community development (in the form of hospitals, schools, employment and infrastructure projects), the company has been perceived by participants in this study to have generally failed to resolve the underlying disputes related to its business activities in West Papua. It is possible that this is one consequence of Freeport's 'distributive' approach to CSR, in which the company has attempted to silence local and international critics through the dispersal of large amounts of money (see Chapter 5). This method has been deemed unsuccessful in promoting peace in West Papua as expressions of 'Papua, Land of Peace' are characterised by claims not just for redistribution but also representation and recognition. Similar to the Bougainville case therefore, Freeport and BP could do well to strike more of a balance between distributive justice and symbolic reparation through their commitments to CSR.

By documenting a thorough record of the injustices which lie at the heart of the West Papua conflict, the Papua Peace Conference has opened an important 'resource opportunity' for Freeport and BP. This opportunity lies in the potential for the '44 indicators' to form the basis of a new 'bottom-up' approach to peaceful development. While the 44 indicators do not in themselves set a clear agenda for the design of corporate–community initiatives, they do 'give tangible content to Papuan aspirations for freedom' (MacLeod, 2011) and could provide a valuable springboard from which the resource companies might begin to reset their relationship with Papuans on a more peaceful, sustainable path. The indicators present Freeport and BP with a unique insight into the types of commitments they could make, which locals might deem meaningful and significant.

The 44 indicators represent a valuable opportunity for Freeport, and BP in particular, as many of the indicators relate to the exploitation of West Papua's natural resources. For example, one indicator that both companies are deeply connected to is, 'management of natural resources is undertaken in a way that protects the environment, respects local wisdom and provides maximal benefits to indigenous Papuans' (ICG, 2011, p. 19). While Freeport may respond to this suggestion by stating that it is already doing this by way of existing commitments to sustainable development, it could be used in a way that seeks to open channels of communication between West Papua and Jakarta on how resources can be used to promote peaceful development, and how effective governance institutions which support this aim can be advanced.

A strategy that used the 44 indicators as a platform to facilitate corporate engagement in the Papuan peace processes could be promoted as 'bottom-up CSR', as it would be Indigenous Papuans setting the agenda. This method forms a stark contrast to the dominant 'top-down CSR' approach that treats Indigenous peoples as passive recipients of better and worse CSR (McKenna & Braithwaite, 2012, p. 334). As we have seen throughout this book, 'top-down CSR' fails companies and communities, with millions of dollars spent on community development projects that do not achieve their aims. An additional advantage to drawing on the 44 indicators in a bottom-up approach to CSR is that it may make it easier to manage local expectations of the companies. This is because the 44 indicators might allow Freeport and BP to identify both 'quick' and 'long-term' contributions they can make towards the promotion of peace building. This would be an attractive option for Freeport and BP as they might be able to develop small (i.e. less 'politically sensitive') contributions towards achieving these indicators, at the same time as demonstrating a commitment to work towards longer-term (i.e. 'politically sensitive') goals. The key point to highlight here is that it would be a long-term process, involving all stakeholders of the resource project, working together with the aim of achieving peaceful development.

As we have seen throughout this book, effective CSR requires more than collaboration between a 'company' and 'society'. It requires security sector reform to achieve indicator no. 2, 'there is no longer stigmatisation of indigenous Papuans as separatists or rebels' (ICG, 2011, p. 19). We saw in Chapter 7 the alleged reluctance of Freeport to engage with this issue due to national stories relating to state sovereignty. Using this indicator as an example, Freeport could arrange a multi-stakeholder dialogue, involving the police and military, to work towards this goal. The positive characteristic of the 44 indicators is that they provide a company like Freeport an opportunity to work towards such a goal without giving an impression that it is attempting to override state sovereignty. In this way, adopting the 44 indicators would significantly challenge Freeport to take action on issues it appears to have traditionally sought to avoid.

There are, however, limitations to what Freeport and BP can achieve in the absence of a broader experience of *merdeka* driven by the state (see Chapter 4). Firms like Freeport and BP can contribute greatly to a fresh start to peace building in West Papua. However, without an experience of *merdeka*, whether based on a referendum for independence, or a more meaningful sense of political freedom to what West Papua was granted through Special Autonomy, no amount of Interdependent Engagement of Freeport and BP is likely to bring sustainable peace with justice. Nonetheless, the presence of MNCs like Freeport and BP could be conceptualised as a necessary condition for peace with justice. For example, Papuan leaders could initiate separate negotiations with Freeport and BP on how they could incorporate the 44 indicators in the context of their resource projects. This type of negotiation could represent an important 'confidence-building' step to a wider transformation towards peace with justice.

Conclusion

A detailed analysis of the roles that corporations have played in specific armed conflicts could be the first step to implementing a conflict-sensitive business strategy. Through a discussion of the contemporary scenarios of resource development on Bougainville and West Papua, it has been argued that BCL, Freeport and BP are faced with important opportunities to participate in reconciliation processes, and shift from a focus on 'top-down' to 'bottom-up' CSR.

For the Bougainville case, we saw the way landowners are engaging in a process of strategically considering the factors that contributed to significant social and environmental problems in the past. They are also contemplating how extractive projects might be undertaken in a way that avoids these problems in the future. This process represents a significant opportunity for BCL to support the empowerment of locals to determine their own future.

The 44 Papua, Land of Peace indicators may present a locally meaningful vision for a peaceful resolution to the West Papua conflict. A similarity in the data collected for both cases, therefore, is the emphasis on the need for an approach to CSR that draws on local voices for the design of appropriate community engagement initiatives. Although these processes differ according to local circumstances, a common theme is the apparent need for a long-term commitment involving all the stakeholders working together with the aim of achieving peaceful development. The following chapter expands on the potential for the Interdependent Engagement approach to enable corporations to understand and transform the complexities associated with natural resource extraction in areas affected by conflict.

Notes

1 Part of this discussion on Bougainville has been published previously in McKenna (2014).
2 See, for example, Regan's (2014, p. 85) discussion of the transfer of mining powers to the ABG.
3 Momis (2014, p. 3) disputes this criticism, arguing that in seeking mine-affected community views, there were extensive consultations, and that over 2,000 landowners voted in elections held to select the executives of the associations. Momis contends that consultations about reopening the mine went beyond landowners, to involve people from all over Bougainville, including '5 Regional Forums … and a Women's Forum in March 2014 involving 200 women from every district in Bougainville' (2014, p. 3).
4 These are only some options that will need to be considered; others include tailings options, status of company assets, logistics, safety, security and others (Taylor, 2014).
5 See also, Regan's (2014, pp. 85–6) discussion of Invincible Resources' Bougainvillean partners and talks held with the ABG.
6 See Business & Human Rights Resource Centre (n.d.).
7 For more on Bougainville's culture of reconciliation, see Regan (2010, pp. 36–44).
8 The *Bel Kol* was anticipated to occur in 2014 but has been delayed until after the 2015 Bougainville elections (Taylor, 2015).
9 One reviewer insightfully noted, however, that it could also push prices up generally in the region, leading to greater exploration at other sites and shift the 'Freeport problem' to other communities.

Bibliography

'ABG pulls out of Panguna mine talks'. 2007. *Post-Courier Online.* <www.postcourier.com.pg/20070312/news03.htm> [accessed 12 March 2007].

Bais, K. & Huijser, M. 2005. *The Profit of Peace: Corporate Responsibility in Conflict Regions.* Sheffield: Greenleaf Publishing.

Banfield, J., Haufler, V. & Lilly, D. 2005. *Transnational Corporations in Conflict Prone Zones: Public Policy Responses and a Framework for Action.* London: International Alert.

Banks, G. 2008. 'Understanding "resource" conflicts in Papua New Guinea', *Asia Pacific Viewpoint*, vol. 49, no. 1, pp. 23–34.

Boege, V. & Franks, D. M. 2011. 'Re-opening and developing mines in post-conflict settings: The challenges of company-community relations', in P. Lujala & S. A. Rustad (eds.), *High-Value Natural Resources and Post-Conflict Peacebuilding.* Peacebuilding and Natural Resources, vol. 1. London: Earthscan, pp. 87–120.

Bougainville Administration. n.d. 'Awareness materials: Establishing representative structures for landowners of BCL mining-related leases'. Unpublished document.

Bougainville Copper Limited. 2013. 'Annual report 2013'. <www.bcl.com.pg/wp-content/uploads/2014/09/1055234_PL_1055234.pdf> [accessed 13 May 2015].

Braithwaite, J., Braithwaite, V., Cookson, M. & Dunn, L. 2010a. *Anomie and Violence: Non-Truth and Reconciliation in Indonesian Peacebuilding.* Canberra: ANU Press.

Braithwaite, J., Charlesworth, H., Reddy, P. & Dunn, L. 2010a. *Reconciliation and Architectures of Commitment: Sequencing Peace in Bougainville.* Canberra: ANU Press.

Business & Human Rights Resource Centre. n.d. 'Rio Tinto lawsuit (re Papua New Guinea)'. <http://business-humanrights.org/en/rio-tinto-lawsuit-re-papua-new-guinea#c9304> [accessed 12 May 2015].

Chauvel, R. 2011. 'The struggle to make Papua a land of peace'. Elsham News Service. <http://elshamnewsservice.blogspot.com.au/2011/08/struggle-to-make-papua-land-of-peace.html> [accessed 12 May 2015].

Goldman, L. 2003. ' "Hoo-ha in Huli": Considerations of commotion and community in the Southern Highlands Province of Papua New Guinea'. State, Society and Governance in Melanesia Discussion Paper, no. 8. <https://digitalcollections.anu.edu.au/bitstream/1885/42124/2/goldman.pdf> [accessed 13 May 2015].

Healy, J. 2011. *Improving Health Care Safety and Quality: Reluctant Regulators.* Farnham: Ashgate.

Howley, P. 2002. *Breaking Spears and Mending Hearts: Peacemakers and Restorative Justice in Bougainville.* London: Zed Books.

Hoyle, R. 2014. 'Rio Tinto considers exiting Papua New Guinea copper mine', *The Wall Street Journal*, 18 August. <www.wsj.com/articles/rio-tinto-weighs-bougainville-copper-stake-1408352487> [accessed 13 May 2015].

International Crisis Group (ICG). 2011. 'Indonesia: Hope and hard reality in Papua'. Asia Briefing no. 126. Jakarta/Brussels.

Jennings, P. & Claxton, K. 2013. 'A stitch in time: Preserving peace on Bougainville'. Australian Strategic Policy Institute, Special Report. <https://www.aspi.org.au/publications/special-report-a-stitch-in-time-preserving-peace-on-bougainville/SR59_bougainville.pdf> [accessed 7 May 2015].

Jubilee Australia. 2014. *Voices of Bougainville.* Sydney: Jubilee Australia.

Kenneth, G. 2011. 'Rebel hits out against mine talks', *Post-Courier Online*, 28 February. <www.minesandcommunities.org/article.php?a=10756> [accessed 15 May 2015].

'Leader denies Bougainville is headed for another crisis'. 2008. *The Sydney Morning Herald*, 9 May. <www.smh.com.au/news/world/leader-denies-bougainville-is-headed-for-another-crisis/2008/05/08/1210131169388.html?s_cid=rss_world> [accessed 13 May 2015].

McKenna, K. 2014. 'Business and peace: Lessons from Bougainville', *Business, Peace and Sustainable Development*, vol. 2014, no. 2, pp. 28–55.

McKenna, K. & Braithwaite, J. 2012. 'Large corporations and obstacles to peace in Papua', in P. King, J. Elmslie & C. Webb-Gannon (eds.), *Comprehending West Papua*. Sydney: Centre for Peace and Conflict Studies, University of Sydney.

MacLeod, J. 2011. 'Comments on ICG's hope and hard reality in Papua', *West Papua Media Alerts*, 24 August. <http://westpapuamedia.info/tag/conflict-resolution/> [accessed 13 May 2015].

Miriori, P. 2010. 'Media Release', 26 March. Unpublished document.

Momis, J. L. 2014. 'Autonomous Bougainville Government office of the president'. <www.jubileeaustralia.org/2013/campaigns/notonmywatch/Momis%2022%20Sept%202014.pdf> [accessed 12 May 2015].

Nisira, P. (Speaker) & Garrett, J. (Presenter). 2011. 'Bougainville consultations on mine re-opening set to widen'. ABC Radio Australia, 31 March. <www.radioaustralia.net.au/pacbeat/stories/201103/s3178057.htm> [accessed 12 May 2015].

Office of the Principal Legal Adviser. 2014. 'Appointing "customary heads" of landowning groups in the Panguna mine lease areas for the purpose of receiving and distributing land rent & compensation'. Buka: Autonomous Bougainville Government. Unpublished document.

Ord River. 2007a. 'Report in Media on Bougainville'. <www.ord.com.au/ASX%20Announcements/130307%20-%20Announcement%20Report%20in%20Media%20on%20Bougainville.pdf> [accessed 7 May 2012].

Ord River. 2007b. 'Update on previous report in media on Bougainville'. <www.ord.com.au/ASX%20Announcements/200307%20Announcement%20%20Update%20on%20Prevous%20Report%20in%20Media%20on%20Bougainville.pdf> [accessed 7 May 2012].

Rabasca, A. 2009. 'The riches of Bougainville', *Within Reach*, vol. 7, no. 2.

Rees, S., Ondawame, J. O. & King, P. 2002. 'Reconciliation and consolidation among Papuans', The West Papua Project, Position Paper 4.

Regan, A. J. 2010. *Light Intervention: Lessons from Bougainville*. Washington, DC: US Institute of Peace Press.

Regan, A. J. 2014. 'Bougainville: Large-scale mining and risks of conflict recurrence', *Security Challenges*, vol. 10, no. 2, pp. 71–96.

Regan, A. J. (Speaker) & Garrett, J. (Presenter). 2011. 'Villagers relocated by Bougainville copper suffer most says peace advisor'. ABC Radio Australia, 4 August. <www.radioaustralia.net.au/pacbeat/stories/201108/s3285078.htm> [accessed 12 May 2015].

Regan, A. J. & Tanis, J. 2010. 'New economic interests and the future of peace-building in Bougainville'. Paper presented for the State, Society and Governance Conference in Melanesia and Resource Management in Asia-Pacific, 15 November, Australian National University, Canberra.

Stempel, J. 2013. 'Rio Tinto wins end to human rights abuse lawsuit in U.S.', *The Star Online*, 29 June. <www.thestar.com.my/story/?file=%2f2013%2f6%2f29%2fworldupdates%2frio-tinto-wins-end-to-human-rights-abuse-lawsuit-in-us&sec=Worldupdates> [accessed 12 May 2015].

Taylor, P. 2014. *Bougainville Copper Limited Annual Report 2013*. <www.bcl.com.pg/wp-content/uploads/2014/09/1055234_PL_1055234.pdf> [accessed 23 July 2015].

Taylor, P. 2015. 'BCL chairman addresses annual general meeting (transcript)'. Bougainville Copper Limited 24. <www.bougainville24.com/bcl/bcl-chairman-addresses-annual-general-meeting-transcript/> [accessed 12 May 2015].

Taylor, P. (Speaker) & Garrett, J. (Presenter). 2011. 'Bougainville's Panguna mine "can be reopened"'. ABC Radio Australia, 17 February. <www.radioaustralia.net.au/asiapac/stories/201102/s3141923.htm> [accessed 12 May 2015].

Tebay, N. 2009. 'Dialogue between Jakarta and Papua: A perspective from Papua'. Pontifical Mission Society, Human Rights Office. <www.europarl.europa.eu/meetdocs/2009_2014/documents/droi/dv/508_nelestebay_/508_nelestebay_en.pdf> [accessed 12 May 2015].

The Devui Committee. 2008. 'Report on the BRDC Inquiry'. The Parliament of the Autonomous Bougainville Government. <http://archives.cap.anu.edu.au/cdi_anu_edu_au/.AP/2009–10/D/2010_01_BGV_Comm_rep/2010_01_BRDC.pdf> [accessed 13 May 2015].

'The Killer Deal'. 2008. Foreign Correspondent, ABC News, 17 June. <www.abc.net.au/foreign/content/oldcontent/s2464812.htm> [accessed 13 May 2015].

Uma, C. & Tanis, J. (Speakers) & Garrett, J. (Presenter). 2011. 'Rebel leader wants to talk about reopening Bougainville copper mine'. ABC Radio Australia, 10 August. <www.radioaustralia.net.au/international/radio/onairhighlights/rebel-leader-wants-to-talk-about-reopening-bougainville-copper-mine> [accessed 12 May 2015].

11 Interdependent Engagement

This book opened with a reflection by one Bougainvillean landowner on the interdependence between large extractive companies and their local host communities:

> In every organisation or company, the management should be connected with us. It took so many years to understand that. Nobody understood that at the time ... but they do now.
>
> (B18, landowner group chairman)

The aim throughout this book has been to explore the possibilities that could emerge through engaging with this interdependence, rather than denying or suppressing it.

Extractive companies have been closely involved with the histories of the Bougainville and West Papua conflicts, yet the potential of this dynamic association to facilitate peace in these areas has been the subject of little analysis. This book begins to redress this lack through an empirical analysis of the crucial sites of interdependence between BCL, Freeport and BP with the grievances at the heart of the two conflicts. These sites of interdependence include:

- historical injustices (Chapter 3);
- state law and customary landownership (Chapter 4);
- revenue distribution (Chapter 5);
- representation (Chapter 6);
- security (Chapter 7);
- social impacts (Chapter 8);
- environmental impacts (Chapter 9);
- local reconciliation (Chapter 10).

The case studies presented reveal some of the opportunities, complexities and constraints that large extractive companies may need to confront if they are to be evaluated locally as taking seriously their social and environmental responsibilities. By confronting these complexities, the data collected for this study suggest large extractive companies might become a powerful conduit for a more socially and environmentally responsive global economy.

Limitations of CSR

Drawing on the theoretical insights of Latour, Fraser and a variety of analysts of CSR, two main limitations of CSR have been identified in the data collected.

(1) The emphasis on pledges over institutional change

The most important limitation of CSR as it currently exists among major resource companies appears to be the emphasis on pledges over institutional change. In other words, CSR seems to be helpful for facilitating corporate contributions to community development which are highly desired and valued by many in the local community, but has demonstrated less capacity to transform the business practices and policies that are considered harmful to societies and ecologies. Chapter 1 identified this as a potential consequence of the fact that corporations tend to underestimate the importance or potential of the 'social' in CSR. As Latour (2005, p. 1) argues, 'problems arise … when "social" begins to mean a type of material, as if the adjective was roughly comparable to other terms like "wooden", "steely", "biological", "economical", "mental", "organizational", or "linguistic"'. Conceptualising the social as an object or fixed domain is unhelpful as it can render invisible the complex range of actors and institutions that influence, and are influenced by, the presence and activities of large corporations.

One consequence of an oversimplified notion of the social analytically is that it can imply that corporations operate somewhere above society in order to then contribute to 'it'. This view can present corporations as 'neutral outsiders' of armed conflicts, rather than players who can at times be deeply implicated with their underlying causes. Consequently, corporations are not encouraged to change business practices, policies and relationships that are deemed harmful to local communities and interests. The Bougainville and West Papua cases reveal that as a potential side effect of this, corporations seem to privilege the distribution of material benefits such as compensation, royalties and trust funds. Drawing on the work of Fraser, it has been argued that corporations might do well to balance the distribution of material benefits with simultaneous efforts towards the 'recognition of people's standing as full partners in social interaction, able to participate as peers with others in social life' (Fraser et al., 2004, p. 377).

A focus on the distribution of material benefits, rather than claims for recognition and representation, may be a rational response by business as these kinds of contributions are relatively easy to document in company reports and websites. It is also possible to calculate how big the discount of profits will be from making the material gesture, decide that profits are still healthy after the payout and then write a cheque. In contrast, it is more difficult to document efforts towards the protection of Indigenous rights and cultural traditions, through, for example, recognising the role of resource development in historical injustices, or the facilitation of regional inequality. While certainly more difficult, the ability to engage with these more complex issues may have the potential to deliver significant benefits for both corporations and communities in terms of minimising the likelihood of violent conflict that may lead to the disruption or total closure of resource projects.

Distinguished scholars of CSR such as Porter and Kramer (2006) have previously highlighted the interrelationship between business and society. However, by focusing on this interaction, Porter and Kramer have framed their analysis according to the profit motive or 'competitive advantage' of firms. This study, in contrast, has been framed according to the justice or peace building potential of engaging with interdependence. While the lack of engagement with the profit motive of firms in this study might be considered to limit the practicality of the Interdependent Engagement model, the prevalence of armed conflict associated with natural resources suggests a need for alternative frameworks. The challenge remains to devise a framework that is likely to be adopted by corporations, yet initiates the reform required to facilitate peace.

A movement towards a politics of recognition that aims to revalue 'unjustly devalued identities' (Fraser, 1996, p. 6) may represent one possibility for the alignment of CSR with peace building. The risk of such an approach, however, is that it could essentialise group difference. As such, corporations seeking to pursue recognition as part of CSR would likely need to engage carefully, and in an ongoing manner, to maintain a balance between recognition of difference and a common or shared language of equity and justice.

Merry (2006, p. 297) discusses the tension between recognition of difference and status equality in relation to human rights reform. In this context, blending international standards completely with the social world includes a risk of losing the radical possibilities that might follow from a mutual engagement of transnational reformers and local communities. It would not be desirable for the elements of human rights ideas to be completely absorbed by local customs, or vice versa. A better aspiration might be for each to be used to strengthen the capacity of the other to achieve sustainable peace and, especially, for Indigenous wisdom to enrich Western practice rather than just the more empirically common influence (according to Merry) in the other direction.

(2) CSR has not empowered alternative visions of justice in the design of voluntary social and environmental initiatives

Acknowledging the importance of a balanced approach, one limitation of existing approaches to CSR is that they have not been considered by participants in this research to empower alternative visions of justice in the design of voluntary corporate social and environmental initiatives. In Latour's words, the data suggest that corporations have not followed '"the actors themselves" … to try to catch up with their often wild innovations in order to learn from them what the collective existence has become in their hands' (Latour, 2005, p. 12). An approach to CSR that enables strong local participation appears desirable; however, there are practical challenges associated with structuring CSR regulation to accommodate the diverse stakeholders of resource development projects.

At the international level, reformers must adhere to standards that apply to all societies to gain legitimacy (Merry, 2006, p. 3). Moreover, if corporations base their community engagement entirely on local terms, there is a risk of jeopardising previously hard-won agreements around human rights, such as international labour standards (Haines, 2005, p. 17). In the worst case, a local indigenous leader might realise that if she or he leads the people to demand (through Interdependent Engagement) less than is their international right, she or he might be paid off with a comfortable salary.

At the local level there are difficulties in determining who in the community wields the power to interpret what is needed (Fraser *et al.*, 2004, p. 375). On the other hand, an argument in favour of the 'unique contribution of place' (Haines, 2005, p. 23) is that cultural flows are not even (Merry, 2006). The cases of Bougainville and West Papua highlight the limitations of universal approaches. An over-emphasis on local engagement in CSR thus raises potential risks in terms of essentialising group differences and sidelining pre-existing global initiatives. However, a framework that balances local and global regulation, and which opens up spaces of dialogue between the two might make a useful contribution by facilitating the injection of local and/or alternative visions of social justice into global circuits (Merry, 2006).

Interdependent Engagement

In an effort to mitigate some of the risks and limitations of CSR identified in the data collected for this study, a new framework for the design of CSR in areas affected by conflict is advanced: Interdependent Engagement. In some ways, the model is not 'new' in the sense that it incorporates CSR measures that are already in place within the extractives industry. Nonetheless the model is unique as it represents an integrated and holistic framework and takes some of these measures further.

Figure 11.1 illustrates the relationship between the work of Fraser and Latour in constructing the Interdependent Engagement model. The vertical axis represents Fraser's theory of justice with recognition at one end of the spectrum, distribution at the other and representation in the middle. The horizontal axis represents Latour's critique of the use of the term 'the social'. The far left of the 'social' axis indicates a concept of CSR in which corporations are thought to be separate or external to the social world in which they operate. Movement to the right of the horizontal axis indicates an increasing level of engagement with the social, or deeper understanding of corporate activity as fundamentally embedded in the social world.

Interdependent Engagement sits on the far end of the social axis, and aims to strike a balance between distribution, recognition and representation in a way that might maximise the potential for peace. Representation is positioned in the middle of the axis since to be effective, both recognition and redistribution require fairness and an equal voice. The dotted line indicates that the required balance between distribution and recognition is likely to be different in

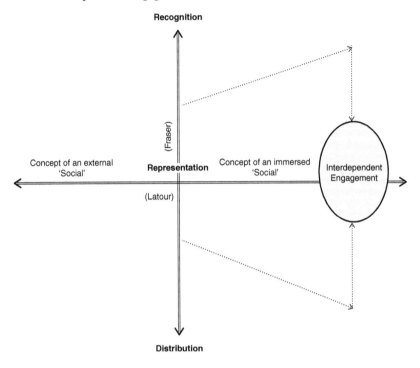

Figure 11.1 Interdependent Engagement theory

every situation and may change over time. It is expected that the optimal balance between distribution and recognition might be one that alters depending on the primary concerns of local affected communities. It is also likely that this balance will need to be revisited at various points during the course of the resource project to respond to changes in local priorities and other external pressures, such as changes in national and global economies.

The logic of the Interdependent Engagement framework is based on the following principles:

The mutual dependence of all stakeholders (state, company, locals, military, shareholders) involved in resource development.

In Chapter 1 we saw that scholars such as Watts (2004, p. 53) have highlighted the normative categories that can be disrupted through natural resource development, such as chieftainship, the space of indigeneity and the nation. Interdependent Engagement builds on this understanding by creating a method that might enable corporations to identify the ways in which they can disrupt local spaces and to consider how they might amend their business practices to promote peace. Interdependent Engagement could have this potential as it highlights the complex, and sometimes conflicting, stakeholder relationships that assemble alongside resource projects. Through engaging with this complexity, this research suggests that corporations might be in a better position to identify the opportunities and constraints facing them as they seek to pursue business development in a manner that safeguards the well-being of the communities and environments in which they operate.

Reflexivity on the consequences of actions.

The Interdependent Engagement framework encourages corporations to critically reflect on their business practices and the detrimental consequences they can have on local communities and environments. This involves not just a consideration of the complexity of the situation, but an active engagement with how corporate actions might facilitate or mitigate the structural injustices that lead to conflict. Moreover, a company with a commitment to Interdependent Engagement might accept the role that resource development can play in either the exacerbation or peaceful resolution of conflict.

The principle of reflexivity, however, points to a limitation of the Interdependent Engagement model. That is, Interdependent Engagement as it currently stands does not engage with issues of enforcement or compliance. As discussed in Chapter 1, a limitation of the data collected for this study is the lack of interviews with members of regulatory agencies in PNG and Indonesia. Nor does it reflect the views of the financial lenders of the resource projects who are increasingly taking on the role of regulating the social and environmental impacts of resource development.

Analysis of why Interdependent Engagement may or may not be adopted by corporations and what may make the model effective in a given economic and political context is therefore somewhat speculative at this stage. Yet the analysis is at least motivated by sensitivity to this warning from the work of Haines (2005). For future research, an engagement with regulatory agencies at international, provincial and local levels could elucidate a more nuanced analysis of the challenges associated with the implementation, enforcement and compliance to the model.

Engagement with local ontologies and the interests of others.

Corporate engagement with local ontologies, however, requires corporations to establish local communities as active participants in the resource project, not just regulatory authorities. By implementing an Interdependent Engagement approach to CSR, corporations could commit to collaborate with locals on the development of a mutually beneficial resource project. This commitment might trigger a process of engagement in which corporations and local communities can participate in two-way learning about the protection of society and the environment. The benefit of this approach is that it could open up new possibilities for Western business practices to be informed, indeed transformed, by local wisdom, spirituality, reconciliation and cultural values.

Flexibility through constant and ongoing responsiveness to situations which
change regularly.

The achievement of mutual engagement necessitates the development of flexible
business strategies that respond to social and environmental problems throughout the life of a resource project. Moreover, the Interdependent Engagement
approach recognises that societies are undergoing continuous processes of change.
Put differently, the social environment in which resource development occurs is
not a temporal vacuum. To be effective, the data collected for this study suggest
that CSR may need to respond to the dynamic nature of the social, political, economic and environmental circumstances in which extractive companies operate.
This may include a commitment to empower locals to determine their own future
vis-à-vis the economic benefits that emerge through resource development.

One element of the principle of flexibility involves a commitment to regularly re-evaluate CSR projects in order to guarantee their ongoing relevance
and effectiveness. It is possible that an initiative agreed to by all stakeholders
as appropriate at the start of a resource project may need to be adjusted or even
abandoned if it does not achieve its intended outcomes, is found to have harmful effects or is no longer considered a priority. The need to respond to changing
circumstances is represented graphically by the dotted lines in the theoretical
diagram of Interdependent Engagement that indicate the potential for movement (Figure 11.1).

Interdependent Engagement works to translate global business regulation into
local justice. This potential is linked to the facilitation of institutional change
through engagement with local particularities. In other words, Interdependent
Engagement is social self-regulation as opposed to asocial self-regulation. By recognising the mutuality that exists between large extractive companies and the
societies in which they operate, the findings of this study suggest that corporations might develop the capacity to move beyond pure self-interest and engage
with the consequences of their business activities on locals.

By engaging with the consequences of business activity on locals, this research
suggests that corporations might also generate a greater capacity to reflect on
how they can amend their practices and relationships in ways that protect the
well-being of society and the environment. In doing so, the data collected suggest that corporations have an important responsibility to ensure that the rights
of local communities are not unjustly compromised by the corporation's profit
motive, its reputation management and/or the state's need to achieve national
economic development.

Interdependent Engagement may provide an ethical framework for how to
engage with complex issues in difficult circumstances. A contrasting limitation
identified in the data collected for this study is that CSR tends to emphasise
distributive justice or the achievement of affirmative action goals. Moreover,
Interdependent Engagement may offer a pathway for proactive engagement and
not just the avoidance of harm or 'business as usual'. As shown in Table 11.1, the
framework sets out a positive formulation for what companies can work towards,

Table 11.1 Interdependent Engagement framework

Site of interdependence	Absence of CSR	Existing CSR models	CSR as Interdependent Engagement
Historical injustice	Corporate entanglement with colonisation and decolonisation processes is ignored		Acknowledges local colonial legacies and corporate involvement in them
State law & customary landownership	State laws (or national stories) are drawn upon to deny local grievances and sideline customary ownership	e.g., Abide by state regulation	Adds checks and balances to state laws and works to engage with customary landownership principles
Revenue distribution	Local communities are treated as homogeneous entities and problems associated with different levels of compensation are overlooked	e.g., Revenue sharing regimes	Acknowledges diversity in the ways local communities are affected by resource development and re-evaluates revenue distribution throughout the life of the project
Representation	Local grievances are dismissed and local people do not have the opportunity to negotiate	e.g., Stakeholder dialogue	Initiates dialogue on the institutional changes required for locals to feel their grievances are heard
Security	Tensions between local communities and official authorities are ignored	e.g., Voluntary Principles on Security & Human Rights	Recognises the hostilities and fears that local communities have of national authorities and seeks to open new spaces of security
Social impacts	Social disruption is maintained and few contributions are made to community development	e.g., Social impact assessments; community development projects	Seeks to alleviate new social problems through community development and ongoing engagement with their relevance and effectiveness
Environmental impacts	Environmental impact assessments are conducted with no local participation and opportunities to contest the results are repressed	e.g., Environmental impact assessments; Sustainable Development	Re-thinks current economic models through engagement with a more holistic understanding of the 'environmental' impacts of resource extraction
Local reconciliation	No attempts to heal symbolically the injustices related to resource development	e.g., Existing CSR measures and the positive benefits of economic development	Nurtures reconciliation based on local customs

rather than simply a list of 'do nots', while in the third column, examples of exist-ing CSR and related models are listed (if identifiable).

The benefit of Interdependent Engagement more broadly

Interdependent Engagement offers a new definition of CSR. It is a process that aims to encourage corporations to be more responsive to the consequences of business activity on the societies in which they operate. The Interdependent Engagement framework, therefore, intends to prompt more effective forms of CSR through place-oriented approaches that acknowledge the primacy of local empowerment, and the importance of all stakeholders working together towards shared goals.

The logic of Interdependent Engagement is not necessarily limited to specific locations (in this case Bougainville and West Papua), or to CSR more generally. The principles of Interdependent Engagement – mutuality, reflexivity, engage-ment and flexibility – are general qualities worth considering in other endeavours that aim to achieve economic development while protecting the well-being of minority groups and environmental sustainability.

The data collected for this study suggest that the peaceful development of nat-ural resources may require the development of new approaches that are respon-sive to bottom-up justice claims. Through engaging with the interdependencies of business activities with the root causes of conflict, it has been argued that Interdependent Engagement is one way this might be achieved. Empowering those who suffer disproportionately from natural resource development is an important step in recognising the struggle of Indigenous peoples for recognition. This is a struggle for identity, to be taken seriously, to share alternative versions of history and for these histories to be acknowledged. Interdependent Engagement could be a powerful vehicle to facilitate this recognition.

It is important to note, however, that the Interdependent Engagement model has developed out of an analysis of three specific companies operating in two resource conflicts located in Melanesia. It is likely that the model would benefit from further development by considering its application to other extractive com-panies operating in other conflict-affected societies and in different cultural con-texts. Interdependent Engagement would also be strengthened by a stakeholder consultation process so that key components of the model can be refined in col-laboration with corporate executives, state officials and landowning communities.

This brings us back to the quote from the opening of the book:

> In every organisation or company, the management should be connected with us. It took so many years to understand that. Nobody understood that at the time … but they do now.
>
> (B18, landowner group chairman)

The goals of Interdependent Engagement link with broader aspirations for a glo-bal economy that is more connected with the impacts of development practices on individuals, societies and environments. This involves an understanding of the delicate balance on which life depends and requires 'an extension of constructs of self-interest in which the needs of others begin to emerge as covalent with one's own' (Macy, 1991, p. 194). This aspiration connects with Escobar's (1995) search for alternatives to development, or development alternatives. The Interdependent Engagement framework may open a space for the destabilisation of dominant modes of knowing, by facilitating opportunities to engage with the ways of knowing of others. As Escobar (1995, p. 225) argues, 'the greatest political promise of minority cultures is their potential for resisting and subverting the axiomatics of capitalism and modernity in their hegemonic form'. In this way, Interdependent Engagement is not a 'development alternative' as such, but it does represent a shift in the processes of development, which may lead to the emergence of alternatives.

Bibliography

Collier, P. & Hoeffler, A. 2005. 'Resource rents, governance, and conflict', *Journal of Conflict Resolution*, vol. 49, no. 4, pp. 625–33.

Escobar, A. 1995. *Encountering Development: The Making and Unmaking of the Third World*. Princeton: Princeton University Press.

Fraser, N. 1996. 'Social justice in the age of identity politics: Redistribution, recognition, and participation'. The Tanner Lectures on Human Values, Stanford University, 30 April–2 May. <http://tannerlectures.utah.edu/_documents/a-to-z/f/Fraser98.pdf> [accessed 11 May 2015].

Fraser, N., Dahl, H. M., Stoltz, P. & Willig, R. 2004. 'Recognition, redistribution and representation in capitalist global society: An interview with Nancy Fraser', *Acta Sociologica*, vol. 47, no. 4, pp. 374–82.

Haines, F. 2005. *Globalization and Regulatory Character: Regulatory Reform after the Kader Toy Factory Fire*. Aldershot: Ashgate.

Latour, B. 2005. *Reassembling the Social: An Introduction to Actor-Network Theory*. Oxford: Oxford University Press.

Macy, J. 1991. *Mutual Causality in Buddhism and General Systems Theory: The Dharma of Natural Systems*. Albany: State University of New York Press.

Merry, S. E. 2006. *Human Rights & Gender Violence: Translating International Law into Local Justice*. Chicago: University of Chicago Press.

Porter, M. E. & Kramer, M. R. 2006. 'The link between competitive advantage and corporate social responsibility', *Harvard Business Review*, vol. 84, no. 12, pp. 78–92.

Watts, M. 2004. 'Resource curse? Governmentality, oil and power in the Niger Delta, Nigeria', *Geopolitics*, vol. 9, no. 1, pp. 50–80.

Appendix 1

Numbers and types of people interviewed, Bougainville case

Data source	Number of interviewees*
Rio Tinto executive – Australia	1
BCL executive	2
Former BCL employee	8
ABG Division Chief Executive Officer (CEO)	3
Civil servant	3
Resident/landowner from a mining-lease area	5
Landowner group chairman	2
Women's leader	5
Me'ekamui Government member	1
Small-scale miner	2
ABG adviser	4
Peacemaker	1
Ex-combatant	2
	Total = 39

* In two cases there was more than one interviewee present for one interview, so the total number of interviews for the Bougainville case was 37.

Appendix 2

Numbers and types of people interviewed, West Papua case

Data source	Number of interviewees*
BP executive – London	1
BP executive – Indonesia	6
Tangguh LNG shareholder company executive	1
BP employees	3
PT Freeport Indonesia employees	4
Former Freeport employees	2
NGO worker	14
Religious leader	6
Journalist	3
MRP (*Majelis Rakyat Papua*/Papuan People's Council) staff member	1
National Commission for Human Rights (*Komnas HAM*) staff member	1
Tongoi Papua (Freeport Union for indigenous workers) member	1
LEMASA (*Lembaga Musyawarah Adat Suku Amungme*/ The Amungme Tribal Council) staff member	1
LEMASKO (*Lembaga Musyawarah Adat Suku Kamoro*/ The Kamoro Tribal Council) staff member	1
LPMAK (*Lembaga Pengembangan Masyarakat Amungme dan Kamoro*/ The Amungme and Kamoro Community Development Organisation) staff member	1
Women's leader	1
	Total = 47

* In one case there was more than one interviewee present for one interview, so the total number of interviews for the Papua case was 41.

Appendix 3

Data collection phases and type

Data phases	Data type	Location	Aims	Findings
1. Fieldwork on CSR and peace building	Interviews at corporate headquarters of extractive companies (not all of which operate in Bougainville and West Papua) Existing academic & civil society literature	London, Paris, Geneva, Beijing Kuala Lumpur, Alberta	Understand how corporate actors conceptualise their commitments, responsibilities, successes, risks and failures in contributing to the objective of peace in their areas of operation Discover how and in what ways the perspectives of corporate executives matched emerging scholarly and activist expectations that corporations adopt new peace building roles.	Corporations would prefer to address issues related to peace building through existing CSR frameworks.
2. Case studies and comparison	Existing case study literature	Desk-based	Explore how specific business practices have intersected with armed conflict and how corporations have responded	Detailed understanding of the relationship between the relevant global corporations and local communities emerged, developed, played out and continue to evolve in these locations.

3. Implementing CSR	Corporate reports & documents Existing case study literature	Desk-based	Understand how well the existing CSR practices of the three companies aligned with the root causes of the two conflicts. Trace the characteristics of the CSR practices to uncover the types of practices that have been, and are currently being, implemented in Bougainville and West Papua.	Draft framework developed for how CSR might be usefully reworked to assist companies to avoid conflict. The draft framework focused on the existence of discrepancies between local perspectives of the problems associated with the resource projects and the focus of existing CSR policies. It also outlined an emerging disjuncture between the visions of social justice held by corporations and local communities.
4. Corporate actors in Bougainville and West Papua	PNG and Indonesia fieldwork Interviews at corporate national head office Consultants Former employees	Port Moresby Buka Arawa Jakarta Jayapura Timika	Trace the translation of global CSR policies into tangible action in two specific locations.	Deeper understanding of the constraints and opportunities of corporate executives in the field of CSR in two locations.

Data phases	Data type	Location	Aims	Findings
5. Local perspectives and expectations	Bougainville and Papua fieldwork Interviews with landowners, NGOs, religious leaders, ex-combatants, women's leaders, etc.	Buka Arawa Jayapura Timika	Understand the extent to which the local communities believed the companies had engaged with their grievances, how this engagement was taking place, as well as the perceived consequences of not engaging. Document community perceptions of the underlying motivations of CSR practices as well as potential roles for the companies in contributing to peaceful development in the future.	Generally speaking, the CSR practices and policies of the case study companies did not align with the grievances and root causes of the conflicts in Bougainville and Papua.
6. Modelling and hypothesising: development of the Interdependent Engagement framework	All of the above	Desk-based	Identify (and potentially extend) areas of connection between companies and the local communities, while also fleshing out some of the other actors and institutions, associated with resource projects.	The data were organised into categories that were labelled according to what I have called the common sites of interdependence between local communities and corporations and are documented in the Interdependent Engagement framework.

Index

Page numbers in *italics* are figures; with 't' are tables.